THE FIRST LAWS OF THE STATE OF RHODE ISLAND

THE FIRST LAWS OF THE
ORIGINAL THIRTEEN STATES

Compiled by: JOHN D. CUSHING

THE FIRST LAWS
OF THE STATE OF
RHODE ISLAND

Volume 2

Michael Glazier, Inc.

Wilmington, Delaware

This edition published in 1983 by MICHAEL GLAZIER, Inc., 1723 Delaware Avenue Wilmington, Delaware

Copyright ©1983 Editorial Note by John D. Cushing

Library of Congress Catalog Card Number: 82-84404
International Standard Book Number
   Series: 0-89453-211-1
   This Volume: 0-89453-224-3

Printed in the United States of America

*An Act to secure to Masters and Mistresses,
and to Apprentices and minor Servants
bounden by Deed, their mutual Privileges.*

Section 1. BE it enacted by the General
Assembly, and by the autho-
rity thereof it is enacted, That minors within the age of twenty-one years may be
bounden by deed as servants and apprentices by their father, and in case of his decease by their mother, when sole, or having
no such parent, and being within the age of
fourteen years, by their guardian, legally
appointed; and if fourteen years of age,
and having no such parent, may of his voluntary accord, with the approbation of his
guardian, or in case of no such guardian, by
and with the approbation of the Town-
Council of the town where such minor belongs or resides, bind himself by deed as an
apprentice or servant; females to the age
of eighteen years, or to the time of their
marriage, within that age, and males to the
age of twenty-one years: *Provided,* that
in every case there shall be two deeds of
the same form and tenor, executed by both
parties, one to be kept by each: *Provided
also,* that all considerations which shall be
allowed by the master or mistress, in any
contract of service or apprenticeship, shall
be secured to the sole use of the minor thereby engaged; and all contracts that shall be
made by any parent or guardian, or by any
for him or herself, pursuant to this act,
shall be good and effectual in law against all
parties, and the minors thereby engaged,
according to the tenor thereof.

Sec. 2. *And be it further enacted,* That
it

Minors may be bounden as servants and apprentices.

For what term.

Proviso.

Contracts made pursuant to this act to be binding.

Parents, &c. of apprentices to protect them from ill usage.

it shall be the right and duty of all parents and guardians, and of Town-Councils, for the time being (where the Town-Council shall give their approbation as aforesaid) binding minors as aforesaid, to enquire into the usage of the apprentices and servants bounden as aforesaid, and to defend them from the cruelty, neglect or breach of covenant of their master or mistress; and such parents, guardians or Town-Councils, for the time being, may complain to the Court of General Sessions of the Peace, in the

May complain therefor to the Court of Sessions.

county where such master or mistress are inhabitants, against him or her, for any personal cruelty, neglect or breach of covenant; and the Court, after having duly notified the party complained against, shall proceed to hear and determine such complaint; and if the same complaint shall be supported, the Court may render judgment that the said minor be discharged from his or her ap-

Who may discharge them, &c.

prenticeship, or service, with cost against the master or mistress, and award execution accordingly; in which case the deed of service or apprenticeship shall be deemed void from the time of rendering judgment, and the minor may be bounden out anew; but if such complaint shall not be supported, the Court shall award costs to the respondent against the parent, guardian or Town-Council (where the complaint of the Town-Council shall be without probable cause) and execution accordingly.

Apprentice absconding, &c. may be apprehended by warrant, &c.

Sec. 3. *And be it further enacted,* That if any servant or apprentice, bounden as aforesaid, shall depart from the service of his or her master or mistress, or otherwise neglect his duty, it shall be lawful for any Justice of the Peace of the county where such servant

or

or apprentice may be found, on complaint made to him by the master or mistress, or by any one in his or her behalf, on oath, to issue his warrant to the Sheriff, his Deputy, or to any Constable within the county, directing him to apprehend such servant or apprentice, and bring him or her before the said Justice, who upon the hearing shall endeavour to reconcile the difference, if he can, and order the said servant or apprentice to be returned to the place of his duty, or to commit him or her to the common gaol of the county, there to remain for a term not exceeding twenty days, unless sooner discharged by his or her master or mistress; and the Justice's warrant for returning such servant or apprentice to the place of his or her duty, directed to any officer or other person by name, shall authorize him to convey any such servant or apprentice to such place, notwithstanding it may be in any other county in this State; and the costs of the process and commitment by said Justice, shall be paid by the master or mistress, to be recovered of the parent or guardian, and the same, with all further costs he may be holden to pay, shall be a proper article of charge in such guardian's account.

By whom to be executed.

Cost, by whom to be paid.

Sec. 4. *And be it further enacted,* That if any servant or apprentice, bounden as aforesaid, shall be guilty of any gross misbehaviour, wilful neglect or refusal of his or her duty, the master or mistress may complain thereof to the Court of General Sessions of the Peace in the county whereof he or she is an inhabitant or resident; and the said Court, after having duly notified such servant or apprentice, and all persons covenanting on his or her behalf, and the

Master may complain to the Sessions, &c.

Apprentice, &c. to be notified.

S s   Town-

Town-Council for the time being of the town, when they shall approve as aforesaid, shall proceed to hear and decide on such complaint; and if the said complaint shall be supported, the Court may render judgment that the master or mistress shall be discharged from the contract of service or apprenticeship, and every article thereof obligatory on him or her, with costs, and award execution for costs accordingly, against the parent, guardian or minor, where the minor shall engage as aforesaid for him or herself; and any servant or apprentice, whose master or mistress shall be discharged as aforesaid, may be bounden out anew.

Court may discharge the master from his contract, &c.

Sec. 5. *And be it further enacted,* That no covenant of apprenticeship entered into by any minor, his parent or guardian, for the purpose of such minor's learning or being instructed in any trade or mystery, and made to any master, the wife of such master, or to the executors, administrators or assigns of such master, shall be binding on such minor, parent or guardian, after the decease of the master; but on the death of such master, the said contract shall be deemed void from that time, and in any such case, any minor may be bounden out anew, in manner as herein before is directed.

Deed of apprenticeship to be void on the death of the master.

1721.

An Act to redress Misemployment of Lands, Goods, and Stocks of Money, heretofore given to certain charitable Uses.

FORASMUCH as certain lands, tenements and hereditaments, and the profits of the same, and also stocks of money, chattels, and the profits thereof, have heretofore been given, limited, appointed and assigned,

by

by several well difpofed perfons, to and for the relief of the poor, and bringing up of children to learning ; which lands, tenements, hereditaments, rents and profits of the fame, and alfo goods, chattels, and ftocks of money, and the profits thereof, neverthelefs have not been employed according to the charitable intent of the givers and founders thereof, by reafon of frauds, breaches of truft, and negligence in thofe who fhould pay, deliver and improve the fame for the ufes defigned :

For redrefs and remedy whereof,

Section 1. *Be it enacted by the General Affembly, and by the authority thereof it is enacted,* That it fhall and may be lawful to and for each refpective Town-Council within this State, as need fhall require, within their refpective jurifdictions, to enquire of all and fingular fuch gifts, limitations, affignments and appointments aforefaid, and of the abufes and breaches of truft, negligence, mifemployments, not employing, concealing, defrauding and mifconverting, or mifgovernment of any lands, tenements, hereditaments, rents, profits, goods, chattels, and ftocks of money, and the profits thereof, heretofore given, limited, appointed, or affigned, to and for any of the charitable and godly ufes aforefaid, yearly, or as often as to them fhall appear requifite and needful.

Town-Councils may enquire into the application of lands, &c. given to charitable ufes.

And after the Town-Council, upon calling the parties entrufted with any fuch lands, tenements, hereditaments, and the rents and profits thereof, or with any fuch goods, chattels, or ftocks of money, fhall make enquiry, they are hereby empowered, upon fuch enquiry, hearing, and examination thereof, to

And make order relative to the fame.

set

set down such orders, judgments and decrees, that the said lands, tenements, hereditaments, rents, goods, chattels, stocks of money, and the profits thereof, may be duly and faithfully employed to and for the charitable uses and intents of the donors and founders thereof; which orders, judgments and decrees, not being contrary or repugnant to the orders, statutes and decrees of the donors

To remain in force until altered by the General Council.

or founders, shall stand firm and good, according to the tenor and purport thereof, and shall be executed by the Sheriff accordingly, until the same be altered or undone by the Governor and General Council of this State, for the time being, upon complaint by the party aggrieved made unto them.

Sec. 2. *And be it further enacted,* That upon the finding any such breach of trust,

Town-Councils may render judgment, and award execution.

negligence, misemployment, mismanagement, or under-renting any such lands, tenements, hereditaments, rents, profits, goods, chattels, or stocks of money, judgments and executions shall be given forth by the said Town-Council, against the misemployers, mismanagers and misimprovers of the same: And the same shall be levied out of their estates; and for want of sufficient estate of theirs to be found to satisfy and pay the same, they shall be committed to gaol, until the same be satisfied and paid, and a just distribution thereof be made, according to the true intent and meaning of the donors or founders.

Appeal granted.

Sec. 3. *And be it further enacted,* That it shall and may be lawful to and for any person or persons aggrieved at any sentence, order, judgment or decree, of any Town-Council, in any of the cases aforesaid, to
appeal

appeal from such sentence, order, judgment
or decree, unto the Governor and Council
of this State, for the time being, as in other
cases is usually allowed; who are hereby
empowered to alter, mitigate, reverse or
confirm such sentence, order or judgment
of such Town-Council, and to give a new
and final judgment and determination in said
case, as they shall think fit and agreeable to
equity and good conscience, according to
the true intent and meaning of the donors
and founders thereof, and shall tax and
award costs of suit, by their directions,
against such persons as they shall find to
complain unto them, without sufficient
cause, of the orders, judgments and decrees
aforementioned. *Provided always*, that the Terms of appeal.
party or parties desiring an appeal from such
Town-Council to the Governor and Council
of this State, do, the same day such order,
sentence, judgment or degree is given, request that such his or their desire be entered
in the records of said Court, and within
ten days after judgment give sufficient bond
to the Clerk of said Council, for the time being, with sufficient sureties, to prosecute his,
her or their appeal with effect, and to stand
and abide such final judgment as shall after-
ward be given in said cause, or otherwise
such person or persons shall lose his, her or
their advantage of appeal as aforesaid.

And in the mean time such sentence, Order of the
order, judgment or decree of such Town- Town-Council is
Council, shall be suspended, and execution the mean time to
be suspended.
stayed thereupon, any thing in this act before
contained to the contrary hereof in any
wise notwithstanding.

An

Towns bodies
corporate.

An Act declaring Towns to be Bodies corporate, establishing Town-Councils, regulating Town-Meetings, and prescribing the Manner of recovering Debts due from Towns.

Section 1. BE it enacted by the General Assembly, and by the authority thereof it is enacted, That the inhabitants of each town within this State are hereby declared to be a body politic and corporate, and as such may commence and prosecute

May sue and be sued.

any suit or action in any Court proper to try the same, and may also defend any suit or action commenced against them; and for this purpose, each town within the State shall have full power and authority to nominate and appoint one or more agents or attornies for that purpose.

May make by-laws.

Sec. 2. *And be it further enacted,* That each and every town within this State shall be and are hereby fully empowered to make and ordain all such acts, laws and orders, for the well directing, managing and ordering all prudential affairs of such town, as to them shall seem most conducive to the welfare and good order thereof, and to inflict

Impose fines, &c.

fines and penalties for the non-observance of the same, not exceeding ten dollars, or one month's imprisonment, for any one offence;

Proviso.

always provided in such cases, that such acts, laws and orders, are not repugnant to the laws of this State.

Town-Meetings to choose a Moderator.

Sec. 3. *And be it further enacted,* That every town-meeting in this State, when legally assembled, shall, by a majority of votes, choose a Moderator, who shall have power and authority to manage and regulate the business of the meeting, and to maintain peace

peace and good order therein; and he is here-by alſo empowered to puniſh by fine not exceeding five dollars, or impriſonment not exceeding ten days, any diſorderly beha-viour, or breach of the peace, that may hap-pen during ſuch meeting.

Who may puniſh for diſorderly behaviour.

Sec. 4. *And be it further enacted*, That the Moderator of every town-meeting in this State, when legally choſen, ſhall, on a mo-tion being made and ſeconded, relative to any buſineſs regularly before ſuch meeting (after having heard ſuch of the freeman as ſhall be deſirous of ſpeaking thereto) cauſe the votes of the freemen to be taken there-on, upon the penalty of being ſuſpended from the office of Moderator, and ſhall for-feit and pay to ſuch town ſeven dollars, to be recovered by an action of debt before any two Juſtices or Wardens of ſuch town ; and another Moderator ſhall be choſen in the room of the Moderator ſo ſuſpended.

Moderator to put queſtions to vote.

On penalty of being ſuſpended, and fined.

Sec. 5. *And be it further enacted*, That ſeven freemen at the leaſt ſhall be neceſſary to conſtitute a legal town-meeting, and all things relating to town affairs ſhall be de-cided by a majority of the votes of the free-men preſent.

Seven freemen to conſtitute a le-gal meeting.

Majority of votes neceſſary.

Sec. 6. *And be it further enacted*, That each and every town in this State ſhall have power and authority, when legally convened, to make ſuch acts and laws in their town, for raiſing ſuch ſums of money as ſhall be by them thought needful for the defraying the incidental charges thereof, or paying the town's debts, by a tax on real and perſonal eſtates, or both, and alſo to order a poll tax in ſuch aſſeſſment, if they ſhall think proper.

Towns may aſſeſs and collect taxes.

Sec. 7. *And be it further enacted*, That no vote ſhall be paſſed in any town-meeting,

No tax to be or-dered, unleſs mentioned in the warrant.

concerning

concerning the difpofing of the town's land, or making a rate, unlefs mention be made, and notice given thereof, in the warrant given out for the warning of fuch meeting ; and that the Town-Clerk of each town fhall grant fuch warrant, unlefs in cafes where the law otherwife directs, which warrant fhall be directed to the Town-Sergeant, or to either of the Conftables of the town.

Which fhall be granted by the Town-Clerk.

Sec. 8. *And be it further enacted,* That when any Town-Clerk fhall be removed by death or otherwife, that then and in fuch cafe the eldeft Juftice or Warden of fuch town fhall grant forth a warrant to warn the freemen to choofe a Town-Clerk in the room of him fo removed, which warrant fhall be directed as aforefaid.

In cafe of his death, the eldeft Juftice to call a meeting.

Sec. 9. *And be it further enacted,* That in each and every town there fhall be annually appointed and conftituted a Town-Council, to confift of the number prefcribed in the act relative to the election of town-officers : That the perfons elected members of faid Council fhall, previous to their entering on the duties of their appointment, be fworn or engaged to the faithful difcharge of their truft : That a major part of faid Town-Council fhall be a quorum : That the faid Town-Council fhall have full power to manage the affairs and intereft of fuch town, to tranfact and determine all fuch matters and things as fhall by law come within their jurifdiction, and to adminifter all neceffary oaths and engagements : And that the Town-Clerk fhall alfo be Clerk of the Council.

Town-Councils to be chofen.

To be fworn.

Their powers.

Sec. 10. *And be it further enacted,* That it fhall be the duty of each Town-Clerk, to caufe the freemen of their refpective towns to be notified of any town-meeting which fhall

Town-Clerk to caufe the freemen to be notified of town-meetings.

shall be prescribed by law, and also of all other town-meetings which shall be legally called : That whenever seven freemen in any town shall make in writing a request for the calling of a town-meeting to transact any business relating to such town, and direct the same to the Town-Clerk, it shall be the duty of such Town-Clerk to cause the freemen to be notified of the time and place when and where the same is to be holden, and of the business proposed to be transacted therein : That the notice to the freemen to meet in town-meeting, when prescribed by law, shall be given by the said Town-Clerk issuing his warrant, directed to the Town-Sergeant, or any Constable of such town, requiring him to post up written notifications, in three or more public places in such town, of the day for said meeting to be holden, and of the business required by law in such meeting to be transacted : That the notice of meetings, when called by request as aforesaid, shall be given by the Town-Clerk issuing his warrant, directed to the Town-Sergeant or Constables, requiring them to give personal notice to the individual freemen of such town of the time when, and the place where, said meeting is to be holden, and of the business therein to be transacted : *Provided always,* that it shall and may be lawful for any town to prescribe by law any other mode for warning the freemen of their respective towns to convene in town-meeting, any thing herein to the contrary notwithstanding.

Sec. 11. *And be it further enacted,* That any Town-Clerk who shall neglect or refuse to issue a warrant as directed by this act, and each Town-Sergeant or Constable who shall neglect

Method of calling town-meetings.

Proviso.

Penalty on the Clerk and Sergeant for neglect of duty.

T t

neglect or refuse to serve the same, as herein
required, shall severally forfeit, for each
neglect, fifty dollars, to be recovered by an
action of debt, one half to the use of the
town, and the other half to the use of the
person who shall sue for the same.

Sec. 12. *And be it further enacted*, That
all persons who shall have any money due
to him or them from any town in this State,

Debts due from
towns, how to
be recovered.

or any demand against such town, for any
matter, cause or thing whatever, shall take
the following method to obtain the same,
to wit : Such person or persons shall present
to the freemen of said town, when legally
assembled in town-meeting, a particular account of his or their debt or demand, and
how contracted; which being done, in case
just and due satisfaction is not made him or
them, by the Town-Treasurer of such town,
within one month after the presentment of
such debt or demand as aforesaid, that then
it shall be lawful for such person or persons
to commence his or their action against such
Town-Treasurer, for the recovery of the
same ; and upon judgment obtained for
such debt or demand, in case the Town-
Treasurer shall not have sufficient of the
town's money in his hands to satisfy and
pay the judgment obtained against him, and
the charges expended in defending such
suit, that then, upon application made by such
Town-Treasurer to any Justice of the Peace
or Warden of such town, such Justice or
Warden shall grant forth a warrant to the
Town-Sergeant of such town, requiring him
to warn the inhabitants of such town to
hold a town-meeting, at such time and place
as shall be appointed, for the speedy ordering and making a rate to be collected for
the

the reimburfement of fuch Town-Treafurer; **Town-Trea-furer's remedy.**
and in cafe fuch town, upon due warning
given them, fhall not take due and effectual
care to reimburfe, pay or fatisfy fuch Town-
Treafurer fuch monies, cofts and charges, by
him expended or recovered againft him, that
then, upon information or complaint thereof
by him made to the next General Affembly
to be holden within the State, fuch order
fhall be given therein for the faid Treafurer's
reimburfement, with allowance for all incidental cofts, charges and trouble occafioned
thereby; and fuch town fhall be fined at the
difcretion of the General Affembly.

An Act eftablifhing the Election of Town 1666.
Officers in each Town within this State. 1680.

Section 1. **B**E it enacted by the General 1747.
Affembly, and by the authority 1753.
thereof it is enacted, That the freemen in each 1754.
town fhall annually, on their town election 1756.
days, choofe and elect fo many town officers 1765.
as by the laws of this State are or fhall be re- 1776.
quired; that is to fay: One Town-Clerk. five 1787.
or feven good and fufficient freeholders for 1792.
a Town-Council, a Town-Sergeant, a Town- 1798.
Treafurer, a Town-Sealer of weights and **What officers to be chofen.**
meafures, an auctioneer, fuch a number of
Affeffors of rates and taxes as may be deemed neceffary (provided that the number be
not lefs than three, nor more than thirteen,
in any town) one or more Collector or
Collectors of taxes, one or more Packer or
Packers of beef, pork and fifh; a Pound-
Keeper, a Sealer of leather, three perfons to
appraife and value eftates, when difputed in
voting, and fo many Conftables, Overfeers
of the poor, Surveyors of highways, Viewers of fences, Gaugers of cafks, and all
                                                    fuch

such other officers as each or any town in this State shall have occasion for: And also one or more person or persons to superintend the building of chimnies, and placing of stoves and stove-pipes, who may, by the said towns respectively, be fully authorized and empowered to take and use such measures as the said towns respectively shall deem effectual and direct, for the removing, if erected or placed, or to prevent the erecting of any chimney, or placing of any stove or stove-pipe, so as to endanger any building or buildings being set on fire by means thereof.

Constable, &c. refusing to serve, to be fined.

Sec. 2. *And be it further enacted,* That whosoever shall be legally chosen and elected to the office of a Constable or Collector of rates, and shall refuse to serve therein, shall forfeit and pay the sum of five dollars to and for the use of the town, to be levied and collected by a warrant of distress from any Justice of the Peace or Warden of such town, directed to the Sheriff of the county, or to his Deputy; and that no person shall be obliged to serve in either of said offices oftener than once in seven years.

Also Town-Sergeant, &c.

Sec. 3. *And be it further enacted,* That whosoever shall be chosen and elected to the office of Town-Sergeant, Overseer of the poor, or Assessor of rates, in any town within this State, and shall refuse to serve therein, shall forfeit and pay seven dollars to and for the use of such town, to be levied and collected as aforesaid; and that no person shall be obliged to serve in either of said offices, oftener than once in seven years.

Town-Sergeants to give bonds.

Sec. 4. *And be it further enacted,* That each Town-Sergeant in this State shall be obliged, at the time of his being sworn into his office, to give bond with sufficient surety ty or fureties, to the Town-Treafurer of the town to which he belongs, in the fum of feven hundred dollars; and each and every Conftable, at the time of his being fworn into office, fhall in like manner be obliged to give bond, with fufficient furety or fureties in the fum of three hundred dollars, both of which bonds fhall be conditioned for the faithful performance of their refpective offices; and each and every Collector of rates, previous to his entering upon the collection of any tax or taxes, fhall give bond, with fufficient fureties, to the Town-Treafurer of the town for which he is chofen, in double the fum of the tax or taxes with the collection of which he fhall be charged, for the faithful performance of fuch truft.

Alfo Conftables,

and Collectors of taxes.

Sec. 5. *And be it further enacted,* That every perfon elected to any town office within this State fhall take the following engagement before he fhall act therein:

Town officers to be fworn.

" YOU A. B. do folemnly fwear (or affirm) that you will be true and faithful unto this State; that you will fupport the Conftitution of the United States, and that you will well and truly execute the office of for the enfuing year, or until another be engaged in your room, or you be legally difcharged therefrom. So help you God. (Or, this affirmation you make and give, upon the peril of the penalty of perjury.")

Form of the oath.

Sec. 6. *And be it further enacted,* That the Governor, Lieutenant-Governor, or either of the Affiftants, fhall not at any time be elected into any of the Town-Councils in this State.

Sec. 7. *And be it further enacted,* That if any town in this State fhall neglect to appoint

Towns neglecting to choofe Affeffors, to forfeit 200 dollars.

point three good fubftantial freeholders to be Affeffors or Rate-makers, fuch town fhall forfeit and pay two hundred dollars, to be recovered by the General-Treafurer by action of debt to be brought againft the Town-Treafurer of fuch town, at the next Court of Common Pleas to be holden in the county in which fuch town may be.

Neglecting to choofe other officers, may be indicted,

Sec. 8. *And be it further enacted*, That if any town in this State fhall neglect, on their town election days, to choofe and elect fo many other town officers as by law are required to be chofen for the management of their prudential affairs, that then fuch towns, upon being prefented by the Grand Jury to the Court of General Seffions of the Peace,

and fined.

and duly convicted, fhall be fined at the difcretion of the Court, not exceeding two hundred dollars, to and for the ufe of the State, and faid Court fhall make an order, directing fuch town to appoint and choofe their town-officers for the refidue of the year, at fuch time as fhall be by them enjoined.

Town-meeting in Jameftown, when to be holden.

Sec. 9. *And be it further enacted*, That the town-meeting of Jameftown for choofing town officers fhall be holden on the fame day, in the month of April annually, on which by law they fhall meet to choofe Reprefentatives, and vote for general officers.

Election to be by ballot, in cafe.

Sec. 10. *And be it further enacted*, That at the election of officers of every defcription, in every town in this State, if any freeman fhall move that the choice fhall be made by ballot or vote in writing, and fuch motion fhall be feconded, it fhall be the duty of the Moderator of the meeting to caufe the fuffrages of the freemen to be taken by ballot or vote in writing. And if any perfon
fhall

shall be chosen to any office otherwise than by ballot, when the same shall be required as aforesaid, such election shall be void.

An Act to prevent the Spreading of the Small-Pox, and other contagious Sickness, in this State.

1743.
1748.
1798.

Section 1. BE it enacted by the General Assembly, and by the authority thereof it is enacted, That no master or commander of any ship or other vessel, who shall come into any port or harbour of this State, and shall have any person or persons on board sick of the small-pox, or any other contagious distemper, or who has had any person sick of such distemper in the passage, or who shall come from any port or place usually infected with the small-pox, or where any other contagious distemper is prevalent, shall presume to bring such vessel to anchor in any of the ports of this State within the distance of one mile of any public ferry, pier or landing place, or permit or suffer any person or persons on board such vessel to be landed, or any person to come on board such vessel without a license first had and obtained from the Governor or Lieutenant-Governor, or in their absence from one or more Assistants of this State, or in his or their absence from two or more Justices of the Peace or Wardens of such town where such vessel shall arrive, on the penalty of forfeiting four hundred dollars to and for the use of the State, to be recovered by the General-Treasurer, by action of debt, in any Court of Common Pleas. And it shall be the duty of such master or commander, on his first arrival in any port in this State, to

No infected vessel to anchor within one mile of any landing place, &c.

Without license.

Penalty.

hoist

hoiſt and keep his colours in the ſhrouds of his ſhip or veſſel, as a ſignal of having come from ſuch infeſted place, or having infection on board.

Sec. 2. *And be it further enacted,* That if any perſon or perſons whoſoever ſhall preſume to land or come on ſhore from on board ſuch veſſel without licenſe firſt had and obtained as aforeſaid, it ſhall be lawful for any Aſſiſtant, Juſtice of the Peace or Warden, to ſend back ſuch offender or offenders immediately on board ſuch veſſel, or confine him or them on ſhore, in ſuch convenient place as to him ſhall appear moſt effectual to prevent the ſpreading of any infection, until the Town-Council of ſuch town ſhall have information and opportunity to remove ſaid offender or offenders, as they are hereafter empowered and directed; and the perſon or perſons ſo offending ſhall ſatisfy and pay all charge that ſhall ariſe thereon, and alſo each of them ſhall forfeit forty dollars, to be recovered in manner as aforeſaid; and if the offender or offenders ſhall not have ſufficient eſtate to pay the ſame, he or they ſhall be confined and ſubjected to hard labour for a term not exceeding two months.

Any perſon coming on ſhore to be ſent back, &c.

And forfeit forty dollars.

Sec. 3. *And be it further enacted,* That the Governor, Lieutenant-Governor, Aſſiſtants, Juſtices and Wardens as aforeſaid, be and they are hereby empowered and directed, to ſend a phyſician or other ſuitable perſon to examine into, and make report to him or them reſpectively, of the true ſtate of ſuch veſſel and the people on board, at the charge of the maſter or commander of ſuch veſſel.

A phyſician to be ſent on board.

Sec.

Sec. 4. *And be it further enacted,* That
the Town-Council of the town where such
vessel shall arrive, be, and they are hereby
empowered and directed, forthwith to put
on board such vessel some suitable person
or persons to secure said vessel, and effectually prevent any communication therewith,
at the expence of the owners.

And persons to take care of the vessel.

Sec. 5. *And be it further enacted,* That
the Town-Council of such town be, and
they are hereby empowered and directed, to
confine on board said vessel, or send to some
hospital or other suitable place, all persons,
mariners or passengers, or others who came
in said vessel, for a convenient time, until
such of them as have, or are liable to have,
the small-pox or other infectious distemper,
are perfectly recovered and cleansed from
said distemper, or have passed a suitable quarantine; and also all other persons who have
gone on board such vessel without license as
aforesaid, at the charge and expence of such
persons respectively; and also all other persons that came in said vessel, until they have
been sufficiently aired and cleansed.

Infected persons to be sent to a hospital, or con-fined on board.

Sec. 6. *And be it further enacted,* That
the Town-Council of the town where such
vessel arrives be, and they are hereby empowered and directed, to appoint two suitable persons to take effectual care that all
goods, wares and merchandizes, imported in
such vessel, which they think liable to hold
and communicate the infection, be landed
on some of the islands in the Narragansett
Bay, and exposed to the sun and air, and
cleansed, not exceeding ten days, nor under
six days, before they are permitted to be
brought into any house, shop or warehouse,
other than where they are cleansed as afore-

Goods imported in such vessel to be cleansed.

U u   said;

said; and when such goods are sufficiently
aired and cleansed, said persons shall give the
owners or possessors thereof a certificate,
and the Town-Council shall allow and order
said goods, wares and merchandizes, to be
delivered to the owner or owners thereof;
and the charge and expence of landing, airing and cleansing such goods, wares and
merchandizes, shall be borne by the respec-

At the expence of the owner. tive owner or owners; and all goods that
are judged by the Town-Council not to be
infected, shall be delivered to the owner or
owners, without delay and expence of airing,
as soon as may be consistent with the safety
of the town in regard to other parts of the

Also goods imported by land. cargo: And all goods, wares or merchandize, imported into any town in this State by
land, from any place infected with the
small-pox or other contagious distemper,
shall be aired and cleansed at the discretion
of the Town-Council of such town, and at
the expence of the owner or owners thereof.

Goods clandestinely landed to be forfeited. Sec. 7. *And be it further enacted,* That
all goods imported in such vessel as afore-
said, that shall be clandestinely landed, or
brought into any house, shop or warehouse,
without a certificate and allowance as aforesaid, or that shall be imported by land as
aforesaid, and not cleansed or aired by order of the Town-Council as aforesaid, shall
be forfeited, one third to and for the use of
the State, and the other two thirds to him
or them who shall inform and sue for the
same, in the Court of Common Pleas in the
county where such offence shall be committed. And all Assistants, Justices and
Wardens, are hereby empowered and required, upon information given them, to
seize and secure all such goods, wares and
merchandizes,

merchandizes, in their refpective jurifdictions, until legal trial.

Sec. 8. *And be it further enacted,* That
the Town-Councils of the refpective towns
be, and they are hereby empowered and
directed, to fix, fettle and adjuft, all wages
and charges demanded by perfons employed
by them to fecure fuch veffel, or to air and
cleanfe fuch goods, or to attend upon and
nurfe fuch perfons as aforefaid. And that
if any owner, freighter, mariner or paffenger as aforefaid, fhall refufe to pay fuch
wages and charges fo fettled, adjufted and
fixed by the Town-Council, that then the
Town-Treafurer of fuch town is hereby empowered and required to fue for and recover fuch wages and charges, if above
twenty dollars, in the Court of Common
Pleas in the county where fuch charges fhall
be adjufted and fettled ; and if twenty dollars or under, then before any one Juftice
or Warden, as in the cafe of other actions ;
and the Judges of fuch Court, where fuch
action is brought. are hereby empowered to
tax double cofts for the plaintiff.

Town-Councils to allow the accounts of perfons employed in cleanfing goods, &c.

How to be recovered.

Court may tax double cott.

Sec. 9. *And be it further enacted,* That
for the better fecuring of the payment of
what charges may arife on the nurfing or attendance upon any failor or mariner belonging to fuch veffel as aforefaid, the mafter
thereof is hereby required to ftop payment
of the wages due to fuch mariner, until certified from the Town-Council that fuch
charges are fully fatisfied and paid, on penalty of paying the fame, fo far as the
amount of the wages fo paid by him : And
no Court in this State fhall make up judgment for any fuch wages, until fatisfaction
be made as aforefaid.

Sailors wages to be ftopped, &c.

Sec.

Penalty for coming from an infected place by land, &c.

Sec. 10. *And be it further enacted,* That when the small-pox or any other infectious distemper shall be prevalent in any place or town in the State of Massachusetts or Connecticut, all persons who shall come from such infected town or place into this State by land, until the expiration of ten days after they shall have left such infected town or place, shall forfeit and pay a sum not exceeding one hundred dollars, nor less than ten dollars, to and for the use of the State, upon legal conviction thereof before any two Justices of the Peace or Wardens, who are hereby empowered to hear and try the same, and also to send back or confine said offenders in some convenient place, not exceeding fifteen days: And the Town-Council in any town in this State are hereby empowered to appoint proper persons at all ferries or places, that to them may seem necessary, to examine, on oath or affirmation, all persons suspected to transgress this law, and on reasonable cause of suspicion, to bring such offenders before said Justices of the Peace or Wardens, that they may be dealt with according to law.

Town-Councils may appoint persons to guard ferries, &c.

Tavern-keepers, &c. to give notice of infected lodgers.

Sec. 11. *And be it further enacted,* That all persons who keep public houses or boarders in their houses, shall immediately acquaint the next Assistant, Justice of the Peace or Warden of the town wherein they dwell, when any person boarding or lodging in their house is taken sick of the small-pox or any other contagious distemper, or suspected to be so, on the penalty of forfeiting twenty dollars to and for the use of the town, to be recovered by the Town-Treasurer before any two Justices of the Peace or Wardens of said town; and the

Assistant,

Affiftant, Juftice of the Peace or Warden, fo notified, is hereby empowered and directed to make proper examination by fome phyfician or other fkilful perfon, and if it be the fmall-pox or other contagious diftemper wherewith fuch fick perfon is vifited, then immediately to fet a proper guard to pre- Guard to be fet. vent the fpreading of the infection, and to fummon the Town-Council of fuch town, who are hereby authorized and empowered Town-Council to remove faid perfon, being an inmate or may remove the boarder in any houfe in any town in this perfon, &c. State, to any fuch place in faid town as they fhall think the moft proper, to prevent the fpreading of the infection, or to continue the faid guard as aforefaid, according as to them fhall feem neceffary; and likewife to confine all fuch perfons as may be by them fufpected to have taken the diftemper, in fome proper place, until they are recovered and cleanfed from the faid diftemper, or have performed a fuitable quarantine.

Sec. 12. *And be it further enacted*, That Expences of when the fmall-pox or other contagious guarding, &c. by diftemper fhall break out in any houfe, and whom to be paid. the infected perfon or perfons be confined to fuch houfe, the town wherein the houfe may be fhall be at the expence of guarding the fame, and the owner at the charge of cleanfing the fame, to be fettled and adjuft- ed by the Town-Council, which charge of cleanfing (upon refufal to pay the fame) fhall be recovered by the Town-Treafurer.

Sec. 13. *And be it further enacted*, That Juftices, &c. in cafe the fmall-pox or other contagious may remove in- diftemper fhall break out in any houfe or fected perfons, family in any town within this State, the houfes to be guarded. Affiftants, Juftices of the Peace or Ward- ens in faid town, together with the Town- Council

Council thereof, be and they are hereby fully empowered to remove any inhabitants of said town, visited with the small-pox or other contagious distemper, to the hospital in said town, or other convenient place, in order to prevent the spreading of the infection, or otherwise, at their discretion, to place a guard round the dwelling-house of the infected person, as to them shall seem necessary.

House infected, not to be entered without licence.

Sec. 14. *And be it further enacted,* That so long as the Town-Council of any town shall endeavour to prevent the spreading of the small-pox, no person whatsoever, under any pretence whatsoever, shall presume to visit any person suspected to have the small-pox, or to go into the house where suspected persons are confined, without a licence first had from the Town-Council, or from one Assistant, or from two or more Justices of the Peace or Wardens of the town, on the penalty of forfeiting, for every such

Penalty.

offence, twenty dollars, one half to and for the use of the town where such offence is committed, and the other half to him or them who shall inform and sue for the same, in the Court of Common Pleas in the county where such offence shall be committed ; and such person or persons, on information of their offence, shall be liable to be confined, until they are suitably aired and cleansed, or have performed a suitable quarantine, at the discretion of the Town-Council, to whom complaint of the same shall be made.

Penalty for wilfully spreading any contagious disease.

Sec. 15. *And be it further enacted,* That any person or persons, who shall be legally convicted of wilfully and purposely spreading the small-pox or other contagious distemper

temper within this State, shall be imprisoned and subjected to hard labour for one
year; and if any person shall die in consequence of the spreading of the small-pox or
other contagious distemper as aforesaid, the
person or persons who shall be legally convicted of wilfully and purposely spreading
the same as aforesaid, shall suffer death.

Sec. 16. *And be it further enacted,* That
it shall and may be lawful for any two or
more Assistants, Justices of the Peace or
Wardens, in any town in this State, having reason to suspect that any person or persons have endeavoured wickedly and wilfully to spread the small-pox or other contagious distemper in any town in this State,
to commit such person or persons to gaol,
there to remain until he, she or they, give
good and sufficient security to appear at the
next Supreme Judicial Court in the county where the offence shall be committed, and
to be of good behaviour during said time:
Provided, nothing in this act shall be construed or understood to extend to such
practitioners in physic as shall be allowed by
the Town-Council to inoculate for the
small-pox, after the said Town-Council
have thought fit to desist their endeavours
to prevent the further spreading of the
same.

Suspected persons may be committed.

Proviso.

Sec. 17. *And be it further enacted,* That
if any physician, surgeon, or any other person or persons, lawfully required by the
Governor or Lieutenant-Governor, or by
any two Assistants, Justices or Wardens, or
by any Town-Council in this State, to do
any duty relating to the preventing of the
spreading of the small-pox, or executing any
part of this act, shall refuse or neglect to
perform

Penalty for phy- sicians, &c. refu- sing to do their duty.

perform the same (the performance whereof being in his or their power) such physician, surgeon, and all and every other person and persons whatsoever, who shall so refuse or neglect, shall for every offence forfeit the sum of forty dollars; to be recovered in the same manner as other fines and forfeitures are herein directed to be recovered.

Town-Councils may permit inoculation.

Sec. 18. *And be it further enacted*, That the Town-Councils of the several towns within this State be, and they are hereby fully authorized and empowered, to grant permission for inoculation for the small-pox in their respective towns, under such conditions and regulations as they shall direct.

Make regulations for the preservation of the health of the inhabitants, &c.

Sec. 19. *And be it further enacted*, That the Town-Councils of the respective towns be and they are hereby fully authorized to make and prescribe such orders and regulations as they may deem prudent and advisable, for the preservation of the health of the inhabitants, by the prevention and removal of nuisances injurious thereto, or any other causes, which in their judgment may originate, or conduce to the spreading of any infectious disease : That they be authorized to annex such pecuniary penalties for the breach of the orders and regulations which they shall make and prescribe, relative to the object aforesaid, as they shall adjudge adequate and necessary to effectuate the same : That said penalties may be prosecuted and recovered by action of debt before any Court proper to try the same, one moiety whereof shall be for the use of the town wherein the offence shall be, and the other moiety for the use of him or her who shall sue for the same : And if such nuisances, or other causes injurious to the health of
the

the inhabitants, as aforesaid, shall not be removed by the person permitting or erecting the same, pursuant to any order or regulation of the Town-Council for the town, it shall be the duty of the Town-Council thereupon, and they are hereby fully authorized and empowered, to adopt such measures as they shall deem effectual for the removal of such nuisances or other causes injurious to the health of the inhabitants, as aforesaid, at the proper charge and expence of the person erecting or permitting the same.   And that the Sheriff, his Deputies, and the Town-Sergeants and Constables of the several towns, shall execute all such precepts and orders as shall be to them directed by said Town-Councils, for carrying this act into execution.

May remove nuisances, &c.

Sheriff, &c. to execute the orders of the Councils.

Sec. 20. *And be it further enacted*, That his Excellency the Governor be and he is hereby authorized and requested, at such times and seasons as occasion may require, to appoint a health officer at each and every port where he shall think such an officer necessary, whose duty it shall be, under the directions of the Governor, to visit all vessels suspected of having contagion on board, and to carry into effect the provisions of this act.

Governor may appoint health officers.

An Act *ascertaining what shall constitute a legal Settlement in any Town in this State.*

1727.
1741.
1748.
1765.
1798.
Settlement, how gained.

Section 1.   **B**E *it enacted by the General Assembly, and by the authority thereof it is enacted*, That legal settlements in any town in this State shall be hereafter gained, so as to oblige such town

X x   to

to relieve and support the persons gaining the same, in case they become poor, and stand in need of relief, by any of the ways and means following, and not otherwise, to wit :

Husband and wife, where settled.

First. A married woman shall always follow and have the settlement of the husband, if he hath any settlement in this State, or any other of the United States ; but if he hath no settlement within this State, or in any other of the United States, the wife shall have and retain her settlement, at the time of her marriage ; and the husband in such case shall follow and have the settlement of his wife.

Legitimate children.

Secondly. Legitimate children shall follow and have the settlement of their father, until they arrive to the age of twenty-one years, if the father shall, before that time, have any settlement within this State, or any other of the United States, and shall retain such settlement until they gain a settlement of their own ; but if the father, before that time, shall not have any settlement within this State or any other of the United States, the children shall, in like manner, follow and have the settlement of the mother.

Illegitimate children.

Thirdly. Illegitimate children shall follow and have the settlement of their mother at the time of their birth ; but neither legitimate nor illegitimate children shall gain a settlement by birth, in the places where they may be born, if neither of their parents shall have a settlement there.

Apprentices.

Fourthly. Any minor, who shall serve an apprenticeship to any lawful trade for the space of four years, in any town, and actually set up the same therein, within three years after the expiration of the said term, being

then

then twenty-one years of age, and continue to carry on the fame for the fpace of five years therein, fhall thereby gain a fettlement in fuch town; but fuch perfon being hired as a journeyman, fhall not be confidered as fetting up a trade.

Fifthly. Any perfon of twenty-one years of age, having an eftate of inheritance or freehold in the town where he fhall dwell and have his home, of the yearly income of twenty dollars, and taking the rents and profits thereof for three years fucceffively, whether he lives thereupon or not, fhall thereby gain a fettlement therein. *Settlement, how to be gained by real eftate.*

Sixthly. Any perfon of twenty-one years of age, having an eftate, the principal of which fhall be fet at two hundred dollars in the valuation of eftates, made by the Affeffors, and being affeffed for the fame in the State and town taxes, and actually paying the fame, for the fpace of five years fucceffively, in the town where he dwells and hath his home, fhall thereby gain a fettlement therein. *By the eftimated value of an eftate.*

Seventhly. Any perfon of twenty-one years of age, who fhall hereafter refide in any town in this State for the fpace of ten years together, and pay all State and town taxes, duly affeffed upon fuch perfon's poll or eftate, for any five years within faid time, fhall thereby gain a fettlement in fuch town. *By paying taxes.*

Sec. 2. *And be it further enacted,* That every legal fettlement, when gained, fhall continue until loft or defeated by gaining a new one. And upon gaining fuch new fettlement, all former fettlements fhall be defeated and loft. *Settlement, how long to continue.*

An

An Act providing for the Relief, Support, Employment and Removal of the Poor.

Towns to support their poor.

Section 1. BE *it enacted by the General Assembly, and by the authority thereof it is enacted,* That every town in this State shall be holden to relieve and support all poor and indigent persons, lawfully settled therein, whenever they shall stand in need thereof; and may vote and raise monies therefor, and for their employment, in the same way that monies for other town charges are raised; and shall also, at their **To choose overseers of the poor.** annual meeting in June, choose any number (not exceeding five) of suitable persons dwelling therein for overseers of the poor.

Their duty.

Sec. 2. *And be it further enacted,* That said overseers shall have the care and oversight of all such poor and indigent persons, so settled in their respective towns, and shall see that they are suitably relieved, supported and employed, either in the work-house, or other tenements belonging to such towns, or in such other way and manner as the inhabitants of the respective towns, at any legal meeting, shall direct, or otherwise at the discretion of said overseers, at the cost of such town.

Fathers, &c. to maintain their children, &c.

Sec. 3. *Provided always, and be it further enacted,* That the kindred of any such poor person, if any he shall have, in the line or degree of father or grand-father, mother or grand-mother, children or grand-children, by consanguinity, living within this State, and of sufficient ability, shall be holden to **May be compelled by the Supreme Court.** support such pauper, in proportion to such ability. And the Supreme Judicial Court, at any term thereof, in any county where
any

any such kindred to be charged shall reside, upon complaint made by the overseer or overseers of the poor of any town, who shall have been at any expence for the relief and support of any such pauper, may, on due hearing, either upon the appearance or default of the kindred, they being summoned, as hereafter prescribed, assess and apportion such sum as they shall judge reasonable therefor, upon such of said kindred as they shall judge of sufficient ability and according thereto, to the time of such assessment, with costs, and may enforce payment thereof by warrant of distress. And the overseer or overseers of any town, complaining as aforesaid, may file their complaint in the Clerk's office of the Court to which such complaint shall be made, and may take out a summons thereon under the seal of said Court, signed by the Clerk thereof, and directed to some proper officer to serve an original summons; which being served by leaving an attested copy thereof with the party to be summoned, or at his last and usual place of abode, twenty days before the sitting of the Court, shall hold him to answer to such complaint: *Provided neverthe-* Proviso. *less,* such assessment shall not extend to any expence for any relief afforded more than six months previous to the filing such complaint. And the said Court may further assess and apportion upon such kindred such weekly sum for the future, as they shall judge sufficient for the support of such pauper, to be paid quarterly, until further order of said Court; and upon application, from time to time, of the overseers of the poor to whom the same shall have been ordered to be paid, the Clerk of said Court shall issue and may

renew

renew a warrant of diftrefs, for the arrears
of any preceding quarter. And the faid
Court may further order with whom of fuch
kindred, who may defire it, fuch pauper
fhall live and be relieved, and for fuch time
with one, and fuch time with another, as
they fhall judge proper, having regard to the
comfort of the pauper as well as the con-
venience of the kindred. And upon fug-
geftion, other kindred of ability not named
in the complaint may be notified, and the
procefs may be continued, and upon due
notice, whether they appear or are default-
ed, the Court may proceed againft. them in
the fame manner as if they had been named
in the complaint ; but if fuch complaint be
not entered, or be difcontinued or with-
drawn, or be adjudged groundlefs, the re-
fpondents fhall recover cofts. And faid
Court may take further order from time to
time in the premifes, upon application of
any party interefted, and may alter fuch
affeffment and apportionment as circumftances may vary.

Sec. 4. *And be it further enacted*, That
faid overfeers be, and they hereby are, empowered, from time to time, to bind out by
deed indented or poll, as apprentices to be
inftructed and employed in any lawful art,
trade or myftery, or as fervants to be employed in any lawful work or labour, any
male or female children, whofe parents are
lawfully fettled in and become chargeable
to their town ; alfo thofe, whofe parents fo
fettled fhall be thought by faid overfeers to
be unable to maintain them, whether they
receive alms, or are fo chargeable or not,
provided they be not affeffed in any town
tax ; and alfo all fuch, who or whofe parents

Overfeers may bind out poor children.

Provifo.

rents refiding in their town are fupported there at the charge of the State, to any citizen of this State; that is to fay, male children until they come to the age of twenty-one years, and females until they come to the age of eighteen, or are married; which binding fhall be as valid and effectual in law as if fuch children had been of the full age of twenty-one years, and had by a like deed bounden themfelves, or their parents had been confenting thereto. And provifion fhall be made in fuch deed for the inftruction of male children fo bounden out, to read, write and cypher, and of females to read and write, and for fuch other inftruction, benefit and allowance, either within or at the end of the time, as to the overfeers may feem fit and reafonable. *Provifion to be made for their education.*

Sec. 5. *And be it further enacted,* That it fhall be the duty of faid overfeers to enquire into the ufage of children, who fhall be bounden out by them by force of this act, and to defend them from injuries; and faid overfeers fhall have the fame remedy in behalf of the perfons fo bounden out as is extended to other apprentices by an act entitled, " An act to fecure to mafters and miftreffes, and to apprentices and minor fervants bounden by deed, their mutual privileges;" and the mafters and miftreffes of fuch apprentices, bounden out by overfeers as aforefaid, fhall have the like remedy againft fuch apprentices, and for the like caufes as are prefcribed in the aforefaid act. *Overfeers to protect them from injury, &c.*

Sec. 6. *And be it further enacted,* That all parties as aforefaid fhall be entitled to an action for the damages they may fuftain for any breach or breaches of contract entered into by fuch deed, and in the fame manner *Action given for breach of covenant.*

as

as is prescribed in and by the aforementioned act.

Sec. 7. *And be it further enacted,* That the said overseers of the poor shall have power to set to work, or bind out to service, by deed as aforesaid, for a term not exceeding one whole year at a time, all such persons residing and lawfully settled in their respective towns, or who have no such settlement within this State, married or unmarried, upwards of twenty-one years of age, as are able of body, but have no visible means of support, who live idly, and use and exercise no ordinary and daily lawful trade or business to get their living by, upon such terms and conditions as such overseers shall think pro-

per: *Provided always,* that any person, thinking him or herself aggrieved by the doings of said overseers in the premises, may apply by complaint to the Supreme Judicial Court in the county where they are bounden, or where the overseers who bound them dwell, for relief; which Court, after due notice to the overseers, and to the master of such person, shall have power, after due hearing and examination, if they find sufficient cause therefor, to liberate and discharge the party complaining from his or her master, and to release him or her from the care of the overseers, or otherwise to dismiss the complaint, and to give costs to either party or not, as the said Court may think reasonable.

Sec. 8. *And be it further enacted,* That if any person shall reside in any town in this State, not being legally settled therein, and shall become or be likely to become chargeable to such town, it shall be lawful for any one of the overseers of the poor of such town to make complaint thereof to the

Town-

Town-Council; and in cafe fuch overfeer
fhall judge it neceffary that an order fhould
be made fooner than the Town-Council are
likely to meet of courfe, he fhall give a notification to the Town-Sergeant to notify the
Town-Council to meet at a time and place
therein named, who upon fuch notification
are required to meet, and are hereby fully
empowered to enquire, either by the oath of
fuch poor perfon or otherwife, in what town
he was laft legally fettled; and upon the beft
information they can obtain to adjudge and
determine to what town or place he lawfully
belongs, or in which he was laft legally fettled; which being done, the Town-Council
fhall make an order, under their feal, to be By order under
figned by their Clerk, for the removal of fuch feal.
perfon to fuch town or place; which order
being directed and given to the Town-Sergeant or one of the Conftables of fuch town,
he fhall proceed forthwith to remove fuch
perfon, and fuch of his family, if any he hath,
as by law ought to be removed with him,
to the town or place to which he is adjudged
by fuch order to belong, and there deliver
him to one of the overfeers of the poor of
fuch town, and leave an authentic copy of
the order with the faid overfeer; and if
fuch overfeer fhall refufe to accept fuch Penalty for re-
poor perfon, he fhall forfeit the fum of fufing to receive
twenty dollars, to be recovered by an action ed.
of debt by the Town-Treafurer of the town
from which fuch poor perfon was fent, to and
for the ufe of the poor of faid town.

Sec. 9. *Provided neverthelefs, and be it
further enacted,* That if any overfeer of the
poor of any town in this State, to which fuch May appeal from
poor perfon or perfons fhall be removed as the order of the
aforefaid, fhall think his town aggrieved Town-Council.

Y y at

at the determination and order of the Town-
Council for the removal of such poor person
or persons, it shall be lawful for him, in behalf of his town, to appeal to the next Supreme Judicial Court to be holden in the
county in which the town, from which such
poor person or persons were removed, lies ;
and the party appealing shall file reasons of
appeal in the Clerk's office of the Court to
which the appeal shall be brought, twenty
days before the sitting of said Court ; and
the Clerk of said Court shall forthwith send
a copy of such reasons of appeal to one of
the overseers of the poor of the town from
which such poor person or persons were
removed ; who upon the receipt of such
copy is hereby fully empowered to appear
at the Court where the appeal is brought,
and to defend and maintain said order of
the Town-Council ; which Court shall have
full power, upon hearing the cause, to confirm or reverse such order, as to them shall
appear agreeable to law ; which judgment
shall be final. And in case the said order
shall be confirmed, the town which appealed
shall pay the whole cost of Court, in which
shall be included the charges of removing
such poor person or persons ; and in case the
said order shall be reversed, then the town
from which such poor person or persons
were removed shall pay the cost of Court,
and also the charges that the town, to which
he or they were removed, shall have been
at, for his or their support between the time
of the removal and the determination of the
appeal ; and such poor person or persons
shall be removed back to said town at the
proper cost and charge thereof, which shall
be

Margin notes:

to the Supreme Court.

Terms of appeal.

What cost, and by whom to be paid.

be levied by an execution againſt the Town-Treaſurer of ſuch town.

Sec. 10. *And be it further enaĉted*, That the Town-Sergeant, or Conſtable, who ſhall be charged with an order for the removal of any poor perſon or perſons as aforeſaid, ſhall have power to go into any town in this State for putting ſuch order into execution, and ſhall make return upon ſaid order to the Town-Council who granted the ſame, at their next meeting, which ſhall be lodged in the Clerk's office ; and he ſhall give copies thereof to any perſon who ſhall deſire them, and ſhall take the ſame fees therefor as in other caſes. And in caſe any Town-Sergeant or Conſtable ſhall refuſe or negleĉt to put ſuch order in execution when delivered to him, he ſhall, for every ſuch refuſal or negleĉt, forfeit the ſum of twenty dollars, to be recovered by the Town-Treaſurer, at the Court of Common Pleas of the county in which the town, where ſaid forfeiture ariſes, lies, or before a Juſtices Court in ſaid town, to and for the uſe of the poor of ſaid town. And the Town-Sergeant or Conſtable, who ſhall remove any poor perſon or perſons as by this aĉt is direĉted, ſhall be allowed and paid, at the diſcretion of the Town-Council, for his trouble, out of the treaſury of the town from which ſuch perſon or perſons ſhall be removed.

Order of removal how to be executed.

Penalty for negleĉt.

Sec. 11. *And be it further enaĉted*, That it ſhall be in the power and at the diſcretion of every Town-Council, to refuſe any bond or certificate which may be offered for keeping their town indemnified from charge, by any perſon who ſhall come into it, of bad fame and reputation, or ſuch as the Town-Council ſhall judge unſuitable perſons to
become

Town-Councils may refuſe bond or certificate of indemnity.

become inhabitants thereof ; and, upon their refusal to accept the bond or certificate offered, to proceed in manner aforesaid to remove such person out of such town for whom bond or certificate may have been tendered and not accepted.

Penalty on paupers for returning.

Sec. 12. *And be it further enacted,* That if any person, who shall be sent out of any town agreeably to this act, shall voluntarily return thither again, without leave first obtained of the Town-Council for so doing, such person shall be fined by the Town-Council not exceeding seven dollars, to and for the use of the poor of such town ; and in default of paying the same, shall be publicly whipped, at the discretion of the Town-Council, not exceeding twenty-nine stripes.

Town-Councils may remove persons of bad fame, &c.

Sec. 13. *And be it further enacted,* That the respective Town-Councils shall have power in their discretion to remove as aforesaid all persons not settled in their respective towns, who are of bad fame and reputation, or such as said Town-Council shall determine to be unsuitable persons to become inhabitants thereof, though such persons shall not, at the time of such removal, have become, or shall not then be likely to become, chargeable to such town. And if such persons shall have no legal settlement in any of the United States, the Town-Council

May bind them out, in case.

shall have a right to warn such persons to depart from such town, within a limited time, and upon their refusal so to do, to bind out such persons to service for one year to any citizen of the United States.

Paupers not settled in the United States to be supported by the State.

Sec. 14. *And be it further enacted,* That if any person, not having a legal settlement in any of the United States, shall become chargeable

chargeable to any town in this State, he
shall be supported at the expence of the
State.

Sec. 15. *And be it further enacted*, That
in case any tavern-keeper, inn-holder, vic-
tualler, or any other person whosoever, inhabiting in any town within this State, shall
entertain or keep in his or her house any
single person or family, being strangers, for
more than one whole week from the time of
their coming into such town, without giving
notice thereof in writing to the President of
the Town-Council, such person so offending
shall forfeit and pay a fine of seven dollars
for every such offence, to be recovered by
the Town-Treasurer of such town, before
any Justice or Warden, to and for the use of
such town.

*Persons enter-
taining strangers
to give notice to
the Town-Coun-
cil.*

Sec. 16. *And be it further enacted*, That
if any person shall bring and leave any poor
and indigent person in any town in this
State, wherein such pauper is not lawfully
settled, unless by an order of removal made
by a Town-Council in this State, knowing
him to be poor and indigent, he shall forfeit
and pay the sum of one hundred dollars for
every such offence, to be sued for and recovered in an action of debt by the Town-
Treasurer, to and for the use of such town.

*Penalty for
bringing paupers
into any town
without an order.*

Sec. 17. *And be it further enacted*, That
if any master or other person, having charge
of any vessel, shall bring into and land, or
suffer to be landed, in any place within this
State, any person before that time convicted,
in any other State or in any foreign country,
of any infamous crime, or of any crime for
which he hath been sentenced to transportation, knowing of such conviction, or having
reason to suspect it, or any person of a notoriously

*For bringing
convicts, &c. into
the State.*

rioufly diffolute, infamous and abandoned life and character, knowing him or her to be fuch, fhall, for every fuch offence, forfeit the fum of four hundred dollars, one half thereof to the ufe of the State, and the other half to the ufe of any perfon, being a citizen of and refiding within this State, who may profecute and fue for the fame by action of debt as aforefaid.

Sec. 18. *And be it further enacted,* That the mafter or any other perfon having the charge of any veffel arriving at any place within this State with any paffengers on board, from any foreign dominion or country, without the United States of America, fhall, within forty-eight hours after fuch arrival, or before landing any fuch paffenger, make a report in writing under his hand of all fuch paffengers, their names, nation, age, character and condition, fo far as fhall have come to his knowledge, to the overfeers of the poor of the town at which fuch veffel fhall arrive. And every fuch mafter or other perfon, who fhall neglect to make fuch report, or who fhall wittingly and willingly make a falfe one, fhall for each of thefe offences forf it the fum of two hundred dollars, to be fued for and recovered by action of debt as aforefaid by the Town-Treafurer, to the ufe of fuch town.

Matters of veffels to report to the overfeers the names, &c. of their paffengers.

Penalty for neglect.

An

An Act empowering the Overseers of the Poor, 1765.
or Work-House, in the Town of Newport, 1798.
more effectually to secure said Town from
Costs and Expences arising from idle and
disorderly Persons.

Section 1. **B**E it enacted by the General *Overseers of the*
Assembly, and by the authority *poor and of the*
work-house may
thereof it is enacted, That the overseers of *commit idle per-*
the poor in the town of Newport, or any *fons.*
two of them, or the overseers of the work-
house in said town for the time being, be
and they are hereby fully empowered to
commit all such idle, indigent persons, as
shall from time to time be found in the said
town, who by their ill courses are likely to
become a town charge, to the work-house.
And for the better enabling said overseers to
perform said service, they are hereby fully
empowered to command the Town-Sergeant,
or any of the Constables of said town, to
assist them as often as occasion shall require.
And said overseers, or any two of them, are
also empowered to grant forth a warrant to
the Town-Sergeant or any of the Constables
in said town, to take up any such person or
persons as cannot give a good account of
themselves, or of their way of living, and
commit them to the work-house. And the
said Town-Sergeant and Constables shall also
have power to command aid, if it shall be
necessary.

Sec. 2. *And be it further enacted*, That *May bind out*
the said overseers be and they are hereby *persons commit-*
ted to the work-
empowered to bind out any such person or *house, and poor*
persons as have been committed to the *children;*
work-house, if it appears they are liable to
become chargeable to the town, for a term
of

of time not exceeding four years. And
the Town-Clerk of faid Newport fhall fign
the indentures for fuch perfons as the overfeers of faid work-houfe fhall order to be
bounden out; and the faid overfeers are
alfo empowered to take up any child or
children who are likely to become chargeable to the town, and bind them out apprentices to fome credible perfon or perfons,
either in or out of the State; and the Town-
Clerk fhall fign the indentures.

take up ftrag-
glers,

Sec. 3. *And be it further enaffed,* That
the faid overfeers of the work-houfe be and
they are hereby fully empowered to take
up any ftraggling perfons who do not belong
to faid town, and if they cannot give a good
account of themfelves, to commit them to
the work-houfe; and in cafe they belong to
any other town in this State, or do not belong to the State, the faid overfeers of the
work-houfe are hereby empowered to fend

and remove
them to the
place of their
fettlement.

fuch perfon or perfons to the town where
they belong, in the manner as hath heretofore been cuftomary, agreeably to law.

May commit
Indians,

Sec. 4. *And be it further enaffed,* That
the overfeers of the work-houfe fhall have
power to take up, or order the Town-Sergeant or Conftables of the town to take up,
any Indian or Indians, who are tippling and
idling their time away about the town, and
commit them to the work-houfe, until
they fhall have a convenient opportunity to
fend them to the town where they belong,

remove them to
the place of their
fettlement,

which fhall be done in the fame manner as
above directed. And in cafe any difpute
fhall arife between the faid overfeers of the
work-houfe, and the overfeers of the poor of
the town where fuch Indian or Indians may
be fent, and faid Indians be returned to the

town

town of Newport, then the ſaid overſeers of the work-houſe ſhall have full power to bind out ſuch Indian or Indians to ſervice, for a term not exceeding four years.

And bind them out, in caſe.

Sec. 5. *And be it further enacted*, That in caſe the overſeers of the poor of any town, to which ſuch perſon or perſons ſhall be removed, ſhall think themſelves aggrieved at the determination and order of the ſaid overſeers of the work-houſe, they ſhall have the ſame liberty of appealing as they now have from a determination of the Town-Council.

Appeal granted from their order.

Sec. 6. *And be it further enacted*, That if any perſon or perſons whoſoever ſhall get into the work-houſe, or attempt to get in, contrary to the orders of the overſeers or keeper of the work-houſe, ſuch perſon ſo offending (ſufficient proof thereof being made) ſhall pay, as a fine, a ſum not exceeding ſeven dollars, to and for the uſe of the town, to be recovered before any two Juſtices of the Peace of ſaid town : And any perſon or perſons in the town of Newport, who ſhall knowingly entertain or harbour any perſon or perſons who ſhall leave the work-houſe, without leave or licenſe had from the overſeers or keeper of the work-houſe, and ſhall not immediately give notice thereof to one of the ſaid overſeers or keeper of the work-houſe, ſhall pay as a fine a ſum not exceeding ſeven dollars, to be recovered and applied in manner as before directed.

Perſons getting into the work-houſe, &c. without licenſe, to be fined.

Sec. 7. *And be it further enacted*, That the freemen of ſaid town of Newport ſhall have full power and authority to make ſuch rules and orders, for the well governing of ſaid work-houſe, and for inflicting corporal

Freemen may make laws for the government of the work-houſe.

Z z   puniſhment

puniſhment on any of the perſons committed
to the ſaid work-houſe, as they ſhall think
fit.

**1796.
1798.**

*An Act for the better ordering of the Police
of the Town of Providence, and of the
Work-Houſe in ſaid Town.*

Regulations for
the government
of the work-
houſe eſtabliſh-
ed.

Section 1. **B**E it enacted by the General
*Aſſembly, and by the autho-
rity thereof it is enacted,* That the regulations heretofore adopted under the authority of the town of Providence, in town-
meeting aſſembled, for the government of
the work-houſe in ſaid town, and to this
act ſubjoined, be and they are hereby eſtabliſhed as regulations for the good government of the ſaid work-houſe.

Sec. 2. *And be it further enacted,* That
the Town-Council of the ſaid town of Providence be, and the ſaid Council is hereby
empowered, from time to time hereafter,
to alter and amend the ſaid regulations, or
expunge ſuch as may ſeem to them erroneous
or unneceſſary, or add ſuch new articles
as may to them ſeem neceſſary.

May be altered
by the Town-
Council.

And whereas by reaſon of the exiſting
laws of ſeveral of the neighbouring States,
it is often attended with great trouble and
expence, and in ſome caſes utterly impoſſi-
ble, to convey perſons rejected by the ſaid
Town-Council to the place of their legal
ſettlement :

Sec. 3. *Be it therefore further enacted,*
That the ſaid Town-Council may, upon the
examination and rejection of any tranſient
perſon or perſons, remove them to the place
of their legal ſettlement, or (if likely to
become

Town-Council
may remove per-
ſons, or commit
them to the
work-houſe.

become chargeable) commit them to faid work-houfe, to be there provided for and kept to labour: And the faid Town-Council is hereby further empowered to commit to the faid houfe, or Bridewell thereto belonging, any perfon, who, having been legally removed from the faid town, fhall return to refide therein, contrary to their order of removal. And in cafe any tranfient perfon, who is ordered to appear, or be brought before the faid Council for examination, fhall fecrete himfelf or herfelf to elude the officer, the faid Council may order the proper officer to take fuch perfon into cuftody, whenever found by him, and commit him or her to the faid work-houfe until his or her examination be legally taken.

May commit perfons who have been removed and returned, &c.

Sec. 4. *And be it further enacted,* That any perfon, an inhabitant of the faid town of Providence, who fhall be convicted before any Court of Juftices in the county of Providence of ftealing or purloining any goods, wares, merchandize or other thing, not exceeding the value of forty dollars, fhall, in default of paying the fine adjudged by the faid Court, be committed to the faid Bridewell for a term of time not exceeding one year: And in default of paying the coft and reftitution adjudged by the faid Court, fuch delinquent fhall be put to hard labour in the faid work-houfe, under the exifting regulations thereof, until he or fhe fhall difcharge faid coft and reftitution, or be otherwife legally difcharged therefrom: But if fuch delinquent be not an inhabitant of the faid town of Providence, but a tranfient perfon, or refident in the faid town without a legal fettlement therein, the faid Court may, at difcretion, fentence him or her as herein before

Perfons convicted of theft may be committed to Bridewell, in cafe.

before provided, or proceed according to the ſtatute in ſuch caſes heretofore made.

Alſo perſons convicted of aſſault, &c.

Sec. 5. *And be it further enacted,* That any perſon convicted before any Court of Juſtices in the ſaid town of Providence of an aſſault or battery, in default of paying the fine adjudged by the ſaid Court, ſhall be committed to the ſaid Bridewell for a term of time, at the diſcretion of the Court. not exceeding ſix months; and in default of paying coſts, ſhall be kept to hard labour in the ſaid work-houſe, under the exiſting regulations thereof, until legally diſcharged therefrom.

Or riotous behaviour.

Sec. 6. *And be it further enacted,* That the Town-Council, or any Aſſiſtant, Judge of a Court, or Juſtice of the Peace in the ſaid town of Providence, may, upon the complaint of a freeholder, or other reſpectable perſon, or from facts within his or their own knowledge, call before him or them any drunken, riotous or diſorderly perſon or perſons, who may be detected in revelling in the ſtreets, committing any ſort of miſchief, quarrelling, or otherwiſe behaving in a riotous and diſorderly manner, to the diſturbance and annoyance of the peaceable. citizens of ſaid town, and him, her or them commit to the ſaid Bridewell, for a time not exceeding twenty-four hours, which commitment ſhall be by a mittimus in writing under hand and ſeal, ſtating the offence, and directed to the Town-Sergeant or Conſtable, to convey, and to the keeper of ſaid work-houſe to receive, the perſon or perſons ſo offending into his cuſtody.

Vagrants, &c. may be committed to the workhouſe.

Sec. 7. *And be it further enacted,* That upon complaint being made to the ſaid Town-Council, or any Juſtice of the Peace

in

in the faid town of Providence, againft any idle vagrant perfon, or any perfon who, having no family, has been examined by the faid Town-Council, and ordered to depart, or any perfon who fhall attempt to procure a living by begging in the ftreets, houfes or elfewhere, the faid Town-Council or Juftice fhall, upon due proof being made, commit fuch perfon to the faid work-houfe, for a term of time not exceeding one month, in manner as aforefaid, there to be kept to labour.

Sec. 8. *And be it further enacted,* That if any officer, to whom any precept fhall be directed as aforefaid, fhall refufe or neglect to execute the fame, upon complaint and due proof of fuch delinquency being made before any one Juftice of the Peace in the faid town, fuch delinquent fhall pay to and for the ufe of the faid town of Providence the fum of twenty dollars, with cofts of profecution. And any freeman of the faid town may fue for and profecute the fame to final iffue : *Provided,* that nothing in this act fhall be conftrued to preclude any perfon from the right of appeal, in any cafe heretofore allowed by law. *And it is further provided,* that no part of the expence attending the government of the faid work-houfe fhall be chargeable on the State, except the maintenance of perfons committed for theft, or affault or battery, who fhall be allowed the fame fupport as is allowed poor prifoners in gaol.

Penalty for officers neglecting to execute precepts.

Provifo.

REGULATIONS for the Government of the Work-Houfe in Providence, by the preceding Act eftablifhed.

Duty of the Overfeers.

The overfeers for the time being fhall meet at the work-houfe ftatedly, on the firft Monday

Monday in June, September, December
and March, and at such other times as
shall be found necessary, as occurrences
may happen. The business of such stated
meetings shall be, to enquire into the state
of the work-house, and, as far as may be,
remedy any inconvenience, settle the keeper's accounts, and do such other business as
the nature of their appointment may require.
The said overseers shall appoint one of their
number, whose duty it shall be to visit the
work-house weekly, and inspect into the conduct of the keeper, and the situation and conduct of those under his charge, which appointment shall continue for such term as
may be agreed upon by the overseers : Which
visiting overseer shall call a special meeting of all the overseers, whenever he may
deem it necessary.

Duty of the Keeper.

The keeper of the work-house shall be
allowed such compensation, together with
such room for the use of his family, as may
be agreed upon by the committee appointed
for that purpose, to be paid out of the
town-treasury quarterly. He shall also be
allowed fifty per cent. of all the neat earn-
ings of those under his care : He shall
carefully inspect into the moral conduct of
the paupers, and whoever may be committed
to his care : He shall enjoin strict attention
to the regulations relative to cleanliness,
sobriety and industry : He shall also, with
the approbation of the overseers, provide
a sufficient stock of materials for the constant
employment of those under his care : He
shall also allot to each one a reasonable task,
according to his abilities : He shall be
careful that no embezzlement take place,
                                        but,

but, by all laudable means in his power, shall make their work as profitable as possible : He shall cause all accounts concerning the maintenance of those put under his care to be entered in a book or books provided for that purpose, taking care to have his accounts so entered as that the expence of each individual may be separately ascertained : He shall keep separate accounts of the stock and materials purchased by him, and shall take proper vouchers whenever money is expended : He shall regularly credit the materials manufactured and sold, mentioning when and to whom disposed of, and at every quarterly meeting of the overseers shall exhibit his accounts and vouchers, for their approbation and allowance : He shall keep an exact register of all persons committed to his charge, noting their particular descriptions, and the time when they were entered and discharged : He shall be responsible for the execution of the several duties herein before mentioned, together with the regulations hereafter expressed, for the fulfilment of which he shall give bond to the satisfaction of the committee.

Rules for the Government of the Poor.

1. The males and females shall be employed and lodged in separate apartments, unless it shall so happen that a husband and his wife shall both be in the work-house at the same time.

2. The paupers shall be constantly employed in such work as the overseers and keeper may consider most profitable.

3. If any person or persons admitted or committed to said house, shall be found remiss or negligent in performing the task allotted to them, they shall be punished by
having

having their allowance of food reduced in
such manner, and for such time, as shall enforce a compliance under the direction of
the visiting overseer.

4. If any one shall refuse to obey the
keeper, or shall be guilty of profane cursing,
swearing, or of indecent behaviour, conver-
sation or expression, or of any assault, quarrel
or abusive words. to or with any other person,
he shall be punished by close solitary con-
finement, together with a reduction of his
allowance; but the keeper, in such cases,
shall have the advice and approbation of the
visiting overseer, who shall with him examine into the case; but in cases where
the security of the house is in danger, or
personal violence offered to the keeper, or
any person or persons acting under him,
they shall use all lawful means to defend
themselves, and secure the authors and abettors of such outrage.

5. The keeper shall not suffer any buying,
selling or bartering, to be carried on by any of
those under his care, either among themselves
or with any other person; neither shall he
suffer any spirituous or fermented liquors to
be introduced, except such as he may use
in his own family, or for medical purposes,
prescribed by the physician who may have
the care of the sick: And if any person under his care shall be detected in dealing
in such liquor, or intoxicated therewith,
he or she shall be proceeded against as
provided in the fourth article.

6. All persons, on their first admission,
shall be separately lodged, washed and
cleansed, together with their clothes, if
found necessary.

7. Any person detected in gaming of any
kind,

kind, fhall be proceeded againft as in the fourth article.

8. Any perfon who fhall demand or exact a garnifh, beg, fteal or defraud, fhall be proceeded againft as in the fourth article.

9. Thofe who fhall diftinguifh themfelves by their attention to cleanlinefs, fobriety and orderly conduct, fhall be reported to the overfeers, and meet with fuch reward as is in their power to grant or procure.

10. The men belonging to the houfe fhall be furnifhed with fuitable bedding, fhall be fhaved twice a week, fhall have their hair cut once a month, change their linen once a week, and regularly wafh their faces and hands every morning; the like attention fhall be paid to the women agreeably to their fex.

11. The houfe fhall be whitewafhed at leaft twice in the year, and oftener if neceffary; the floors fwept every morning, and wafhed on Wednefdays and Saturdays, from the twentieth of May to the firft of October, and once a week for the remainder of the year.

12. The phyfician appointed annually to attend the poor, fhall keep a regifter of all the fick, their diforders and his prefcriptions, and fhall render his accounts for the examination and allowance of the overfeers at each of their quarterly meetings.

An Act for filling up certain low Grounds, covered with ftagnant Water, in the compact Part of the Town of Providence. 1797.

WHEREAS it hath been reprefented unto this Affembly, that certain low grounds in the compact part of the town of Providence are covered with ftagnant water, to the great prejudice of the inhabitants in the vicinity of such places:

For remedy whereof;

Section 1. *Be it enacted by the General Assembly, and by the authority thereof it is enacted,* That upon information being given of any such place or places to the Town-Council of the said town, the said Town-Council shall appoint a committee to examine the place or places so complained of, and make report thereof to them; that if, on the report of such committee, it shall be the opinion of the said Town-Council that such place or places ought, for the security of the inhabitants, to be filled up, they shall by their Sergeant, or other proper officer, notify the owner or owners of such lands, or, if non-residents, his, her or their agent or attorney, that they fill the same within a time to be limited by the said Town-Council; and that upon the refusal or neglect of such owner or owners, his, her or their agent or attorney, to fill up such low grounds with earth, within the time limited as aforesaid, the said Town-Council shall appoint a proper person or persons to fill the same with earth, of such depth as they may think necessary.

Town-Council to cause ground covered with water to be filled up.

Sec. 2. *And be it further enacted,* That the accounts for all such services, as aforesaid, shall be presented to the Town-Auditors of the said town, and be by them audited, and the sums allowed certified; that the owner or owners of such lot or lots of land, or his, her or their agent or attorney, shall be notified of the same. in the manner herein before provided; and that upon the refusal or neglect of such owner or owners, his, her or their agent or attorney, to pay the

Accounts therefor to be audited, and paid by the Town-Treasurer, in case.

the bills fo audited, the faid Town-Council fhall give an order or orders on the Town-Treafurer of the faid town for the amount of the fame, who is hereby authorized to pay the amount of fuch bills out of the Town-Treafury.

Sec. 3. *And be it further enacted,* That the faid Town-Treafurer, upon his accept- Town-Treafurer ance of fuch order or orders, fhall be and to profecute for hereby is authorized and empowered to fue the fame. for and recover the amount of the fame, with cofts, in an action of debt, to be commenced and profecuted by him againft the owner or owners of fuch lots or places fo filled up ; that the writ in fuch action of debt may and fhall be levied upon fuch lots or places fo filled up ; and the fame fhall and may be fold on execution, to fatisfy the judgments which may be obtained in fuch actions of debt, according to law : That if, after fatis-fying fuch executions, any furplus arifing from the fale fhall remain, fuch furplus fhall be paid to fuch owner or owners, his, her or their agent or attorney, by the Sheriff, he taking his, her or their receipt for the fame. And if fuch owner or owners, agent or at-torney, are not to be found within this State, or fhall refufe to receive the fame, the Sheriff fhall lodge fuch furplus in the town-trea-fury of the faid town, to be paid to fuch owner or owners, or to his, her or their agent or attorney, or other proper reprefent-ative.

Sec. 4. *And be it further enacted,* That if, in the opinion of the faid Town-Council, it fhall Town-Council be neceffary to carry a ditch, drain or fink, may order drains. for the general accommodation of any part of the faid town, through any lots or lands, the proprietors of fuch lots or lands fhall pay

for

for the expence of doing the ſame, in proportion to the advant.ges they ſhall derive
therefrom ; to be aſſeſſed by a committee to
be appointed by the ſaid Town-Council, and
to be collected in the manner herein before
provided.

_____

1752.
1769.
1786.
1792.
1795.
1798.

On the examina-
tion of an unmar-
ried woman, with
child, a warrant
to be iſſued a-
gainſt the perſon
accuſed.

To whom direct-
ed.

An Act regulating the Proceedings in Caſes
of Baſtardy.

Section 1. BE *it enacted by the General*
          Aſſembly, and by the autho-
rity thereof it is enacted, That upon the examination of any unmarried woman, taken
on oath in writing, in conſequence of a
complaint made under the hand of one or
more of the overſeers of the poor of the
town where ſuch unmarried woman ſhall reſide or belong, that ſhe is with child, it ſhall
be lawful for any Juſtice of the Peace or
Warden of either of ſuch towns, to grant
forth a warrant or ſummons againſt the perſon whom ſhe ſhall ſo charge with getting
her with child ; which warrant or ſummons,
in caſe the perſon ſo charged ſhall live or
may be found in any other town in the
county than the town liable to become
chargeable for the ſupport of ſuch child,
when born, ſhall be directed to the Sheriff
of the county, his deputy, or to the Town-
Sergeant of the town where ſuch unmarried
woman ſhall reſide or belong, who are hereby authorized and empowered to execute
ſuch warrant or ſummons, in any town in
ſuch county ; but if the perſon ſo charged
ſhall live in the ſame town with ſuch unmarried woman, the warrant or ſummons may be
directed for ſervice to the Sheriff, his deputy, or to the Town-Sergeant, or to either of
the

the Conftables of fuch town; that when the party accufed fhall appear before any fuch Juftice of the Peace or Warden, if he can offer no fatisfactory reafon that he is innocent, he fhall enter into a recognizance with one or more fureties, at the difcretion of fuch Juftice of the Peace or Warden, to appear at the next Supreme Judicial Court to be holden in and for the county in which fuch complaint may have originated; and if he fhall refufe to enter into fuch recognizance, the Juftice of the Peace or Warden fhall commit him to the common gaol, there to remain until he fhall be by due courfe of law difcharged therefrom; and that the faid Supreme Judicial Court, if recognizance be entered into, and the woman be not delivered, may order a continuance of the recognizance to their next term, and fo on from Court to Court, until the woman fhall be delivered, to the end that an order may be made.

Person accufed to be recognized.

On refufal, to be committed.

Sec. 2. *And be it further enacted,* That after any baftard child fhall be born in any town in this State, whether fuch child be born alive, or be ftill born, or, being born alive, fhall die before an order be made, and no examination had before the birth of fuch child, it fhall be lawful for any two or more Juftices of the Peace or Wardens, living in the town where fuch child fhall be born, upon examination of the woman, by them taken on oath, and upon the complaint of the overfeers of the poor for fuch town, to grant forth a warrant for the perfon whom the mother of the child fhall charge on oath with begetting fuch child; or in cafe the mother, before the birth of fuch child, fhall have charged any perfon upon oath,

On the birth of a baftard child, the mother to be examined.

oath, as aforeſaid, with begetting the ſame,
then, upon the birth of ſuch child, a warrant
ſhall be iſſued in like manner againſt the perſon ſo accuſed; *provided* he ſhall live or
may be found in the ſame county; which
warrant or warrants ſhall be directed and
ſerved as is herein before directed; that
when the accuſed perſon ſhall appear, if the
woman, on being examined anew on oath,
ſhall continue conſtant in her accuſation, and
no plea or proof be produced ſufficient to
ſatisfy the Juſtices or Wardens, who ſhall
have taken cognizance of the caſe, that he
is innocent, they ſhall adjudge him to be the
putative or reputed father of the child, and
make an order for its maintenance, if living,
or if dead, for payment of the expences
accrued before and at its death and in-
terment; and that if the perſon accuſed ſhall
be diſſatisfied with the order, he may appeal therefrom to the Supreme Judicial
Court, at the term thereof next to be holden
in the county in which the child ſhall have
been born, upon paying down the coſts that
ſhall have then accrued, and entering into a
recognizance with one or more ſureties, at
the diſcretion of ſuch Juſtices or Wardens,
for his appearance, and abiding by ſuch order as ſhall be made by the ſaid Supreme
Judicial Court; and in default of ſuch order to be then made or taken by the ſaid
Supreme Judicial Court, to perform the
order already made; but if he ſhall not pray
an appeal, the Juſtices or Wardens, who
ſhall have iſſued the order, are hereby empowered and directed to commit him, if he
ſhall refuſe or neglect to give bond to perform their order.

Sec. 3. *And be it further enacted,* That

if

if the perſon accuſed doth not live in the county wherein complaint ſhall be made, before or after the birth of ſuch baſtard child as aforeſaid, or is not there to be found, it ſhall be lawful for any Juſtice of the Court of Common Pleas in the county where complaint ſhall be made as aforeſaid, having firſt examined the mother of ſuch child upon oath, to grant forth a warrant, directed to the Sheriff of the county or his deputy, in which the accuſed perſon dwells or reſides, to apprehend the ſaid perſon, and him bring to the town where ſuch complaint ſhall be made, before the birth of any baſtard child, or after ſuch child ſhall be born; and when he appears, the Juſtice who ſhall have granted the warrant or ſummons as aforeſaid, ſhall order him into the cuſtody of the Town-Sergeant, or ſome Conſtable of that town; and is hereby fully empowered, in conjunction with any one Juſtice or Warden living in the ſaid town, to take cognizance of the cauſe, and proceed therein, in the manner directed in the two preceding ſections, with concurrent powers, and ſimilar forms preſcribed therein to the Juſtices or Wardens, whether on complaint that any unmarried woman ſhall be with child of a baſtard child, or ſuch child be born alive, or be ſtill born, or, being born alive, ſhall die before an order be made, and no examination had before the birth of ſuch child, reſpect being had to the local juriſdiction of the different authorities created by this act.

The accuſed perſon living out of the county, warrant by whom to be iſſued.

Proceedings thereon.

Sec. 4. *And be it further enacted,* That the order to be made for the maintenance of a baſtard child ſhall be in ſubſtance of the following form, to wit:

WHEREAS

WHEREAS due proof hath been made before us, A. B. and C. D. Eſquires, inhabiting
in the town of N. in the county of N. upon
the oath of E. F. of   mother of a
          baſtard child, born the   day
of   in the town aforeſaid, that G. H.
of   did beget the ſaid baſtard child,
which child is likely to become chargeable
to the ſaid town of N.   We, the ſaid
upon examination of the ſaid E. F. and the
cauſe and circumſtances of the premiſes, do
adjudge the ſaid G. H. to be the putative
father of the ſaid baſtard child ; and thereupon do order, as well for the relief of the ſaid
town of N. as for the keeping and maintaining of ſaid child, that the ſaid G. H. ſhall
forthwith, upon ſight of this our order,
pay, or cauſe to be paid, to the overſeers of
the poor of the ſaid town, for the time being,
the ſum of   for the firſt four weeks
from the birth of the ſaid child, for defraying the charge of the lying in of the ſaid E.
F. and after the expiration of the ſaid four
weeks, the ſaid G. H. ſhall likewiſe pay, or
cauſe to be paid, to the overſeers of the
poor of the town aforeſaid, weekly and every week, the ſum of   for and towards the maintenance of the ſaid baſtard
child, for ſo long time as the ſaid child ſhall
be chargeable to the ſaid town : And further
we do hereby order, that the ſaid E. F. ſhall
every week, for ſo long time as the ſaid
child ſhall be chargeable as aforeſaid, and
ſhe ſhall not keep the ſame, pay or cauſe to
be paid unto the overſeers of the poor of
the town of N. aforeſaid, for the time being, the ſum of   for and towards the
further maintenance of ſaid child.

Laſtly. We order that the ſaid G. H. do,
upon

upon notice of this our order, give ſufficient ſecurity to the overſeers of the poor
of the town of N. aforeſaid, for the performance of this our order. In witneſs
whereof we have hereunto ſet our hands and
ſeals, this

Sec. 5. *And be it further enaſted,* That
when any order, made in manner as aforeſaid for the maintenance of a baſtard child,
ſhall be brought before the ſaid Supreme
Judicial Court by appeal, the ſaid Court be
and hereby is fully empowered to alter or
amend the ſame, if it ſhall appear to be extravagant or any way defeſtive ; but ſhall
not quaſh or reverſe it, unleſs it be made to
appear that there is no ſufficient reaſon to
adjudge the perſon charged with the maintenance of the child to be the putative father thereof, any law, cuſtom or uſage, to
the contrary in any wiſe notwithſtanding.

Order may be altered by the Supreme Court.

And whereas it ſometimes happens that
the perſons charged as the reputed or putative fathers of baſtard children, with the
maintenance thereof, are of little or no
eſtates, and are committed to gaol for non-
performance of orders made againſt them,
or for not giving ſecurity to perform the
ſame, and make the towns liable with their
ſupport in gaol :

Sec. 6. *Be it therefore further enaſted,* That
when and ſo often as any man ſhall ſtand
committed to any of the gaols in this State,
for the non-performance of any final ad-
judication and order in baſtardy made up
againſt him, the Town-Council, for the time
being, wherein ſuch order originated, ſhall
and may bind out and give and take indentures of ſervitude of ſuch priſoner, for ſuch
length of time, and for ſuch wages or ſum,

*Perſons commit-
ted for refuſal to
perform an or-
der, may be
bound out.*

as the Town-Council ſhall think convenient and requiſite, which indenture ſhall be ſigned and ſealed by the Council-Clerk, in behalf of the Council ; and that ſo much of the wages or money ariſing from ſuch ſervice as ſhall be neceſſary to fulfil the order, and all incidental charges, ſhall be ſo applied, and the reſidue, if any there be, ſhall remain to and for the uſe of the perſon ſo charged.

Their wages how to be applied.

Sec. 7. *And be it further enaɛted,* That in caſe ſuch baſtard child ſhall die, or ceaſe to be chargeable to the town in which born, the Juſtices, Wardens, or other authority empowered by this aɛt, ſhall make a juſt eſtimate of all reaſonable expences that ought to be paid by the perſon bound, and be and hereby are fully empowered to iſſue a warrant for colleɛting the ſame ; but in caſe the perſon againſt whom ſuch order ſhall be made ſhall be diſſatisfied with ſuch eſtimate, he may appeal to the ſaid Supreme Judicial Court to be next holden in the county wherein ſuch town lieth, which Court ſhall be, and hereby is, empowered to hear and finally determine between the parties.

Child dying, the Juſtices to aſcertain all expences, &c.

Appeal granted.

Sec. 8. *And be it further enaɛted,* That in all caſes where complaint has been made and ſubſtantiated to the authority aforeſaid, after the birth of a baſtard ſtill born child as aforeſaid, the words, in the form of the order preſcribed by this aɛt, ſhall be varied as follow, to wit :

Form of the order when the child is ſtill born.

After the words, " And thereupon do order, as well for the relief of the ſaid town of N." the following words ſhall be inſerted, inſtead of thoſe, " For the future maintenance of the child," to wit : " As for paying

paying the neceffary charges which have accrued for the expences and trouble which
have arifen for rendering comfort and fuf-
tenance to the mother of fuch ftill born
child, and of decently interring the fame,
that the faid G. H. fhall forthwith, upon
fight of this order, pay or caufe to be paid
to the overfeers of the poor of faid town,
for the time being, the fum of   in
fatisfaction for the expence and trouble
aforefaid." All the other parts of which
order, in fuch cafe, fhall be of the form of
the order above recited.

Sec. 9. *And be it further enacted,* That
if any woman on her examination, after the
birth of a baftard child, fhall refufe to charge
any perfon on oath or affirmation with being
the father of the child, the Juftice to whom
complaint fhall have been made as aforefaid
fhall fentence fuch woman to be committed
to gaol, at any time after one month from
her delivery, there to remain until fhe fhall
charge as aforefaid the perfon who fhall
have gotten her with child. And if fuch
woman fhall not have wherewith to fupport herfelf in gaol, fhe fhall be fupported at
the expence of the town wherein fuch complaint fhall have been made. *Provided neverthelefs,* that if fufficient fecurity fhall be
proffered to the overfeers of the poor, in
any cafe of complaint as aforefaid, and to
their fatisfaction, to indemnify fuch town for
the fupport of fuch child, it fhall be the duty
of fuch overfeers to accept fuch fecurity,
and the woman, on fuch fecurity being given,
fhall be difcharged on payment of cofts.

The mother of a baftard, refufing to declare the father, may be committed.

How to be fupported.

Provifo.

An Act for regulating the Affize of Bread.

1763.

Town-Councils
to regulate the
affize of bread.

BE it enacted by the General Affembly, and by the authority thereof it is enacted, That the Town-Council in each town in this State, be and they are hereby empowered to make laws and regulations for fettling the affize of bakers bread in the refpective towns to which they belong, and the fame to regulate monthly. And that the faid Town-Council be and they are hereby fully empowered to carry fuch laws and regulations by them made into execution, to all intents and purpofes.

An Act for laying out Highways.

1715.
1725.
1731.
1741.
1752.
1772.

Proprietors to lay
out highways.

Section 1. BE it enacted by the General Affembly, and by the authority thereof it is enacted, That the proprietors of the lands in each and every town in this State, fhall lay out fuitable, neceffary and convenient highways within their refpective proprieties, from town to town, and to mills and markets, and generally wherever they may be wanted. And all highways duly laid out and approved by fuch proprietors, and recorded in their records, fhall be good, binding and valid, as though laid out and eftablifhed in any other manner whatfoever.

Town-Councils
may order high-
ways to be laid
out.

Sec. 2. *And be it further enacted,* That if it be found neceffary that other highways be laid out in any town, befides fuch as have been or fhall be laid out by the proprietors as aforefaid, in every fuch cafe it fhall be lawful for the Town-Council of fuch town, to order a highway to be laid out fo far, and through fuch part of the fame town, as they may

may judge neceſſary. And for the due
marking out ſuch highway, the Town-Council ſhall appoint three ſuitable and indifferent men, not intereſted or concerned in the
land through which ſuch highway is to paſs,
who ſhall be ſworn by the Town-Council
for the faithful diſcharge of that truſt; which
three men, being accompanied by one Juſtice
of the Peace and one Conſtable, or the Town-
Sergeant of the town, to be named by the
ſaid Town-Council for that purpoſe, ſhall go
to the place where ſuch highway is ordered
to begin, and from thence proceed to ſur-
vey, bound and mark out a highway, con-
formably to the direction of the Town-
Council; always taking care to lay it in
ſuch manner as may be moſt to the advantage of the public, and as little as may be
to the injury of the owners of the land
through which it paſſeth: And ſhall alſo
agree with the owners for the damage they
ſhall ſuſtain, by means of ſuch highway's
paſſing through their land: And in caſe they
cannot agree with the owners, then the
Town-Council ſhall value and appraiſe the
damage. And having thus proceeded and
finiſhed laying out ſuch highway, they ſhall
cauſe an exact draught or plan thereof to be
made, which, together with a proper return
of their whole doings in writing, under their
hands and ſeals, ſhall be by them preſented
to ſuch Town-Council, who thereupon ſhall
cauſe notice to be given to all parties concerned to appear before them, if they ſhall
ſee cauſe, and be heard for or againſt receiving ſuch report; and after ſuch hearing,
the Council ſhall proceed to receive or re-
ject ſuch report, as to them ſhall appear juſt
and right: And if the report be approved
and

How to be done.

and received, then they fhall caufe the fame to be recorded, and fuch highway to be eftablifhed and laid open ; and the land, with all charges of laying out the fame, fhall be paid out of the town-treafury.

Sec. 3. *And be it further enacted,* That the feveral Town-Councils in this State be and they are hereby empowered to lay out drift-ways in their refpective towns, in fuch places and of fuch widths as they fhall think neceffary, as fully as by law they are empowered to lay out highways: That fuch drift-ways be laid out in the fame manner, and be under the fame regulations in every refpect, as highways are : That the damage fhall be afcertained by the Town-Council in the fame manner as in laying out highways : That it fhall be in the power of the Town-Council to order and direct who fhall be at the charge of maintaining gates and bars, where any fuch drift-way or driftways fhall be laid out, and alfo whether the fame fhall be furnifhed with gates or bars : And that when a committee fhall be appointed to lay out any highway or drift-way, fuch committee may be fworn by the Town-Council, or the Juftice of the Peace appointed to attend upon them.

Sec. 4. *And be it further enacted,* That if any perfon through whofe land fuch highway or drift-way is laid fhall be aggrieved by the doings of fuch committee or Town-Council, he fhall have liberty to appeal to the next Court of General Seffions of the Peace to be holden for the county, giving bond to profecute his appeal, and producing an attefted copy of the whole proceedings to fuch Court of Seffions, and filing his reafons of appeal with the Clerk of fuch
Court

Court ten days before the fitting thereof; where an order fhall be made for his appearing to profecute his appeal, requiring the Sheriff of the county to impannel a jury of twelve good men, not being inhabitants of, or having intereft in, the town where fuch highway or drift-way is laid; which jury, being duly fworn for that purpofe, fhall go and re-examine the laying of the highway or drift-way, and the damages given and allowed to the owners of the land through which it paffeth, and make fuch alterations in either or both as to them fhall feem juft and right, or totally annul and reverfe all fuch proceedings, if they fhall fee caufe, relating to the laying of any fuch highway or drift-way; and fhall, under their hands and feals, make return of their doings to faid Court of Seffions, which being accepted by fuch Court, fhall be recorded, and be final. And the faid Court of Seffions fhall tax fuch cofts as fhall accrue by the proceedings aforefaid, againft the appellant, in cafe the Jurors fhall make no alteration in the doings of the committee or Town-Council refpecting faid highway. But if the Jury fhall make any alteration in, or fhall reverfe and annul fuch doings of the faid committee or Council, then cofts fhall be taxed againft the town where fuch highway fhall have been laid.

A jury to re-examine the highway.

Cofts by whom to be paid.

Sec. 5. *And be it further enacted,* That all fuch damages as fhall be agreed for or adjudged to any perfon through whofe land fuch highway or drift-way is laid, either by the committee, Town-Council or Jurors, fhall be paid to fuch perfon by the Town-Treafurer of the town in which the highway or drift-way is laid; and if he fhall refufe or neglect to pay the fame, an action may be brought

Damages to the owners of land to be paid by the Town-Treafurer.

brought and maintained for fuch money by the perfon to whom the fame is due and payable.

Town-Council mav change highways.

Sec. 6. *And be it further enacted,* That the Town-Council of each town within this State fhall have full power and authority, in manner as aforefaid, to lay out new highways inftead of any which they fhall judge to be inconvenient or ufelefs, and fhall have power and authority to fell and difpofe of any fuch inconvenient or ufelefs highway, for the beft advantage of the town in which they are, and to make and pafs a · deed or deeds of conveyance, in the name of themfelves and fucceffors in faid office ; which deed or deeds fo made, fhall create in the purchafer or purchafers thereof a good and lawful eftate in fee-fimple, and the money arifing upon the fale of any fuch highway, fhall be by the Town-Council immediately

Provifo.

paid into the town-treafury of fuch town for the ufe thereof. *Provided,* that no Town-Council fhall have power to alter or change any highway which hath been, or hereafter fhall be, laid out by the General Affembly.

An Act for the Mending of Highways.

1745.
1747.
1750.
1759.
1760.
1771.
1773.
1780.
1786.
1794.
1798.

Surveyors to warn perfons to work on the highways.

Section 1. BE it enacted by the General Affembly, and by the authority thereof it is enacted, That all perfons chofen and engaged to the office of furveyors of highways within this State, fhall warn and give timely notice (two days at leaft) to each and every houfeholder and labourer within his diftrict, to work one day in a year, or more if need require, between the firft day of April and the firft day of October. And thofe who are of ability, or keep teams,

fhall,

shall, between the first day of April and the first day of October, work four days or more, and shall find a team, with two able hands, if need require; and if no team be required, they shall send two able bodied men, and common labourers shall send one hand; and on refusal or neglect to work as aforesaid, if warned to appear with a cart and four oxen or two horses, and two able hands, the delinquent shall pay as a fine three dollars per day; and if warned with a cart and two oxen, or one horse and one hand, two dollars per day; for two hands, one dollar and fifty cents per day; and for one hand, seventy-five cents per day.

Fines of delinquents.

Sec. 2. *And be it further enacted,* That all delinquents who shall not make a reasonable excuse within twenty days, shall be fined as aforesaid, by complaint of the surveyors to a Justice of the Peace or Warden of the town where any such person shall dwell, to be levied by warrant of distress on the delinquent's goods; which warrant shall be directed to the Town-Sergeant or either of the Constables of said town.

How collected.

Sec. 4. *And be it further enacted,* That when and so often as it shall be necessary to erect or repair a bridge or bridges for the conveniency of passing in the public roads or highways of any town in this State, it shall be the duty of the surveyor or surveyors in whose district the said bridge or bridges to be erected or repaired shall be, to apply to the owner or occupant of any lot or lots of timber or woodland within such district, for the purchase of so much timber or other materials as may be necessary to build or repair such bridge or bridges.

Timber, &c. for erecting or repairing bridges; how to be procured.

C c c   But

But if the said surveyor or surveyors cannot agree with such owner or occupant for said purchase, on such terms as to the said surveyor shall appear reasonable, in such case the said surveyor or surveyors shall be and they are hereby empowered to call into his or their assistance two substantial freeholders of his or their district, and by and with their advice to cause so much timber or other materials to be cut and carried off from the lot or lots of timber or woodland within such district, as shall be sufficient for said purpose, having due regard to the cutting of the same in such places, and in such proportions, as shall in their opinion do the least injury and waste on the respective lands where the same shall be so taken.

and paid for.

Sec. 5. *And be it further enacted*, That in case of disagreement between the said surveyor or surveyors, and the owner or occupant of the timber or woodland as aforesaid, the said surveyor or surveyors, together with the persons called into his or their assistance as aforesaid, shall make a just and true appraisal of the value of tho timber or other materials taken and applied as aforesaid, certifying the name or names of the real or supposed owner or owners of the said lot or lots under their hands, which certificate and appraisal the said surveyor or surveyors shall lodge in the Town-Clerk's office of such town, that the owner or owners of such lands may receive the amount of such appraisal out of the treasury of such town.

Surveyors to keep the roads open in the winter.

Sec. 6. *And be it further enacted*, That it shall be the duty of every surveyor of highways within this State, to cause the roads and highways within his district

trict to be kept open and paffable with fleds and fleighs in the winter feafon : That for this purpofe, whenever any highway or road fhall be obftructed with fnow, the furveyor thereof be and is hereby empower-ed to notify all the inhabitants who live within his diftrict immediately to repair to fuch obftructed road or highway with one or more hands, and with fuch horfes and oxen as they can furnifh ; and the inhabitants fo notified fhall be obliged to repair to fuch road or highway, and caufe the fame to be made paffable as aforefaid, under the direction of the faid furveyor, in the fame manner, and under the fame penalty, as by law they are obliged, at any other feafon of the year, which fhall be collected in the fame way, and for the fame ufe.

Sec. 7. *And be it further enacted,* That all fines and forfeitures, collected as afore- said, fhall be laid out towards the mending of the highways in the diftrict in which they may arife, in the beft manner, at the difcretion of the furveyor, and he fhall be obliged to render an account of his pro-ceeding to the Town-Council of the town to which he belongs, within one month's time after the year for which he is chofen fhall expire.

Fines, how to be appropriated.

Sec. 8. *And be it further enacted,* That when and fo often as any of the highways in this State fhall be fo far neglected by the furveyor, within whofe proper diftrict the fame fhall lie, that the fame fhall want mend-ing and repairing, it fhall and may be law-ful for any perfon to complain thereof to any Juftice of the Peace, living in the town where fuch highway fhall lie, or any Juftice of the Court of Common Pleas with-in

Surveyors ne-glecting to repair highways, how to be proceeded against.

in the county where the fame fhall be, or
any Juftice of the Supreme Judicial Court;
and the faid Juftices refpectively fhall thereupon iffue forth an order to the furveyor
within whofe diftrict fuch highway lies. directing him to caufe the fame to be fufficiently mended and repaired within ten days
from the delivery of fuch order; which
order may be delivered by the perfon complaining, or any other fuitable perfon, at
the difcretion of fuch Juftice; and if fuch
furveyor fhall neglect or refufe to caufe fuch
highway to be fufficiently repaired and
mended, agreeably to fuch order, that then
fuch Juftice fhall iffue forth his warrant,
directed to the Town-Sergeant or either of
the Conftables of faid town, commanding
him to caufe fuch furveyor to appear before him, then to find fureties for his appearance at the next Court of General Seffions of the Peace, to be holden in the county where the offender lives, there to anfwer
for his neglect and contempt aforefaid,
where he may be profecuted by information or a bill of indictment; and no plea
of non-acceptance of fuch office fhall be
admitted, unlefs he fhall bring from the
Town-Treafurer a certificate of his having
paid his fine for refufing to ferve in faid office; and if found guilty, fhall be fined by
faid Court not exceeding thirty-five dollars, nor lefs than feven dollars, one moiety
whereof fhall be for the ufe of the town
where fuch offence fhall be committed, and
the other moiety fhall be for the ufe of him
who fhall complain as aforefaid; and fhall
alfo pay cofts of profecution and conviction.

Sec. 9. *And be it further enacted,* That the
Town-

Town-Council of every town in this State, once in every year, at their meeting next after the election of town-officers, fhall appoint and determine the diftricts or portions of highways which fhall belong to each furveyor in the town, taking care that each furveyor's diftrict be in proportion to the number and ability of the people he may have to work under him.

Town-Council to appoint the diftricts.

Sec. 10. *And be it further enacted*, That if any perfon fhall be chofen furveyor of highways, and fhall refufe to take his oath or engagement to the faithful difcharge of his office, he fhall be fined the fum of three dollars, to be recovered by a warrant of diftrefs from any Juftice or Warden of the town where the party refufing dwells, which warrant fhall be directed to the Town-Sergeant or either of the Conftables of faid town; and the fine fo collected fhall be paid into the town-treafury, for the ufe of the town.

Surveyors refufing to ferve, to be fined.

Sec. 11. *Provided always, and be it further enacted*, any thing in the firft fection of this act to the contrary notwithftanding, That inftead of the mode therein prefcribed, each and every town may, when legally convened, order a tax to be levied and affeffed on the rateable eftates and polls in faid town, and to be applied towards repairing the highways in fuch town, under fuch regulations and reftrictions as the faid town may prefcribe.

Towns may repair their roads by taxes.

Sec. 12. *And be it further enacted*, That any town which fhall neglect to keep in good repair its highways, fhall be liable to be indicted therefor, and on conviction before any Court of General Seffions of the Peace of fuch neglect, fhall be fined to the

Neglecting to repair their roads, may be indicted.

ufe

use of the State in a sum not less than fifty nor more than five hundred dollars, and execution shall issue therefor against the Town-Treasurer of such town: And it shall be the duty of the Attorney-General, on complaint to him made by any freeholder, to prefer a bill of indictment against such town.

1718.

An Act enabling the Surveyors of the Highways of the Town of Newport, to recover the Charges of paving before the Land in said Town owned by Persons who live out of the State.

Owners of land in Newport to pay for paving the streets before the same.

BE it enacted by the General Assembly, and by the authority thereof it is enacted, That whosoever hath, or shall have, any lands in the body of the town of Newport, and it shall be found convenient to pave before the said lands, and the owner or owners of such lands shall not inhabit within this State, and do not, within three months after such paving shall be done, satisfy and pay for the same, that then it shall and may be lawful for the surveyors of the highways of said town to apply themselves to the Justices of the Peace of said town, or any two of them, and give in under oath or affirmation the charges of such paving; and such Justices are empowered and authorized to grant forth a warrant of distress to any of the Constables of said town, to seize and distrain so much of the goods and chattels of the tenant or tenants of such person or persons within the town of Newport, as will satisfy and pay the said charge, and the other reasonable charges accruing thereon; which shall be by such tenant or tenants discounted with the

the owner or owners **of** said land, out of the rents and profits of such lands by him or them hired ; and if such owner or owners shall refuse so to do, he shall have no action at law for the same.

An Act to prevent the Pavement laid in Queen- 1752. *Street, in Newport, from the State-House to the East Side of Thames-Street, from being damaged by loaded Carts or Trucks.*

BE it enacted by the General Assembly, and Loaded carts, by the authority thereof it is enacted, &c. not to be That every person who shall drive a loaded driven on the pavement in cart or trucks upon any part of the pavement Queen-Street. lately laid in Queen-Street, in Newport, from the State-House to the east side of Thames-Street, shall forfeit and pay a fine of two dollars for every offence, to be recovered by the Town-Treasurer before any two Justices of the Peace of said town, for the use of the Town.

An Act enabling the Town-Councils of each 1728. *Town in this State to grant Licenses for* 1747. *retailing strong Liquors, and to prevent* 1762. *the selling of the same without License,* 1770. *and against the keeping up of Signs at* 1798. *unlicensed Houses.*

Section 1. BE it enacted by the General Town-Councils Assembly, and by the autho- to grant license rity thereof it is enacted, That the Town-Councils of the respective towns in this State shall have the power of granting licenses for keeping taverns and ale-houses, and retailing wines or strong liquors within their several towns, and shall take for each license granted

granted difcretionally, not exceeding twenty dollars, nor lefs than four dollars, which money fhall be paid into the town-treafury where fuch licenfe is granted, for defraying the charges of the town.

Penalty for felling without licenfe. Sec. 2. *And be it further enacted*, That if any perfon or perfons fhall fell, or fuffer to be fold, in their dwelling-houfes or poffeffions, by their wives, children or fervants, or other perfons whomfoever, any rum, wine, or ftrong liquors whatfoever, by retail, in any lefs quantity than a gallon, without licenfe firft had and obtained from the Town-Council, and be thereof convicted, either by his, her or their confeffion, or by the teftimony of one or more credible witnefs or witneffes, on oath or affirmation, before any two Juftices of the Peace or Wardens, in any town where fuch offence fhall be committed, he, fhe or they fhall forfeit and pay as a fine the fum of twenty dollars, one half thereof to him who fhall inform and fue for the fame, and the other half to and for the ufe of the town where fuch offence fhall be committed.

Appeal granted. Sec. 3. *And be it further enacted*, That when any perfon or perfons fhall be aggrieved by any judgment given againft them by any Juftices or Wardens, for the breach of this act, he, fhe or they may appeal therefrom to the next Court of General Seffions of the Peace, to be holden in the county where fuch judgment appealed from fhall be given: *Always provided*, that fuch **Terms of the appeal.** appeal be afked at the time fuch fentence or judgment fhall be given, and that he, fhe or they fo appealing, pay down the cofts taxed by the Court appealed from, and enter into recognizance in the fum of thirty dollars,

lars, with one fufficient furety, for profecuting fuch appeal with effect, and paying
fuch further cofts as may be taxed, if judgment be affirmed, and to be of good behaviour in the mean time. *Provided alfo,*
that the appellant file his reafons of appeal
ten days before the fitting of the Court appealed to, as in other cafes.

Sec. 4. *And be it further enacted,* That
if any innholder or tavernkeeper fhall
hereafter truft or give credit to any perfon
inhabiting in the fame town where they are
trufted, or to any perfon whofe place of
abode is within five miles diftance from fuch
inn or tavern, for victuals or drink, for
more than two dollars, fuch innholder or
tavernkeeper fhall lofe all fuch fums fo
trufted ; and all actions hereafter brought
for fuch debt or debts fhall be utterly ex-
cluded and barred ; and the defendant in
fuch action may plead the matter fpecially,
or give it in evidence under the general
iffue. *Provided always,* that nothing in this
fection fhall be conftrued to prohibit any
licenfed retailer from giving credit on fales
of liquor exceeding one quart.

Tavernkeepers not to give credit for more than two dollars.

Provifo.

Sec. 5. *And be it further enacted,* That
each Town-Council fhall take bonds, from
all perfons to whom they fhall grant licenfes,
for their maintaining good order in their
houfes, and conforming themfelves to the
regulations of law refpecting taverns and
public houfes.

Tavernkeepers, &c. to give bonds.

Sec. 6. *And be it further enacted,* That
it fhall and may be lawful for the Town-
Council of each town, upon any perfon's
being convicted of keeping a diforderly
houfe, or irregular tavern, or houfe
of entertainment, contrary to the bond

Town-Council may withdraw licenfes, &c.

D d d   by

by him given, immediately to withdraw
ſuch perſon's licenſe, and further proſecute ſuch offender according to law.

Sec. 7. *And be it further enacted*, That
if any perſon whoſoever in this State ſhall
preſume to erect, or keep up any ſign before erected, for the keeping of a public
houſe, without firſt obtaining a licenſe from
the Town-Council of the town where he lives,
he ſhall forfeit for the firſt offence to the ſaid
town the ſum of twenty dollars, to be recovered by the ſaid Town-Council, to and
for the uſe of ſaid town, by due courſe of
law ; and for every offence afterwards, he
ſhall pay as a fine the ſum of forty dollars,
to be recovered and appropriated in manner as aforeſaid. *Provided neverthelefs*, that
all ferry-houſes be and they are hereby excepted out of this act.

*Penalty for keep-
ing up ſigns with-
out licenſe.*

Proviſo.

1721.
1725.
1798.

An Act to prevent Drunkenneſs.

Section 1.   BE *it enacted by the General
Aſſembly, and by the autho-
rity thereof it is enacted*, That it ſhall and
may be in the power of the Town-Council
of each town within this State, upon complaint unto them made, that any perſon
dwelling within the limits of ſuch town
doth practiſe the odious and deſtructive
vice of drunkenneſs, to order prohibitions
to be poſted in ſuch and ſo many places,
within the town where ſuch perſon belongs,
as to them ſhall ſeem needful ; thereby ſtrict-
ly prohibiting all retailers of ſtrong liquors,
as well as others, from ſelling any kind of
ſtrong liquors, directly or indirectly, to any
ſuch perſon as ſhall be mentioned in ſuch
prohibition.

*Town-Councils
to prohibit the
ſelling of liquors
to drunkards, by
poſting them.*

Sec,

Sec. 2. *And be it further enacted,* That the Town-Council of each and every town as aforeſaid, after they ſhall have poſted any perſon as a common drunkard as above required, may notify the Town-Councils of the neighbouring towns, who, upon ſuch notifications, are required to poſt the ſame in ſome convenient place or places in their reſpective towns : Whereupon the inhabitants of ſuch town ſhall be reſtrained from ſelling to ſuch perſon ſo poſted any kind of ſtrong liquor whatſoever, as much as the inhabitants of ſuch towns are, where ſuch poſted perſon belongs. And if any perſon ſhall preſume to do contrary hereunto, upon conviction thereof, he ſhall ſuffer the ſame penalties as in this act are laid upon ſuch offender or offenders, and to be recovered in the ſame manner. And in caſe any retailer of ſtrong liquor, or other perſon, ſhall preſume contrary to this act to ſell or vend any kind of ſtrong liquor to any perſon as aforeſaid, and ſhall be duly convicted thereof, before any two Juſtices of the Peace or Wardens in ſuch town, either by his own confeſſion, or by the teſtimony of one or more credible witneſs or witneſſes, ſuch perſon ſo offending ſhall forfeit, to the uſe of the poor of the town in which ſuch offence ſhall be committed, the ſum of four dollars for the firſt offence, and for every offence in the premiſes afterwards, the ſum of eight dollars, to be levied by warrant of diſtreſs, to be granted by ſuch Juſtices or Wardens in ſuch town before whom the offender ſhall be convicted, and the perſon ſo convicted ſhall alſo pay coſts.

May be poſted in the neighbouring towns.

Penalties for offending.

An

An Act enabling the Secretary of the State to appoint a Deputy.

1730.

Secretary may appoint a Deputy.

BE it enacted by the General Assembly, and by the authority thereof it is enacted, That it shall and may be lawful for the Secretary of the State for the time being to appoint a Deputy under him, who being duly sworn before the Governor, Lieutenant-Governor, or one or more of the Assistants, for the faithful discharge of his office, is hereby authorized and empowered to act and do, in the absence of the Secretary, all things by law required of him, as fully and amply, and to all intents and purposes, as the Secretary himself might or could do. And that the Secretary shall be responsible and liable in the law, for all and every misconduct, neglect, or default of such Deputy.

An Act for registering public Letters.

1753.
1757.
1798.

Public letters to be registered.

BE it enacted by the General Assembly, and by the authority thereof it is enacted, That the Secretary of this State do register all public letters, sent from this State to any public person or officers, in a book to be kept for that purpose; and also all such public letters as shall be sent to this State, from the Secretary of State or other public persons or officers, in another book to be kept for that purpose.

An

An Act requiring the General-Treasurer to give Bond.

BE it enacted by the General Assembly, and by the authority thereof it is enacted, That the General-Treasurer for the time being shall, previous to his entering upon the execution of the duties of his office, give bond, with sufficient sureties, to the Secretary of this State, and to his successors, for the use of the State, in the sum of forty thousand dollars, for the true and faithful discharge of the duties of his said office.

An Act directing the Duty of the Attorney-General.

BE it enacted by the General Assembly, and by the authority thereof it is enacted, That the Attorney-General for this State shall give his attendance at the Supreme Judicial Court, and Courts of General Sessions of the Peace, in this State, for the service thereof; and shall give unto such Courts due advice and information concerning any criminal matters, breaches of the peace, or wrong done to the State, or any of the citizens thereof, that shall come to his knowledge, and draw up and present to such Courts all informations and indictments, or other legal process, against any such offenders, as by law is required; and diligently, by a due course of law, prosecute the same to final judgment and execution.

An

1705.
1751.
1792.
1798.
Notaries Public
to be appointed.

An Act for the Appointment of public Nota-ries.

BE it enacted by the General Assembly, and by the authority thereof it is enacted, That a public Notary be annually appointed for each of the counties within this State; and that the Secretary of the State, and his Deputy, for the time being, shall also be public Notaries for the counties wherein they shall reside, and that they are severally hereby empowered and authorized to act, transact, do and finish all matters and things relating to protests or protesting bills, as are by law required, or other matters within their offices, and that they be severally engaged to the faithful performance of their offices.

1747.
1749.
1752.
1753.
1769.
1798.
Eldest Justice
to be Coroner.

An Act appointing Coroners.

Section 1. BE it enacted by the General Assembly, and by the authority thereof it is enacted, That the eldest Justice of the Peace or Warden in each town in this State, be and he is hereby constituted Coroner in and throughout the town in which he dwells; and that he take the Coroner's oath or engagement before a Justice of the Peace.

Or in his ab-
sence, the next
in order.

　　Sec. 2. *And be it further enacted*, That whenever the eldest Justice or Warden of any town in this State shall be absent or unable to attend, the next Justice or Warden in order, who shall be present, shall have full power to execute the office of Coroner in all its parts as prescribed by law, in the same manner as such eldest Justice or Warden

en could or might do. if prefent; and fhall
be fworn into faid office accordingly, to officiate upon fuch fpecial occafion.

Sec. 3. *And be it further enacted,* That
if any inquifition fhall be had on the body
of any deceafed perfon, who left no eftate,
the charges of inquifition fhall be paid out
of the town-treafury of the town where the
dead body is found: *Provided neverthelefs,*
that the parent or mafter of any child or
fervant, upon whofe body an inquifition
fhall be taken, fhall pay the charges thereof,
if of ability.

Coft of inquifition, by whom to be paid.

Sec. 4. *And be it further enacted,* That
where the deceafed fhall have effects in any
perfon's hands, the Coroner who made the
inquifition may demand of fuch perfon the
whole amount of the lawful fees attending
fuch inquifition, and on his neglect or refufal to pay and difcharge faid fees, fuch
Coroner may fue fuch perfon for the fame,
if not exceeding twenty dollars, at a Juftices
Court, and if more than twenty dollars, at
the Court of Common Pleas in the county
where fuch inquifition was made; and upon
recovering and receiving the fame, with the
cofts of profecution, the Coroner fhall pay
the Jury and all others concerned in fuch
inquifition their lawful demands.

May be demanded of perfons holding property of the deceafed.

Sec. 5. *And be it further enacted,* That
if any perfon fhall be returned as a Juror to
ferve on an inquifition on a dead body, and
fhall refufe or neglect to ferve, fuch perfon,
(unlefs he be exempted by law) fhall be fined
five dollars; and on his refufal to pay the
fame, the Coroner fhall iffue forth a warrant
of diftrefs, directed to the Sheriff of the
county, or his deputy, or to any Town-
Sergeant or Conftable in fuch town, who
fhall

Jurors may be fined.

shall levy the same, in the same manner as other Jurors' fines are levied and collected; which fines shall be for the use of the town where such dead body shall be found.

Who exempted.　Sec. 6. *And be it further enacted,* That such persons, and no others, shall be exempted from serving as Jurors on any inquisition, as are by the laws of this State exempted from serving as Jurors in other cases.

An Act relating to Sheriffs, Deputy-Sheriffs and Gaolers.

Sheriffs to be elected.　Section 1. BE it enacted by the General Assembly, and by the authority thereof it is enacted, That there shall be annually appointed by the General Assembly one Sheriff for each county: That every person who shall be elected to the office of Sheriff shall, at the time of his election, be a freeholder and an inhabitant of the county for which he is elected, and shall, previous to his entering on the duties of his office, be sworn or affirmed to the faithful performance thereof, and shall moreover give bond, with two sufficient sureties, to the General-Treasurer, in the sum of six thousand dollars, for the due and faithful execution of his office according to law.

Members of Assembly not eligible, &c.　Sec. 2. *And be it further enacted,* That no member of either house of Assembly shall be eligible to the office of Sheriff, or hold a deputation under him; nor shall any Sheriff, Deputy-Sheriff or Gaoler, be eligible as a member of either house of Assembly.

Sheriffs may appoint Deputies.　Sec. 3. *And be it further enacted,* That each Sheriff be authorized to appoint as many Deputies, being freeholders and inhabitants of the county, as he shall deem necessary

neceſſary for his aſſiſtance in the due performance of the duties of his office ; and
that the appointments of ſuch Deputies
ſhall be in writing, under the hand and ſeal
of the Sheriff, and ſhall be lodged and Deputations to
recorded in a book to be kept for that purpoſe in the office of the Clerk of the Court
of Common Pleas in the county for which
they are appointed, previous to their entering on the duties of their office ; and that
they ſhall be ſworn or affirmed in like manner as the Sheriffs, and give bonds with
ſufficient ſureties to the Sheriff, in the ſum
of three thouſand dollars, for the faithful
execution of their office : That each May appoint
Sheriff moreover ſhall be authorized to ap- Gaolers.
point a Gaoler or keeper of the priſon in
his county, who ſhall be ſworn to the faithful performance of the duties of his office,
and ſhall alſo give bond in the ſame manner
as Deputy-Sheriffs are by this act required
to do : That the oath of office for the Sheriff
and his Deputies ſhall be in the form following, to wit :

" I A. B. do ſolemnly ſwear (or affirm) Oath of Sheriff,
that I will faithfully execute all lawful pre- &c.
cepts iſſued under the authority of the State
of Rhode-Iſland and Providence Plantations, and to me directed and delivered, and
true returns make, and in all things well
and truly, and without malice or partiality,
perform the duties of the office of Sheriff
of the county of   (or *Deputy-Sheriff,*
as the caſe may be) during my continuance
in ſaid office, and take my lawful fees
only. So help me God."

And that the Sheriffs ſhall have the power May revoke de-
of revoking any deputations by them given ; putations.
provided ſuch revocation be entered in the
E e e   book

book for recording deputations as aforesaid.

May appoint special Deputies.

Sec. 4. *And be it further enacted,* That every Sheriff shall be authorized to appoint a special Deputy for the service of any writ or precept to him directed, *provided* the same be done upon the back of such writ or precept, and such special Deputy be sworn before any Judge or Justice of the Peace, duly and faithfully to execute said writ or precept, and the same be certified by said Judge or Justice under such deputation.

Liable for neglect of their Deputies.

Sec. 5. *And be it further enacted,* That each and every Sheriff shall be responsible and accountable for any neglect or misfeasance in office of his Deputies or Gaoler ; and that in all cases where any person shall be entitled to an action for any neglect or misfeasance in office of any Deputy-Sheriff or Gaoler, he shall have his election to bring the same either against the Sheriff himself, or such Deputy or Gaoler.

Sheriff's duty.

Sec. 6. *And be it further enacted,* That it shall be the duty of the Sheriffs to attend the General Assembly, when sitting in their respective counties, and also the Supreme Judicial Court, the Courts of Common Pleas, and Courts of General Sessions of the Peace, when holden in their several counties ; and moreover it shall be the duty of the Sheriffs and their Deputies to execute, within their respective counties, all lawful precepts directed to them, and issued under the authority of this State, and they shall have power to command all necessary assistance in the execution of their duty.

Deputies may act after the decease of their principal.

Sec. 7. *And be it further enacted,* That in case of the death of any Sheriff, his Deputy or Deputies and Gaoler shall continue

tinue in office, unless otherwise removed, as herein provided, and shall execute the same in the name of the deceased, until another Sheriff shall be appointed and sworn or affirmed ; and the neglects or misfeasances of such Deputy and Deputies and Gaoler, in the mean time, as well as before, shall be a breach of the condition of the bond given as before directed by the Sheriff who appointed them ; and the executors or administrators of the deceased Sheriff shall have the like remedy for the defaults and misfeasances in office of such Deputy or Deputies and Gaoler, during such interval, as they would have been entitled to if the Sheriff had continued in life, and in the exercise of his office, until his successor was appointed and sworn or affirmed : And every Sheriff who shall not be re-elected when his term of office expires, or whose office shall become vacant by removal or resignation, shall have power, notwithstanding, to officiate as such until his successor shall be sworn into office.

Their neglects to be a breach of the bond, &c.

Sec. 8. *And be it further enacted,* That it shall be the duty of the Sheriffs to furnish the General Assembly, when sitting in their respective counties, with copies of the laws and other proceedings of the General Assembly, which shall, from time to time, be transmitted to them, as by law provided ; and also to deliver commissions, proclamations, schedules, and all other public acts, to the persons to whom directed, in their respective counties, without expence to the State.

Sheriffs to furnish the Assembly with the laws, &c.

Sec. 9. *And be it further enacted,* That it shall be the duty of the Sheriff of the county of Providence to attend the celebration of the Commencement of the University

Sheriff to attend the Commencement at Providence.

or

or College in this State annually, and to preſerve the civil peace, good order and decorum, during the ſame.

Supreme Court, &c. may remove Deputies, &c.

Sec. 10. *And be it further enacted,* That the Supreme Judicial Court, and the Courts of Common Pleas, in their reſpective counties, on complaint to them made, ſhall be authorized to remove any Deputy-Sheriff or Gaoler for miſdemeanor in office.

1754.

An Act empowering the Sheriffs to ſell and give Deeds of Lands mortgaged and forfeited to the State.

Lands mortgaged to the State, how to be ſold.

Section 1. BE it enacted by the General Aſſembly, and by the authority thereof it is enacted, That the Sheriff, after having levied execution on any land mortgaged to the State's Truſtees, for which a judgment of Court has been obtained, ſhall ſet up notifications in three or more public places in the town, and one notification on or near the door of the court-houſe in the county in which the land lies, for the ſpace of three months after execution is levied, and before the land is expoſed to ſale, notifying all perſons concerned of the whole proceedings, that the mortgageor of the ſaid land, his heirs and aſſigns, may have time and notice to come in and redeem the ſame ; and if no perſon appears to redeem the ſaid land, then the Sheriff ſhall ſell the ſame at public auction, and a deed thereof by him given ſhall make to the buyer a good eſtate againſt the ſaid mortgageor, his heirs or aſſigns. And the money ariſing

Proceeds, where to be paid.

by the ſale, after all lawful coſts and charges are deducted, ſhall, within three months after the ſale, be paid by the Sheriff into the

the Grand Committee's office, and be ac-counted for and burnt at the next enfuing audit; and a receipt of the keeper of the faid office fhall be a full difcharge to the Sheriff for the fum fo paid; and if the faid fum was more than was due on the mort-gage of the land for principal and intereft, the overplus fhall remain in faid office, and be paid upon demand (exclufive of the in-tereft due to the State, which intereft fhall be paid into the General-Treafurer's office) to the mortgageor, his heirs or affigns, he or they giving a receipt for the fame.

Sec. 2. *And be it further enacted,* That in all lands, mortgaged and fold as aforefaid, the mortgageor fhall be foreclofed of all other equity of redemption; and all actions brought for the recovery of fuch lands, or any part thereof, by the mortgageor, his heirs or affigns, fhall be barred in all Courts of Judicature in this State. *Equity of re-demption fore-clofed.*

Sec. 3. *And be it further enacted,* That if the Sheriff who fold the land fhall neglect to pay the money arifing on the fale within the time aforefaid, he fhall forfeit the whole fum the land fold for; and the keeper of the Grand Committee's office, for the time be-ing, is hereby fully authorized and em-powered to fue for and recover the fame, by an action of debt, in which the defend-ant fhall not be allowed to make any plea, but only to iffue. *Sheriff neglect-ing to pay the money, liable.*

Sec. 4. *And be it further enacted,* That deed or deeds given for fuch lands fhall be of the following form, to wit:

To

To all People to whom thefe Prefents fhall
come. I, A. B. Efq; Sheriff of the Coun-
ty of   in the State of Rhode-Ifland,
&c. fend greeting.

Sheriff's deed.   WHEREAS there is an act of the General
Affembly, made and paffed at their feffion
holden at Newport, within and for faid
State, on the fecond Monday of June, A. D.
1754, entitled, " An act empowering the
Sheriffs to fell and give deeds of lands mortgaged to the State," by virtue of which act
the lands or real eftate of   mortgaged to the State's Truftees, and for which
they obtained judgment at a Court of Common Pleas holden at   within and for
the county of   on the   Monday of   an execution hath been levied on the fame, have been fold at public
auction, for the fatisfaction of the faid execution to   who was the higheft bidder, for the fum of   which the faid
               hath fince well and truly paid me,
the faid Sheriff, and all the fteps of the aforementioned act of Affembly hitherto exact-
ly purfued : Now know ye, that by force
and virtue of the faid act, I, the faid Sheriff,
in confideration of the fum of money paid
unto me as aforefaid, do, by thefe prefents,
bargain, fell, affign and fet over, unto the
faid   his heirs and affigns forever,
all and every the aforefaid lands, tenements
and hereditaments, with their and every of
their appurtenances, as the fame are above
defcribed, with all the eftate, right, title,
intereft, property, freehold and inheritance
of the faid   of, in and to the faid premifes
and appurtenances to the faid   his
heirs and affigns forever.   In witnefs

An

An Act regulating the affefsing and collecting 1696.
of Taxes. 1702.

1747.

Section 1. **B**E *it enacted by the General* 1755. Secretary to
B *Affembly, and by the autho-* 1757. fend
rity thereof it is enacted, That when any tax 1758. copies
of acts
is ordered to be affeffed and levied on the 1761. for affeffing
inhabitants of this State, or any eftates with- 1763. taxes to
in the fame, the Secretary of the State, for the 1764. the
Town-
time being, fhall forthwith fend a copy 1781. Clerks.
thereof unto each of the Town-Clerks in 1782.
the State, to be by them immediately deli- 1785. To be
deli-
vered to the Affeffors of taxes for their re- 1798. vered
fpective towns: And that the Affeffors of the Affeffors.
each town fhall affefs and apportion the fame
on the inhabitants of fuch town, or the rateable eftates within the fame, by the time
expreffed in fuch act of Affembly. And Who are to notify the inhabi-
the Affeffors of each town, or the major tants to exhibit a
part of them, fhall, ten days before they lift of their
eftates.
affefs or apportion the fame, fet up three
notifications under their hands, requiring
the inhabitants of their towns to bring in
unto them in writing, under their hands, an
exact lift of their rateable eftate, by fuch
time as fhall be therein prefixed, who are
hereby required to give and make oath
or affirmation before any one of the affeffors,
who is hereby empowered to adminifter
the fame; which oath or affirmation fhall be
in the following form, to wit:

"You A. B. do folemnly fwear (or affirm) that the account or lift now exhibited
by you, contains, to the beft of your knowledge and judgment, a true and full account
of all your rateable eftate. So help you
God. (Or, and this affirmation you make
and

and give, upon the peril of the penalty of perjury.")

On neglect, to have no remedy if over taxed.

Sec. 2. *And be it further enacted,* That whosoever shall refuse or neglect to render and give in an account of his rateable estate as aforesaid, if he be over taxed, shall have no remedy for the same.

Taxes, how to be assessed.

Sec. 3. *And be it further enacted,* That the Assessors shall, before they apportion the tax among the inhabitants, make a list containing the value of each person's rateable estate by him given in ; and likewise a list containing the value of all such person's estates, according to the best judgment and estimate of the Assessors, who neglect or refuse to give in an account thereof agreeably to law, and of the number of rateable polls, and deduct the sum that the polls will raise from the sum to be assessed and levied ; and the assessors shall cast the rateable estates, and thereby find how much per centum it will be, and they shall apportion the tax accordingly :

Proviso.

Provided nevertheless, that when any person shall give in an account of his rateable estate, and the assessors, or either of them, know that such account is not just and true, in such case the Assessors shall estimate such person's estate at such a value in said list as

Party aggrieved may petition the Court of Sessions.

they shall think it worth : And if any person shall think himself aggrieved thereby, he may petition to the next Court of General Sessions of the Peace for the county in which the supposed grievance shall happen ; and

Proceedings therein.

the Sessions, on receiving such petition, are hereby required to grant a citation for the Assessors, against whom such complaint is made, to appear before them to answer thereunto : And if it shall appear, on trial,

before

before the said Court of Seffions, that the party complaining did fecrete or omit any part of his ratable eftate in giving in his lift or account, they fhall give judgment againft him, and the Affeffors fhall recover double coft, and the faid Court fhall award execution for the fame: But if on trial it fhall appear to the faid Court that a true lift was given in, then they fhall give judgment for the complainant, that the fum in which they fhall judge him to be over-taxed, together with his coft, be deducted from his tax: A copy of which judgment being produced to the Collector of taxes of the town, he fhall deduct fuch fum over-taxed as aforefaid, and coft, from fuch perfon's tax, in cafe the fame be not levied and collected, and the town fhall pay into the general-treafury fuch fum deducted; but in cafe fuch tax fhall have been fully paid before the producing to the faid Collector of taxes a copy of fuch judgment, then the complainant fhall prefent the fame to the Town-Treafurer, who fhall refund to him the fum over-taxed, and coft, out of the town-treafury. And in cafe fuch fum over-taxed, and coft, fhall amount to more than fuch perfon's tax, then the balance fhall be paid him out of the town-treafury, on producing to the Town-Treafurer a copy of the judgment as aforefaid. And no fuch appeal or complaint to the Court of Seffions fhall, during the procefs thereof, and before judgment obtained as aforefaid, ftay or prevent the collection of the tax of the appellant or complainant.

Sum over-taxed, how to be deducted.

Sec. 4. *And be it further enacted*, That the Affeffors of taxes in the feveral towns in this State, in affeffing taxes for real eftates,

Taxes for real eftates to be affeffed on the occupants.

F f f

tates, affefs the fame upon the perfons who
hold and occupy the real eftates in the
refpective towns ; and that the real and
perfonal eftates of fuch tenants or occupants, on whom the fame are affeffed, fhall
be liable for the payment and fatisfaction
of the taxes which fhall be affeffed as afore-
Provifo. faid : *Provided neverthelefs*, that if the tenants or occupants of real eftates as aforefaid are not poffeffed, in their own rights, of
eftates real or perfonal fufficient to fatisfy
the taxes affeffed againft them as aforefaid,
the faid real eftates by them holden and oc-
cupied as aforefaid fhall be liable for the
payment and fatisfaction of the faid taxes.

Lift of ratable   Sec. 5. *And be it further enacted*, That the
eftates, how
made. Affeffors fhall, in making the faid lift or eftimate of ratable eftates, diftinguifh therein
thofe perfons who give in an account or lift
of their eftates, from thofe who neglect fo to
do ; and fhall alfo diftinguifh all taxes affeffed for real eftates from thofe affeffed for
perfonal eftates, making in the tax-bill a
diftinct and feparate column for each ; and
fhall deliver the faid eftimate to the Town-
Clerk with the faid tax-bill.

Affeffors to de-   Sec. 6. *And be it further enacted*, That
liver the tax-bill
to the Town- the Affeffors fhall, immediately upon their
Clerk. affeffing and apportioning any tax to them
committed to affefs, fend a true bill or lift
thereof to the Town-Clerk of the town to
which they refpectively belong, under their
Who fhall fend hands ; and if it be a State tax, the Town-
the fame to the
General-Trea- Clerk fhall, upon receipt thereof, draw an
furer. exact copy under his hand, and fend the
fame to the General-Treafurer, with the
names of the Town-Treafurer and the Collector of taxes for his town ; but if it be
a town tax, he fhall deliver the fame to the
Town-

Town-Treafurer of faid town. And the
General-Treafurer, on receipt of fuch copy, fhall iffue forth his warrant to the
Collector of faid town, and affix the fame to
the tax-bill, commanding him, in the name
of the State, to collect the feveral fums of
money therein expreffed againft each perfon's name, by fuch time as by law is limited, and when collected, to pay the fame
unto him or his fucceffor in faid office.

General-Trea-
furer to iffue his
warrant.

Sec. 7. *And be it further enacted,* That
if any perfon in this State, being legally
taxed in any town, fhall neglect or refufe
to pay fuch tax, it being by the officer to
whom fuch tax fhall be committed to collect
legally demanded of him, in cafe no eftate,
real or perfonal, can be found by fuch
officer, to attach or diftrain, fufficient for
the payment thereof, he fhall be by fuch
officer committed to the gaol of the county,
there to remain (without any allowance for
his fupport) until he fhall pay the fum affeffed on him, with the coft.

Perfons neglect-
ing to pay their
taxes, may be
committed, in
cafe.

Sec. 8. *And be it further enacted,* That
when any perfon fhall be taxed in one town,
and remove into another, before his tax
fhall be collected, then it fhall be lawful
for the Collector of taxes to follow fuch
perfon into any town in the State, and there
levy and collect fuch tax as fully and effectually, to every intent and purpofe, as if
fuch perfon had not removed out of the
town wherein he was taxed.

Removing out of
the town, may
be followed by
the Collector.

Sec. 9. *And be it further enacted,* That the
feveral Collectors of taxes in this State be
and they are hereby empowered, to remove
flock, or other property by them diftrained,
for the non-payment of taxes, to any part
of the State where the fame may be fold to
the

Collectors may
remove property
to any town for
fale.

the beft advantage ; and that a fale thereof
at public auction in fuch place to which the
fame fhall be removed as aforefaid, after
due notification, fhall be as good and valid
in law as though the fame had been fold in
the town where the faid ftock or property
was diftrained.

Sec. 10. *And be it further enacted*, That
the taxes affeffed upon all unimproved
lands within this State, the owner or owners whereof do not refide within the fame,
and upon all improved lands whereof neither the owner nor occupant lives within
this State, fhall be levied by fale of fo much
of the faid land as will pay the faid tax, after
public notice hath been given twenty days
in one of the news-papers printed in this
State, neareft to the lands fo affeffed, by the
Collector of taxes of the town in which
fuch unimproved land lies. And if the
owner or owners thereof neglect to pay the
tax fo affeffed and levied upon his or their
lands, with the coft of notification, by the
time limited in the notification in faid news-
paper, then, and in fuch cafe, the Collect-
or of taxes fhall fell fo much of the faid
land at public auction, to the higheft bidder,
as will be fufficient to pay faid tax, and the
coft of notification.

**Taxes on un-
improved lands,
&c. to be levied
by fale thereof.**

Sec. 11. *And be it further enacted*, That
if any perfon, being legally taxed in any
town in this State, fhall go to fea or depart
out of the State, leaving no property whereby his faid tax may be fatisfied, it fhall and
may be lawful for the Collector of fuch
town to cite the attorney, agent, factor,
truftee or debtor of any fuch abfent perfon,
before any Juftice or Warden of the Peace
in fuch town, to declare, on oath, how
much

**Collectors may
cite the agent,
&c. of abfent
perfons before a
Juftice, in cafe.**

much of the eftate of fuch abfent perfon he
or fhe hath, if any, in his or her poffeffion.
And fuch attorney, agent, factor, truftee
or debtor, fhall forthwith pay to the faid
Collector the tax of fuch abfent perfon,
with the coft of citing as aforefaid, if he
hath fufficient property in his poffeffion, or
fhall deliver unto the faid Collector all or fo
much of the property of fuch abfent perfon as will be fufficient to difcharge his faid
tax, and coft.

Sec. 12. *And be it further enacted*, That
if any attorney, agent, factor, truftee or
debtor, of fuch abfent perfon as aforefaid,
fhall neglect or refufe, on being cited to
appear before any Juftice or Warden as
aforefaid, to declare on oath how much, if
any, of the property of fuch abfent perfon
he or fhe hath in his or her poffeffion, or
having declared on oath as aforefaid, fhall
neglect or refufe to pay the tax of fuch abfent perfon, or to deliver to the Collector all
or fo much of the property of fuch abfent
perfon as will be fufficient to pay the fame,
with the cofts, fuch Juftice or Warden
fhall forthwith grant unto the faid Collector
his warrant of diftrefs againft the proper
goods and chattels of fuch attorney, agent,
factor, truftee or debtor; and the faid Collector is hereby authorized and empowered
to feize and diftrain the fame, or fo much
thereof as will be fufficient to pay and difcharge faid tax, with the coft.

Neglecting to pay fuch abfent perfon's tax, his goods may be diftrained, in cafe.

Sec. 13. *And be it further enacted*, That
if any attorney, agent, factor, truftee or
debtor, fhall pay the tax of any fuch abfent
perfon, or fhall deliver unto the Collector
the property of fuch abfent perfon for that
purpofe, or fhall have his goods and chattels

Such diftraint, &c. to be a bar againft the ab- fent perfon.

tels diftrained for the payment of fuch abfent perfon's tax in manner as aforefaid, it fhall be a good and fufficient bar to
any aftion which fhall or may be brought
for the fame by fuch abfent perfon, againft
fuch attorney, agent, faftor, truftee or
debtor.

Sec. 14. *And be it further enacted,* That
the General-Treafurer, for the time being,
is hereby empowered and directed to call
Special Courts upon every Colleftor of
taxes and his fureties, who fhall negleft to
pay into the general-treafury the proportion
of any tax to him committed to colleft, by
the time limited for collecting the fame;
and the Town-Treafurers of the refpeftive
towns fhall, on requeft, deliver the bonds
of fuch delinquent Colleftor or Colleftors
unto the General-Treafurer, for that purpofe.

General-Trea-
furer may call
Special Courts
on delinquent
Colleftors.

Town-Trea-
furers to deliver
their bonds for
that purpofe.

Sec. 15. *And be it further enacted,* That
in all executions iffuing on any judgment
obtained by the General-Treafurer as aforefaid, againft any delinquent Colleftor of
taxes and his fureties, the words " or real
eftate," fhall be inferted in the mandatory
part of faid execution immediately after
the words "goods and chattels :" That the
Sheriff to whom the faid execution fhall be
delivered, fhall, immediately on receipt of
the fame, attach and take into his poffeffion
all the eftate, real and perfonal, within his
precinft, belonging to fuch Colleftor, and
fhall immediately after fuch attachment ad-
vertife the faid eftate, real and perfonal,
to be fold at public auftion, within twenty
days thereafter; and fhall caufe fo much of
faid eftate to be fold as will be fufficient to
pay and fatisfy the amount of fuch execution, and all incidental expences and cofts.

Executions, how
to iffue.

To be levied on
real and perfonal
eftate.

Sec.

Sec. 16. *And be it further enacted,* That in cafe of accidents or extraordinary ftorms or tempefts, by reafon whereof few or no pur-chafers may attend, it fhall and may be lawful for the Sheriff to adjourn the fale of the eftates fo attached, from one day to the next, and fo for three adjournments, and no longer.

Sec. 17. *And be it further enacted,* That in cafe any delinquent Collector of taxes as aforefaid fhall have eftates in two counties, the execution fhall be directed to the She-riffs or their Deputies of the faid refpective counties, and the faid eftates in both coun-ties fhall be attached and proceeded againft in manner as aforefaid.

Sec. 18. *And be it further enacted,* That if the eftate, real and perfonal, of fuch de-linquent Collector, which fhall be fold as aforefaid, fhall not be fufficient to difcharge the amount of the execution, with the coft of levying the fame, an *alias* execution fhall be immediately iffued againft the fure-ties of fuch Collector for levying and col-lecting the remainder, which execution fhall be levied on the eftate, real and perfonal, of the fureties, in manner as above directed, and fhall be returnable in fourteen days from the date thereof.

Sec. 19. *And be it further enacted,* That if any Town-Treafurer fhall neglect or re-fufe to deliver to the General-Treafurer, as herein required, the bond of any delinquent Collector to be profecuted in manner as aforefaid, the General-Treafurer fhall im-mediately iffue a warrant of diftrefs againft fuch Town-Treafurer, directed to the She-riff or his Deputy of the county in which
fuch

such Town-Treasurer shall reside; and the said Sheriff or Deputy shall, on receipt of the same, attach and take into his possession all the estate, real and personal, of such Town-Treasurer, and sell the same at public auction, in the same manner he is above directed to sell the estates of delinquent Collectors. And if the estate of such Town-Treasurer, attached and sold as aforesaid, shall not be sufficient to discharge the tax for which such delinquent Collector is in arrear, together with the cost of executing said warrant of distress, the body of said Town-Treasurer shall be committed to gaol, there to remain until such tax and cost are fully paid and satisfied.

Real estate, how to be sold.

Sec. 20. *And be it further enacted,* That in all cases where, by virtue of this act, real estates are liable for the payment of taxes, and the manner of selling the same, and executing deeds thereof is not herein prescribed, the same shall be sold at public auction to the highest bidder, notifications thereof having been set up in two or more public places in the town where such land lies, twenty days, at least, previous to such sale; and a deed or deeds thereof made and executed by the Sheriff or Collector who shall sell the same, shall vest in the purchaser or purchasers all the estate, right and title the owner or owners thereof had in and to such real estate, at the time the same was first notified for sale as aforesaid.

Sec. 21. And whereas the Collectors of taxes have in many instances endeavoured to depreciate orders drawn on the general-treasury, whereby they might purchase the same at a discount: *Be it therefore further enacted,*

enacted, That the General-Treasurer shall not receive of any Collector of taxes any order on the treasury, or certificate for the payment of money out of the same, in payment or discharge of any tax, unless the same be in the name of such Collector, or the Collector hath received the same at the full value thereof, agreeably to the sum expressed in said order or certificate : And in order to ascertain the truth, the said General-Treasurer shall, previous to his receiving the same in payment or discharge of any tax, administer the following oath or affirmation unto such Collector :

"YOU A. B. do solemnly swear (or affirm) that the orders or certificates by you here presented, have been received by you at the full value or sum as is in said order or certificate expressed ; and that you have not made any discount on the same, directly or indirectly, to lessen the value thereof. So help you God. (Or, and this affirmation you make and give, upon the peril of the penalty of perjury.") *Oath of the Collector.*

Sec. 22. *And be it further enacted,* That if any Collector of taxes shall purchase or receive of any individual any order or certificate as aforesaid for a less sum than is in said order or certificate expressed, in order to make gain or lucre thereby, and shall be thereof lawfully convicted by indictment before any Court of Record in this State, such Collector shall forfeit double the amount of such order or certificate by him so purchased or received, to and for the use of the State; and shall be forever thereafter incapable of sustaining any office in the State, civil or military ; *provided* such pro- *Penalty for receiving orders at a discount.*

G g g secution

fecution be had againft fuch Collector in one year after the offence committed.

Sec. 23. *And be it further enacted,* That all town taxes which fhall be affeffed on any town in this State, fhall be affeffed, levied and collected, in the fame manner as the State taxes are, or by this act ought to be; and the Town-Treafurer of each town fhall have the fame power of calling Special Courts on delinquent Collectors and their fureties, and of levying execution on their eftates, real and perfonal, as the General-Treafurer hath by this act.

Town taxes how to be affeffed, collected, &c.

Sec. 24. *And be it further enacted,* That all warrants that fhall be granted for collecting taxes, fhall continue and remain in full force until the whole of each refpective tax fhall be collected.

Warrants for collecting taxes, how long to continue in force.

Sec. 25. *And be it further enacted,* That the Affeffors fhall be allowed one and one quarter per cent. for apportioning each tax, and the Town-Clerk for copying the tax-bills fhall be paid as for other copies, and the Collector fhall be paid for collecting at the rate of five per cent. unlefs he fhall have agreed with the town therefor for a lefs fum, which fees fhall be paid out of each town-treafury.

Affeffors, Collectors and Clerks fees.

Sec. 26. *And be it further enacted,* That when and fo often as any tax fhall be ordered by the General Affembly to be affeffed upon the inhabitants of this State, and any or either of the towns therein fhall neglect or refufe to affefs fuch tax upon the inhabitants of their refpective towns, agreeably to fuch order of the Affembly, fuch town fo neglecting or refufing fhall pay a fine of double their proportion of faid tax into the general-treafury, to be recovered by the General-Treafurer

Penalty for neglecting to affefs taxes.

Treasurer by an action of debt against the Town-Treasurer of such delinquent town, in either of the Courts of Common Pleas in this State. And further, that any such delinquent town, notwithstanding their being fined, shall be obliged to pay their proportion of the tax.

Sec. 27. *And be it further enacted,* That all estates, real or personal, granted or appropriated to religious uses, or to the use of schools or seminaries of learning, within this State, be and the same are hereby exempted from taxation.

Lands granted for the use of schools, &c. exempted from taxation.

An Act for introducing the Dollar and its Parts, as the Money of Account within this State.

1795.

Section 1. BE *it enacted by the General Assembly, and by the authority thereof it is enacted,* That the money of account of this State shall be the dollar, cent and mille ; and all accounts in the public offices and other public accounts, and all proceedings in the Courts of Justice and in the Town-Councils, shall be kept and had in conformity to this regulation.

The dollar and its parts established as the money of account.

Sec. 2. *And be it further enacted,* That the forms of writs or processes, or instruments used in the Courts of Justice or Town-Councils, or in any public office in this State, in which any sum or sums are now required to be expressed in pounds, shillings and pence, shall and may be altered to an equivalent sum in dollars and parts of a dollar, expressed as above mentioned.

Forms of writs, &c. to be altered.

Provided, That this act shall not be understood to vitiate or nullify any account, charge or entry, originally made or to be made, or

Proviso.

any

any note, bond or other inftrument, expreff-
fed, or which fhall be expreffed, in any
money of account exifting at the time of paffing this act; but the fame fhall be reduced to
dollars and parts of a dollar, as herein before
directed, in any fuit or declaration thereupon.

---

*An Act declaring how Mortgages and Bonds,
given by the feveral Perfons who borrowed
of this State the Paper Money Bills, of the
Emiffion of May, A. D. 1786, fhall be difcharged.*

Mortgages, and
bonds given for
paper money,
how to be dif-
charged.
B E it enacted by the General Affembly, and
by the authority thereof it is enacted,
That the feveral perfons who borrowed of
the State the paper bills of the emiffion of
May, A. D. 1786, and for fecuring the payment thereof, with the intereft, gave their
mortgages and bonds, be allowed to difcharge them by paying in the amount thereof in the faid paper currency, or in gold or
filver, at and after the rate of one dollar in
filver money for every four pounds ten
fhillings fpecified in fuch mortgage or bond,
at the refpective periods when the fame fhall
become due. And in cafe of an action being commenced for the recovery thereof,
judgment fhall be entered up for the fame
accordingly, together with any intereft that
may have accrued thereon.

---

*An Act regulating the Manner of drawing
Money out of the General-Treafury.*

No money paid
out of the trea-
fury without an
order.
B E it enacted by the General Affembly, and
by the authority thereof it is enacted,
That no money be paid out of the general-
treafury of this State to any perfon, unlefs
he produce an order therefor from the
General Affembly, certified by the Secretary.
Provided

Provided nevertheless, That the Governor   of this State, for the time being, fhall have power to draw upon the General-Treafurer for payment for any particular fervices or expences of a public nature, to the amount of twenty dollars, at any one time: *And pro-vided alfo,* that all accounts paffed by the Supreme Judicial Court, or either of the Courts of General Seffions of the Peace within this State, in favour of thofe who have in faid Courts obtained allowances for fervices rendered in bringing criminals to juftice, and for other incidental expences ; and alfo all certificates for any officer's or Juror's attendance on faid Court according to law, fhall be paid by the General-Trea-furer on the certificate of the Clerk of faid Court.

An Act to prevent the Detention of Fines from the proper Offices.   1752. 1765.

Section 1. **B**E it enacted by the General 1794. Affembly, and by the autho-rity thereof it is enacted, That all officers   who fhall receive any fine or fines, forfeit-ures or penalties, fhall forthwith pay the fame into the proper office where by law they ought to be paid ; and that if any officer, judicial, executive or minifterial, fhall refufe or neglect, for the fpace of three months, to pay over any fine, forfeiture or penalty, or any part thereof which may have come to his hands, to the proper officer to whom by law the fame ought to be paid or delivered, he fhall forfeit and pay treble the   value or amount of the fine, forfeiture or penalty, fo withholden or not paid over, to be recovered by action of debt before any

Court

Court proper to try the fame ; one moiety thereof to the ufe of the perfon who fhall fue for the fame, and the other moiety to and for the ufe of the State.

Officers to profe-
cute for the fame.

Sec. 2. *And be it further enacted, That* it fhall be the duty of the officers from whom any fines, forfeitures or penalties may be withholden or detained, to collect the fame in the due courfe of law, and to profe-cute for the breaches of this act in manner aforefaid.

Juftices to make
return of fines to
the General-
Treafurer.

Sec. 3. *And be it further enacted, That* every Juftice of the Peace and Warden fhall annually, at the May feffion of the General Affembly, make return to the General-Trea-furer whether he hath collected any fines due to the State during the laft year, and until that time, and the amount and circum-ftances of fuch fines, if any, by him collected,

On neglect, ren-
dered ineligible.

and fhall pay over the fame to the General-Treafurer ; and that if any Juftice of the Peace or Warden fhall neglect to make re-turn as aforefaid, or fhall neglect to pay over the fines by him collected, he fhall be ineligi-ble to the faid office of Juftice of the Peace or Warden.

An Act to organize the Militia of this State.

WHEREAS by the Conftitution of the United States, the Congrefs have power to provide for organizing, arming and difciplining the militia, and for govern-ing fuch part of them as may be employed in the fervice of the United States ; referv-ing to the States refpectively the appoint-ment of the officers, and the authority of training the militia according to the difci-

pline

pline prefcribed by Congrefs: And whereas 1776.
the Congrefs did, on the eighth day of May, 1777.
A. D. 1792, pafs an act, entitled, "An act 1779.
more effectually to provide for the national 1794.
defence, by eftablifhing an uniform militia 1796.
throughout the United States;" which act 1798.
is in the words following, to wit:

"An Act more effectually to provide for the
national Defence, by eftablifhing an uni- Act of Congrefs.
form Militia throughout the United States.

1. *BE it enacted by the Senate and Houfe
of Reprefentatives of the United States of
America, in Congrefs affembled,* That each
and every free able bodied white male citi- Who fhall be en-
zen of the refpective States, refident therein, rolled.
who is or fhall be of the age of eighteen
years, and under the age of forty-five years,
(except as is herein after excepted) fhall
feverally and refpectively be enrolled in the
militia, by the Captain or Commanding
Officer of the company within whofe bounds
fuch citizen fhall refide, and that within
twelve months after the paffing of this act.
And it fhall at all times hereafter be the duty
of every fuch Captain or Commanding
Officer of a company, to enrol every fuch
citizen as aforefaid, and alfo thofe who fhall,
from time to time, arrive at the age of eighteen years, or being of the age of eighteen
years, and under the age of forty-five years,
(except as before excepted) fhall come to
refide within his bounds; and fhall without
delay notify fuch citizen of the faid enrolment, by a proper non-commiffioned officer
of the company, by whom fuch notice may
be proved; that every citizen fo enrolled
and notified fhall, within fix months thereafter.

after, provide himfelf with a good mufket of firelock, a fufficient bayonet and belt, two fpare flints, and a knapfack, a pouch, with a box therein, to contain not lefs than twenty-four cartridges, fuited to the bore of his mufket or firelock, each cartridge to contain a proper quantity of powder and ball; or with a good rifle, knapfack, fhot-pouch and powder-horn, twenty balls fuited to the bore of his rifle, and a quarter of a pound of powder; and fhall appear, fo armed, accoutred and provided, when called out to exercife, or into fervice, except that when called out on company days to exercife only, he may appear without a knapfack. That the commiffioned officers fhall feverally be armed with a fword or hanger and efpontoon, and that from and after five years from the paffing of this act, all mufkets for arming the militia, as herein required, fhall be of bores fufficient for balls of the eighteenth part of a pound. And every citizen fo enrolled, and providing himfelf with arms, ammunition and accoutrements, required as aforefaid, fhall hold the fame exempted from all fuits, diftreffes, executions or fales, for debt, or for the payment of taxes.

2. *And be it further enacted,* That the Vice-Prefident of the United States; the officers, judicial and executive, of the government of the United States; the Members of both Houfes of Congrefs, and their refpective officers; all cuftom-houfe officers, with their clerks; all poft-officers and ftage-drivers, who are employed in the care and conveyance of the mail of the Poft-Office of the United States; all ferry-men employed at any ferry on the poft-road;

road ; all infpectors of **exports** ; all pilots ; all mariners actually employed in the fea fervice of any citizen or merchant within the United States, and all perfons who now are or may hereafter be exempted by the laws of the refpective States, fhall be and are hereby exempted from militia duty, not-withftanding their being above the age of eighteen, and under the age of forty-five years.

3. *And be it further enacted*, That within one year after paffing of this act, the militia of the refpective States fhall be arranged into divifions, brigades, regiments, battalions and companies, as the Legiflature of each State fhall direct ; and each divifion, brigade and regiment, fhall be numbered at the formation thereof, and a record made of fuch numbers in the Adjutant-General's office in the State ; and when in the field, or in fervice in the State, each divifion, brigade and regiment, fhall refpectively take rank according to their numbers, reckoning the firft or loweft number higheft in rank. That if the fame be convenient, each brigade fhall confift of four regiments ; each regiment of two battalions ; each battalion of five companies ; and each company of fixty-four privates. That the faid militia fhall be officered by the refpective States as follows : To each divifion one Major-General, and two Aids-de-Camp, with the rank of Major ; to each brigade, one Brigadier-General, with one Brigade Infpector, to ferve alfo as Brigade Major, with the rank of a Major ; to each regiment, one Lieutenant-Colonel Commandant ; and to each battalion, one Major ; to each company, one Captain, one Lieutenant, one Enfign, four Serjeants,

Militia, how to be divided,

and officered.

H h h four

fout Corporals, one Drummer, and one Fifer or Bugler. That there shall be a regimental staff, to consist of one Adjutant, and one Quarter-Master, to rank as Lieutenants; one Paymaster, one Surgeon, and one Surgeon's Mate; one Serjeant-Major, one Drum-Major, and one Fife-Major.

Companies of grenadiers, &c. to be formed, &c. 4. *And be it further enacted,* That out of the militia enrolled, as is herein directed, there shall be formed for each battalion at least one company of grenadiers, light infantry or riflemen; and that to each division there shall be at least one company of artillery, and one troop of horse: There shall be to each company of artillery, one Captain, two Lieutenants, four Serjeants, four Corporals, six Gunners, six Bombardiers, one Drummer, and one Fifer. The officers to be armed with a sword or hanger, a fusee, bayonet and belt, with a cartridge-box, to contain twelve cartridges; and each private or matross shall furnish himself with all the equipments of a private in the infantry, until proper ordnance and field artillery is provided. There shall be to each troop of horse, one Captain, two Lieutenants, one Cornet, four Serjeants, four Corporals, one Saddler, one Farrier, and one Trumpeter. The commissioned officers to furnish themselves with good horses of at least fourteen hands and an half high, and to be armed with a sword and pair of pistols, the holsters of which to be covered with bearskin caps. Each dragoon to furnish himself with a serviceable horse, at least fourteen hands and an half high, a good saddle, bridle, mail-pillion and valise, holsters, and a breastplate and crupper, a pair of boots and spurs, a pair of pistols, a sabre, fabre, and a cartouch-box, to contain twelve cartridges for piſtols : That each company of artillery, and troop of horſe, ſhall be formed of volunteers from the brigade, at the diſcretion of the Commander in Chief of the State, not exceeding one company of each to a regiment, nor more in number than one eleventh part of the infantry, and ſhall be uniformly clothed in regimentals, to be furniſhed at their own expence ; the colour and faſhion to be determined by the Brigadier commanding the brigade to which they belong.

5. *And be it further enacted,* That each battalion and regiment ſhall be provided with the State and regimental colours by the field officers, and each company with a drum and fife, or bugle-horn, by the com- miſſioned officers of the company, in ſuch manner as the Legiſlature of the reſpective States ſhall direct.

Colours, &c. to be provided.

6. *And be it further enacted,* That there ſhall be an Adjutant-General appointed in each State, whoſe duty it ſhall be to diſtri- bute all orders from the Commander in Chief of the State to the ſeveral corps ; to attend all public reviews, when the Com- mander in Chief of the State ſhall review the militia, or any part thereof ; to obey all orders from him relative to carrying into execution and perfecting the ſyſtem of military diſcipline eſtabliſhed by this act ; to furniſh blank forms of different returns that may be required, and to explain the principles on which they ſhould be made ; to receive from the ſeveral officers of the different corps throughout the State returns of the militia under their command, report- ing the actual ſituation of their arms, accoutre- ments

Adjutant-Ge- neral, his duty.

ments and ammunition, their delinquencies, and every other thing which relates to the general advancement of good order and discipline: All which the several officers of the divisions, brigades, regiments and battalions, are hereby required to make in the usual manner, so that the said Adjutant-General may be duly furnished therewith; from all which returns he shall make proper abstracts, and lay the same annually before the Commander in Chief of the State.

Rules of discipline.

7. *And be it further enacted*, That the rules of discipline, approved and established by Congress, in their resolutions of the twenty-ninth of March, one thousand seven hundred and seventy-nine, shall be the rules of discipline to be observed by the militia throughout the United States, except such deviations from the said rules as may be rendered necessary by the requisitions of this act, or some other unavoidable circumstances. It shall be the duty of the Commanding Officer, at every muster, whether by battalion, regiment or single company, to cause the militia to be exercised and trained agreeably to the said rules of discipline.

Rank.

8. *And be it further enacted*, That all commissioned officers shall take rank according to the date of their commissions; and when two of the same grade bear an equal date, then the rank to be determined by lot, to be drawn by them before the Commanding Officer of the brigade, regiment, battalion, company or detachment.

Disabled soldiers.

9. *And be it further enacted*, That if any person, whether officer or soldier, belonging to the militia of any State, and called out into the service of the United States,

be

be wounded or difabled while in actual
fervice, he fhall be taken care of and provided for at the public expence.

10. *And be it further enacted,* That it fhall
be the duty of the Brigade Infpector to attend the regimental and battalion meetings of the militia compofing their feveral
brigades, during the time of their being
under arms ; to infpect their arms, ammunition and accoutrements ; fuperintend their
exercife and manœuvres, and introduce
the fyftem of military difcipline before defcribed throughout the brigade, agreeable to
law, and fuch orders as they fhall, from
time to time, receive from the Commander
in Chief of the State ; to make returns to
the Adjutant-General of the State, at leaft
once in every year, of the militia of the
brigade to which he belongs, reporting
therein the actual fituation of the arms,
accoutrements and ammunition of the feveral corps, and every other thing which in
his judgment may relate to their government, and the general advancement of good
order. and military difcipline ; and the Adjutant-General fhall make a return of all
the militia of the State to the Commander
in Chief of the faid State, and a duplicate
of the fame to the Prefident of the United
States.

And whereas fundry corps of artillery,
cavalry and infantry, now exift in feveral of
the faid States, which by the laws, cuftoms
or ufages thereof, have not been incorporated with. or fubject to, the general regulations of the militia :

11. *Be it further enacted,* That fuch corps
retain their accuftomed privileges, fubject
neverthelefs to all other duties required
by

*Brigade Infpect-
or, his duty.*

*Independent
companies.*

by this act, in like manner with the other militia.

And whereas the reservations contained in the said Constitution, relative to the militia of the States respectively, render it necessary that provision should be made in the premises by the Legislature of this State:

Section 1. *Be it therefore enacted by this General Assembly, and by the authority thereof it is enacted,* That the whole militia of this State shall be arranged into one division; that the said division shall constitute four brigades; that the militia in the counties of Newport and Bristol shall form one brigade; the militia in the county of Providence, one brigade; the militia in the county of Washington, one brigade; and the militia in the county of Kent, one brigade: That the brigade in the counties of Newport and Bristol shall consist of three regiments; the brigade in the county of Providence, of six regiments; the brigade in the county of Washington, of three regiments; and the brigade in the county of Kent, of two regiments: And that each regiment, whose numbers, in the opinion of the field officers, will admit of it, shall be divided into two battalions.

Sec. 2. *And be it further enacted,* That the regiments aforesaid be constituted as follows, to wit: That the towns of Newport, Portsmouth, New-Shoreham, Jamestown and Middletown, constitute one regiment; and the towns of Tiverton and Little-Compton, one regiment: That the towns of Bristol, Warren and Barrington, constitute one regiment: That the towns of Providence and North Providence constitute

Militia divided into brigades,

and regiments.

Regiments constituted.

stitute

ftitute one regiment; the towns of Smithfield and Cumberland, one regiment; the
town of Scituate, one regiment; the town
of Glocefter, one regiment; the towns of
Cranfton and Johnfton, one regiment; and
the town of Fofter, one regiment : That the
towns of Wefterly, Charleftown and Hopkinton, conftitute one regiment; the towns
of North-Kingftown and Exeter, one regiment; and the towns of South-Kingftown
and Richmond, one regiment : That the
towns of Warwick and Eaft-Greenwich
conftitute one regiment; and the towns of
Weft-Greenwich and Coventry, one regiment.

Sec. 3. *And be it further enacted,* That there
be four companies of militia in the town of
Newport, five in the town of Providence,
two in the town of Portfmouth, three in
the town of Warwick, four in the town of
Wefterly, one in the town of New-Shoreham, four in the town of North-Kingftown,
four in the town of South-Kingftown, two
in the town of Eaft-Greenwich, one in the
town of Jameftown, four in the town of
Smithfield, four in the town of Scituate,
fix in the town of Glocefter, two in the
town of Charleftown, three in the town of
Weft-Greenwich, four in the town of Coventry; three in the town of Exeter, one in
the town of Middletown, one in the town of
Briftol, three in the town of Tiverton, two
in the town of Little-Compton, two in the
town of Warren, three in the town of Cumberland, two in the town of Richmond,
three in the town of Cranfton, four in the
town of Hopkinton, two in the town of
Johnfton, two in the town of North-Providence, one in the town of Barrington, and
four

Companies cen-
ftituted.

four in the town of Foster: And that the aforesaid division, brigades, regiments, battalions and companies, be officered agreeably to the above recited act of Congress, and that the officers be engaged according to law.

Sec. 4. *And be it further enacted*, That in addition to the persons exempted from military duty by the act of Congress herein before recited, there shall be, and hereby are, exempted from such duty, the following persons, to wit: All persons who have holden the offices of Governor or Lieutenant-Governor; all persons who sustained any military commission or commissions, previous to the last day of February, A. D. 1796, and took their engagement thereupon according to law; all persons who after the said last day of February, A. D. 1796, shall hold any military commission or commissions for the space of five years successively, and take their engagements thereupon according to law; and all persons, who after the said last day of February, A. D. 1796, shall hold any military commission or commissions, and shall take their engagements thereupon according to law, and shall be therefrom suspended or left out by any election of the General Assembly.

Sec. 5. *And be it further enacted*, That persons of the following description, so long as they shall continue of said description, shall be, and hereby are, exempted from military duty, to wit: The members of both Houses of the Legislature, the Justices and Clerks of the Supreme Judicial Court, the Justices and Clerks of the Court of Common Pleas, the Secretary, the Attorney-ney-General, the General-Treasurer, the High-Sheriff of each county, Justices of the Peace, one Ferryman at each stated ferry, who usually attends the same; one Miller at each grist-mill, who usually attends the same; every settled or ordained Minister of the gospel, the President, Professors, Tutors, Students and Steward of Rhode-Island College; Town-Council men, Town-Treasurers, Town-Clerks, Town-Sergeants, practising Physicians, Surgeons, Apothecaries, Preceptors and Ushers of Academies and schools, Enginemen, and every member of a chartered independent military body, who shall deliver, once for all, a certificate from the Commanding Officer of said body, that he is a member of such body, and completely equipped according to law, and the rules and regulations of said body.

Sec. 6. *And be it further enacted,* That whenever any member of any such chartered independent military body shall cease, otherwise than by death or removal out of the State, to be a member thereof, it shall be the duty of the Commanding Officer of such body forthwith to give notice thereof to the Commanding Officer of the militia company within the bounds of which the said member shall then reside.

Notice to be given of leaving a chartered company.

Sec. 7. *And be it further enacted,* That every person liable by this act to do military duty, shall be deemed and adjudged to have notice of his being enrolled by the Captain or Commanding Officer of the company of militia, within the bounds of which he shall reside; *provided* that such person shall have resided three months in the town in which such company shall be.

Notice of enrolment.

Sec. 8. *And be it further enacted,* That

Return

I i i   it

it fhall be the duty of the Commanding Of
ficer of every company to make a return of
the fame to the Commandants of their refpective regiments, who fhall make returns
of their refpective regiments to the Briga-
dier-Generals : And where faid companies
or regiments are not refpectively attached
to any regiment or brigade, returns fhall be
made to the Adjutant-General. And it
fhall be the duty of the Brigade-Major of
fuch brigade, to form a brigade return, and
tranfmit the fame to the Adjutant-General,
who fhall, from the feveral returns thus
made, form a general return, and prefent
the fame to his Excellency the Commander
in Chief of the State, and a copy thereof to
the Major-General; and tranfmit another
duplicate thereof to the Prefident of the
United States; and that the general return
aforefaid, and the copies thereof, be made,
prefented and tranfmitted as aforefaid, on
or before the firft day of January, annually.

Times, &c. of
training.

Sec. 9. *And be it further enacted,* That
on the firft Wednefday in April, and on the
fecond Wednefday in September, in every
year, the militia of this State fhall meet by
companies (unlefs the weather on thofe
days fhall be foul, in which cafe they fhall
meet on the next fair day) for the purpofe of training, difciplining and improving
them in martial exercife; and in the month
of October, in every year, in regiment or
battalion; and that the places of rendez-
vouzing by companies be appointed by the
Commanding Officers of the refpective companies; the places of regimental or battalion rendezvous, by the Commandants of
the regiments refpectively ; and the days of
regimental

regimental or battalion rendezvous, by the refpective Brigadiers.

Sec. 10. *And be it further enacted,* That it fhall be the duty of the Brigade-Major of each brigade, to furnifh a copy of all orders for mufter to the Commandants of regiments within each refpective brigade; and of the Adjutant of each regiment to furnifh a copy of all orders for mufter from the Commandants thereof, to the Commanding Officers of the refpective companies.

Orders for muftering, by whom to be furnifhed.

Sec. 11. *And be it further enacted,* That whenever the Commanding Officer of any company fhall receive orders from his Brigadier, or the Commandant of his regiment, he fhall iffue his warrant for the affembling of his company, at leaft ten days before the time appointed for mufter, directed to one or more non-commiffioned officer or officers, private or privates, by him fpecially appointed, requiring him or them to warn the men of faid company, either in general or in diftricts, to be by him affigned, to affemble, at the time and place appointed therein, equipped according to law. And the warning officer aforefaid fhall warn the men as aforefaid, either by perfonal notice, or by leaving word at their ufual places of abode, fix days before, and fhall return his warrant, with the name of every man fo warned, to the faid Commanding Officer, one day before the day of affembling, as aforefaid.

Companies, how to be warned.

Sec. 12. *And be it further enacted,* That the Commanding Officers of the feveral companies of militia in this State fhall take poft according to the dates of their refpective commiffions, and that their companies fhall

Poft of captains and companies.

shall take post with them in the same station when on parade.

Sec. 13. *And be it further enacted,* That when the militia, or any part of them, shall be assembled together for review or training, it shall be in the power of the Commanding Officer present to punish all disorders, or breaches of military order and discipline, whether in non-commissioned officers or privates, by immediately putting the offender under guard, for a space of time not exceeding twelve hours, or by fining him, not exceeding six dollars, at the discretion of the said Commanding Officer; which fine shall be certified by the officer inflicting the same, to some one Justice of the Peace, and collected, paid over and appropriated, in the manner prescribed by the fifteenth section of this act. And if any commissioned officer shall behave in a disorderly or insolent manner, when the militia, or any part of them, shall be assembled as aforesaid, the said officer shall be liable to be arrested and tried for such behaviour by a Court-Martial, and if found guilty, shall be broken.

Sec. 14. *And be it further enacted,* That every non-commissioned officer or private, who shall neglect to appear (being first legally warned) at the regimental or battalion rendezvous, shall forfeit two dollars for every day of such neglect; and every one who shall neglect to appear (being first legally warned) at the company parade, shall forfeit one dollar and fifty cents for every

day of such neglect; and if he shall not be armed and equipped according to the said act of Congress, when so appearing. in case he shall have resided in this State six months, and

and shall not, within ten days after such rendezvous or parade, produce to the Commanding Officer of his company a certificate from the Clerk of the Town-Council of the town, that he had been adjudged by said Town-Council unable to arm and equip himself, he shall, for appearing without a gun, forfeit twenty-five cents; without a bayonet and belt, eight cents; without a cartouch-box and cartridges, eight cents; without a knapsack, four cents; and without flints, priming-wire and brush, four cents.

Sec. 15. *And be it further enacted,* That at the expiration of ten days after such rendezvous or parade, the Commanding Officer of every company shall deliver to some one Justice of the Peace, residing in the same town, a copy of his warrant, and of the return of the warning officer thereon, together with a list of the delinquents, in not appearing at the rendezvous or parade as aforesaid, and of the delinquents, in not being equipped in the articles enumerated in the preceding section of this act, and of the articles of equipment aforesaid in which they shall have been deficient, and of such offenders as he shall fine, or shall incur a fine, by virtue of the provisions of the thirteenth or eighteenth section of this act, who shall not have paid their fines to said Commanding Officer, or shall not have rendered to him a satisfactory excuse for their delinquencies; and the said Justice of the Peace shall, within ten days after he shall have received such copy and list from such Commanding Officer, issue his warrant against each of such delinquents or offenders, directed to the Town-Sergeant or either of the Constables of said town,

Fines, how collected.

town, requiring them to levy, of the goods and chattels of such delinquent or offender, the fine or fines aforesaid, together with twenty-five cents for said warrant, and all the said Justice's proceedings thereon, and such fees as are allowed by law for serving the same; and for want of such goods or chattels to be found, to commit the body of such delinquent or offender to gaol, and to return the said warrant in twenty days from the date thereof. And in case such delinquent or offender shall be within age, and live with his father, mother or guardian, or shall be an apprentice or indented servant, the said Town-Sergeant or Constable shall be required by said warrant to levy the same upon the goods and chattels of said father, mother, guardian, master or mistress, as the case may be; and the said Town-Sergeant or Constable shall be allowed, for serving said warrant, the same fees as are allowed by law for serving an execution. And if said warrant shall be returned *non est inventus,* the said Justice is hereby authorized to issue an *alias* warrant at any time after.

How appropriated. And the money so levied, and the money paid as a commutation hereafter mentioned, shall be paid to the said Captain or Commanding Officer of the company, at the return of said warrants, to be appropriated to pay the expence of warning said company, and that of music *(provided* the expence of music shall not exceed per day one dollar to the drummer, and one dollar to the fifer) and to purchase colours; and the residue thereof, if any, shall be paid to the Town-Councils of the several towns, to be by them appropriated to the arming and equipping of those who are not able to arm

and

and equip themselves. And the Commanding Officer of the company shall allow a
sum not exceeding the rate of one dollar per
day, to the warning officer aforesaid, for
each and every day that he shall or ought
to be employed in warning said company, to
be judged of by the Commanding Officer
aforesaid.

Sec. 16. *Provided nevertheless, and be it*
further enacted, That the said Captain or
Commanding Officer shall excuse from the
payment of his fine for one year any of the
delinquents aforesaid, *provided* such delinquent shall annually produce to said Captain
or Commanding Officer a certificate of his
belonging to the society of Friends, from
the Clerk of said society, and pay three
dollars as an annual commutation, or annually produce a certificate from any Judge or
Justice of the Peace, that such delinquent
hath made oath or affirmation before said
Judge or Justice, that he is conscientiously
scrupulous against bearing arms, and shall
pay three dollars as an annual commutation.

Sec. 17. *And be it further enacted*, That
it shall be the duty of the Commanding Officer of every company of militia in this
State, to make return of all the fines and
commutations by him collected, and how
disposed of, to the Commandant of his regiment, on or before the first day of January,
in every year.

Sec. 18. *And be it further enacted*, That
every non-commissioned officer or private,
who shall neglect or refuse to warn the men
of his company, when thereto required, as
provided in the eleventh section of this act,
without sufficient excuse, shall forfeit the
sum of five dollars, to be levied and collected

ed after the day appointed for rendezvous or parade, in the manner prescribed for the collection of fines by the fifteenth section of this act.

Sec. 19. *And be it further enacted,* That

Officers neglect-
ing to parade, to
be tried.

every commissioned officer, who shall neglect or refuse to appear on parade with his company, when duly notified, and not having sufficient excuse, shall be tried by a Court-Martial; and if found guilty, shall be broken, and reduced to the ranks.

Sec. 20. *And be it further enacted,* That

Regimental
Court-Martial.

every regimental Court-Martial shall consist of at least five commissioned officers, one whereof at least being a Captain, and shall be appointed by the Commanding Officer of the regiment, who is empowered to confirm, mitigate or disapprove, any sentence by them

General Court-
Martial.

given. And that every General Court-Martial shall consist of at least thirteen commissioned officers, one whereof to be a General or Field Officer, and none under the grade of a Captain, to be appointed by the Major-General, or in his absence by the next officer present in command, who is empowered to confirm, mitigate or disapprove, any sentence by them given.

Sec. 21. *And be it further enacted,* That

Divisions of com-
panies.

the divisions of companies, as now existing in the several towns, be continued, subject however to such alterations as their present numbers or future increase or diminution may, in the judgment of the Field Officers of the regiments respectively to which they belong, from time to time render necessary or expedient.

Sec. 22. *And be it further enacted,* That

Militia subject to
the articles of
war.

whenever the military force of this State, or any part thereof, shall be called into actual
service,

fervice, it fhall be fubject to the articles
of war, prefcribed by Congrefs, for the
government of the troops of the United
States.

Sec. 23. *And be it further enacted,* That
in addition to the officers to be appointed
purfuant to the afore recited act of Congrefs, there be alfo appointed for the militia of this State, one Director and Purveyor-
General of the military hofpital, one Quar-
termafter-General, one Commiffary-Ge-
neral, with the power of fubftitution as
occafion may require, and that the Adjutant-
General fhall have the rank of Lieutenant-
Colonel Commandant.

Commiffary-
General, &c. to
be appointed.

Sec. 24. *And be it further enacted,* That
all officers of the militia, deriving their
appointments from the General Affembly,
fhall hold their refpective appointments for
and during the term of one year from the
time of their refpective appointments, except
in cafe of refignation, or being removed
by the Legiflature for mifdemeanor, or
broken by a fentence of a Court-Martial.

Officers to be ap-
pointed annually.

Sec. 25. *And be it further enacted,* That
the militia of New-Shoreham and Jameftown fhall not be obliged to rendezvous in battalion or regiment, but in
company only, and then the militia of
New-Shoreham on the ifland of Block-
Ifland, and the militia of Jameftown on the
ifland of Connanicutt.

Militia of James-
town, &c. to
rendezvous in
company.

Sec. 26. *And be it further enacted,* That
whenever it fhall happen that any Surveyor
of the highways fhall have warned the men
of his diftrict to work on the highways,
on the fame day that is or fhall be affigned for training, purfuant to this act,

Warned to train
and work on
the highways,
fame day, &c.

the

the faid warning to work upon the highway, fhall be confidered as fuperfeded.

Sec. 27. *And be it further enacted,* That this act fhall be read once in every year, at a company training of every company of militia in this State.

An Act to eftablifh the Senior Clafs.

Section 1. BE it enacted *by the General Affembly, and by the authority thereof it is enacted,* That all perfons exempted from military duty in the militia, by virtue of the act entitled, " An act to organize the militia of this State," be and they are hereby formed into a feparate corps, to be called and known by the name of the Senior

Clafs : That the feveral companies and regiments of fenior clafs be officered in the fame manner as the militia, and be under the command of the Brigadiers of the militia in the diftricts refpectively wherein they fhall be formed.

Sec. 2. *And be it further enacted,* That the fenior clafs of the town of Providence conftitute one company ; that of the town of Cranfton, one company; that of the town of Johnfton, one company ; that of the town of North-Providence, one company ; that of the town of Smithfield, one company ; that of the town of Cumberland, one company ; that of the town of Scituate, one company ; that of the town of Glocefter, one company ; that of the town of Fofter, one company ; which faid companies fhall form one regiment : That the fenior clafs of the town of Wefterly conftitute one company ; that of the town of Charleftown, one company ; that of the

town

town of Hopkinton, one company; that
of the town of North-Kingſtown, one company; that of the town of Exeter, one
company; that of the town of South-
Kingſtown, one company; that of the town
of Richmond, one company; which ſaid
companies ſhall be formed into one regiment: That the ſenior claſs of the towns of
Briſtol, Warren and Barrington, conſtitute
one company; that of the town of Tiverton, one company; that of the town of
Little-Compton, one company; that of the
towns of Newport and Jameſtown, one
company; that of the towns of Portſmouth
and Middletown, one company; which
companies ſhall be formed into one regiment: And that the ſenior claſs of the towns
of Warwick and Eaſt-Greenwich conſtitute
one company; that of the town of Weſt-
Greenwich, one company; and that of the
town of Coventry, one company; which
companies ſhall be formed into one regiment.

Sec. 3. *And be it further enacted,* That When to meet.
the ſenior claſs ſhall meet once in every
two years, on the ſecond Wedneſday in
September, by companies, for the purpoſe
of training, improving and diſciplining them
in martial exerciſe, and of being inſpected by the Captain or Commanding Officer
of the Company: And every member of the How to be equip-
ſenior claſs ſhall provide himſelf with arms ped.
and accoutrements, in like manner as the
members of the militia of this State are by
law required to do; and ſhall be liable to
be called out, in caſe of the invaſion of the
State.

Sec. 4. *And be it further enacted,* That
the Colonels of the ſeveral regiments of
ſenior

senior class shall make returns of their regiments respectively to the Commander in Chief of the State, once in every two years.

Sec. 5. *And be it further enacted,* That the senior class hereby established shall be governed by the same rules and regulations, and be subject to the same fines and penalties, as are established by law for the government of the militia of this State, except as in this act is otherwise provided.

An Act ascertaining Damages on protested Bills of Exchange.

Section 1. BE it enacted by the General Assembly, and by the authority thereof it is enacted, That when any foreign bill of exchange is or shall be drawn or indorsed within this State, for the payment of any sum of money, and such bill is or shall be returned from any place or country without the limits of the United States, protested for non-acceptance or non-payment, the drawer or indorser shall be subject to the payment of ten per centum damages thereon, and charges of protest ; and the bill shall carry an interest of six per centum per annum, from the date of the protest, until the money therein drawn for shall be fully satisfied and paid.

Sec. 2. *And be it further enacted,* That it shall be lawful for any person or persons, having a right to demand any sum of money upon a foreign protested bill of exchange as aforesaid, to commence and prosecute an action for principal, damages, interest, and charges of protest, against the
drawers

drawers or indorsers, jointly or severally,
or against either of them separately; and
judgment shall and may be given for such
principal, damages and charges, and interest
upon such principal, after the rate aforesaid, to the time of such judgment, together
with costs of suit.

Sec. 3. *And be it further enacted*, That when any inland bill of exchange shall be drawn or indorsed within this State, for the payment of any sum of money without the same, and such bill shall be protested for non-acceptance or non-payment, the drawer or indorser shall be subject to the payment of five per centum damages thereon, and charges of protest; and the bill shall carry an interest of six per centum per annum from the date of the protest, until the money therein drawn for shall be fully satisfied and paid.

Damages on inland bills.

An Act concerning Promissory Notes.

Section 1. BE it enacted by the General Assembly, and by the authority thereof it is enacted, That when any person or body corporate, by themselves, or by any person by them lawfully authorized for the purpose, shall hereafter make or sign any promissory note, whereby such person or body corporate shall promise to pay to any other person or body corporate, any sum of money or specific article mentioned in such note, the same shall be taken and construed to be by virtue thereof due and payable to such person or body corporate; and such person or body corporate may maintain an action for the same, against the

Actions may be maintained on promissory notes.

person

perfon or body corporate who fhall have made the fame.

Sec. 2. *And be it further enacted,* That a note made as aforefaid, containing a promife for the payment of money only, made payable to order or bearer, fhall be affignable or indorfable over, in the fame manner as bills of exchange are or may be, according to the cuftom of merchants ; and the affignee or indorfee of fuch negotiable note may maintain an action againft the maker of fuch note, or any prior indorfer, for the recovery of the money due thereon.

Sec. 3. *Provided neverthelefs, and be it further enacted, any thing in this act to the contrary notwithftanding,* That all actions which fhall be brought on any promiffory note, payable to order or bearer, made prior to the paffing of this act, fhall be commenced and profecuted in the name of the original payee of fuch note, or in cafe of his death, in the name of his legal reprefentatives, otherwife fuch action fhall abate.

Sec. 4. *And be it further enacted,* That all actions commenced on any promiffory note, in the name of an affignee or indorfee, againft the original promifor, fhall be commenced in the fame county wherein fuch action ought by law to have been commenced, if no affignment or indorfement of fuch note had been made; and that no more cofts fhall be taxed in any fuch action than would be by law taxable, if the fame had been commenced in the name of the original promifee.

A Law,

A Law, made and passed by the General Assembly, at South-Kingstown, the fifth Day of November, A. D. 1791.

An Act to incorporate the Stockholders in the Providence Bank.

WHEREAS the President and Directors of the Bank established at Providence, on the third day of October last, have petitioned this General Assembly for an act to incorporate the Stockholders in said Bank: And whereas well regulated banks have proved very beneficial in several of the United States, as well as in Europe: Therefore,

Sec. 1. *Be it enacted by this General Assembly, and by the authority thereof it is hereby enacted,* That the Stockholders in said Bank, their successors and assigns, shall be, and are hereby created and made, a corporation and body politic, by the name and stile of *The President, Directors and Company, of the Providence Bank.* And by that name shall be and are hereby made able and capable in law to have, purchase, receive, possess, enjoy and retain, to them and their successors, lands, rents, tenements, hereditaments, goods, chattels and effects, of what kind or nature foever; and the same to sell, grant, demise, aliene or dispose of; to sue and be sued, plead and be impleaded, answer and be answered, defend and be defended, in Courts of record, or any other place whatsoever; and also to make, have and use a common seal, and the same to break, alter and renew, at their pleasure; and also to ordain, establish and put in execution, such by-laws, ordinances and regulations, as shall seem necessa-

The Stockholders incorporated.

ry

ry and convenient for the government of the said Corporation, not being contrary to law, or to the constitution of said Bank ; and generally to do and execute all and singular acts, matters and things, which to them it shall or may appertain to do.

And whereas the said Stockholders, on the said third of October, formed and adopted a constitution for said Bank, in the words following, to wit :

Constitution of the Bank.

"TAUGHT by the experience of Europe and America, that well regulated banks are highly useful to society, by promoting punctuality in the performance of contracts, increasing the medium of trade, facilitating the payment of taxes, preventing the exportation of specie, furnishing for it a safe deposit, and by discount rendering easy and expeditious the anticipation of funds on lawful interest, advancing at the same time the interest of the proprietors :

"We the subscribers, desirous of promoting such an institution, do hereby engage to take the number of shares set against our names respectively, in a Bank to be established at Providence, in the State of Rhode-Island, on the following plan, to wit :

" I. That a subscription be now opened for two hundred and fifty thousand dollars, in six hundred and twenty-five shares, of four hundred dollars each ; and that fifty thousand dollars thereof, being one hundred and twenty-five shares, be reserved for the United States, to be subscribed by the Secretary of the Treasury, or the Directors of the national Bank, which may first happen, and fifty shares for the State of Rhode-Island, should they choose to subscribe for the same

between

between this and the ending of the second seffion of Congrefs after this time.

"II. That faid fubfcription be paid into the hands of the Directors, to be this day chofen, at the periods and in the proportions following, to wit : Two fifth parts of the whole fum to be in filver and gold, and three fifth parts in the fix per cent. funded debt of the United States; or any fubfcriber, not having the whole in fix per cents, may pay any part in the three per cents of faid funded debt, at the rate of two dollars for one, with liberty to exchange them within twelve months from the firft day of January next ; twenty-five dollars in filver or gold to each and every fhare to be paid down, or as foon as the Directors are ready to receive the fame, and fifteen dollars more to each fhare, in not exceeding thirty days, with intereft from this day till paid, which make one quarter part of the filver or gold; the fecond quarter of fpecie is to be paid by the fecond Monday of January next ; the third quarter by the fecond Monday of April next; and the fourth and laft quarter by the fecond Monday of July next. And the faid funded fecurities, with their intereft, reckoned up to the firft of January next. are to be paid, one half of the whole amount on or before the fecond Monday of faid January next; one quarter by the fecond Monday of April next ; and the fourth and laft quarter by the fecond Monday of July next.

"III. The number of votes to which each Stockholder fhall be entitled in the choice of Directors, or any other bufinefs concerning the inftitution, fhall be according to the number of fhares he, fhe or they

L. ll   fhall

shall hold, in the proportion following; that is to say, for one share, and not more than two shares, one vote; for every two shares above two, and not exceeding ten, one vote; for every four shares above ten, and not exceeding thirty, one vote; for every six shares above thirty, and not exceeding sixty, one vote; for every eight shares above sixty, and not exceeding one hundred, one vote; for every ten shares above one hundred, one vote; but no person, copartnership or body politic, shall be entitled to a greater number than thirty votes.

"IV. That all Stockholders shall be entitled to vote by themselves, agent or proxy, duly appointed; and their votes to be counted in proportion to the shares they hold, as above expressed.

"V. That there be nine Directors chosen by a majority of such voters present, in person or by proxy, from among those who are entitled to vote; and the same number of Directors shall, after the first choice, be annually elected; and as often as any vacancy shall happen by death or otherwise, if, in the opinion of the remaining Directors, it shall be necessary to fill up such vacancy before the period of a general election, they shall call a general meeting of the Stockholders for that purpose. The Directors shall, at their first meeting after being elected, and after every general election, choose one from among them to act as President, which general election shall be held annually on the said first Monday of October in every year.

"VI. That there be a meeting of the Directors quarterly, for the purpose of regulating the affairs of the Bank; any five of

of the Directors to make a Board, or a less
number may adjourn from time to time,
and meet at any other time when they may
think it necessary.

" VII. That the Board of Directors determine the manner of doing business, and
the rules and forms to be pursued ; appoint
and pay the various officers which they may
find necessary; dispose of the money and
credit of the Bank for the interest and benefit of the proprietors, and make, from time
to time, at least once in every six months,
such dividends out of the profits as they
may think proper; provided they shall in
no instance do any act contrary to the regulations made by the Stockholders.

" VIII. That the Board shall, at every
quarterly meeting, choose three Directors to
inspect the business of the Bank for the en-
suing three months ; and that the Inspectors
so chosen, or some one of them, shall once
a week at least examine into the state of the
cash account, and of the notes issued and
received, and shall see that those accounts
are regularly balanced, and the balances
transferred.

" IX. That application be made to the
Legislature to incorporate the subscribers,
under the name of *The President, Directors
and Company, of the Providence Bank*, and to
pass laws to secure the Bank notes from being counterfeited, and also to prevent any
President, Director, Inspector, or other officer of the Bank, from converting any property, money or credit, of said Bank to his
own use ; and to pass such other laws as will
best promote the speedy recovery of any
debt that may be due to or from said Bank,
as the strictest punctuality will be absolutely

necessary,

neceffary, as well with the Managers of faid Bank, as all who may deal therewith.

" X. That any Director or officer of the Bank, who fhall commit any fraud or embezzlement touching the money or property of the Bank, fhall forfeit all his fhare or ftock to the Company, and be profecuted to the utmoft rigour of the law.

" XI. That no Director fhall be entitled to any pecuniary advantage for his attendance on the duties of his office, as Director, or as Prefident or Infpector, unlefs the profits arifing from the Bank ftock fhall exceed fix per cent. per annum clear of all charges, and an alteration in this refpect fhall hereafter be made by the confent of a majority of Stockholders, at an annual meeting.

" XII. If any fubfcriber fhall anticipate the fecond, third or fourth payment of his, her or their fubfcription, of the fpecie part, fo that the Bank may be benefited by the ufe thereof before the time ftipulated as above, the lawful intereft upon fuch fum fo paid fhall be allowed up to the time when fuch fubfcription becomes due, and be deducted from the faid fubfcription. But if any fubfcriber fail of making payment at the periods fixed, he, fhe or they, fhall forfeit the fum or fums by him, her or them, previoufly paid.

" XIII. All fums of money offered fhall be received into the Bank for fafe keeping, and delivered out to the order or check of the proprietor, at his, her or their pleafure, without any charge for the receiving, keeping and delivering the fame.

" XIV. That the Directors may at all times know the Proprietors of the Bank, no fale

fale or conveyance whatever of any fhares in the Bank fhall be deemed good, but fuch as may be entered on the Bank books.

" XV. Every Cafhier, or Treafurer, or Clerk, before he enters on the duties of his office, fhall be required to give bond, with one or more fureties, to the fatisfaction of the Directors, in a fum not lefs than five thoufand dollars for the Cafhier, with conditions for his good behaviour, and not lefs than one thoufand for each Clerk.

" XVI. That the Bank ftock may be increafed at any time hereafter, when a majority of the Stokholders may find it neceffary for the public utility, to any fum not exceeding five hundred thoufand dollars ; and that one-fifth part of the whole capital be referved for the Congrefs of the United States, or their Secretary of the Treafury, or the Directors of the national Bank, to fubfcribe.

" XVII. That in cafe the Directors may be of opinion that the laft payment may be fafely fufpended, they are authorized to fufpend the payment thereof, by giving public notice for the fpace of ninety days, for fuch period as they may judge proper. And the Stockholders fhall be held to make punctual payment, on the within penalty, at fuch period by the Directors afcertained."

Sec. 2. *Be it further enacted, and by the authority of this General Affembly it is hereby enacted and declared,* That the articles aforefaid are and fhall be the conftitution of the faid Bank ; with this alteration and provifo, that no fecurity given before the paffing of this act fhall be received in the faid Bank, fubject to the operation of the laws of the faid Bank ; and that no fecurities given after the granting this charter, which are not made

Conftitution eftablifhed.

Provifo.

made payable to the said Bank, excepting those commonly called bills of exchange, shall be considered in the operation of the laws of the said Bank.

Sec. 3. *And be it further enacted by the authority aforesaid,* That no Stockholder or Member of said Corporation shall be answerable for any losses, deficiencies or failure, of the capital stock of the said Corporation, for any more or larger sum or sums of money whatsoever, than the amount of the stock, stocks or shares, which shall appear by the books of the said Corporation to belong to him at the time or times when such loss or losses shall be sustained.

Stockholders how far answerable.

Sec. 4. *And be it further enacted by the authority aforesaid,* That in case any person indebted to said Bank, on any bond, bill or note, by him duly executed or indorsed, with an express consent, in writing, that the same should be negotiable at the Bank, shall fail of making payment at the time therein specified, the President, or in his absence the three Directors to be quarterly appointed, shall cause a demand of payment to be made, in writing, on the person of the said delinquent or delinquents, having consented as aforesaid, or if not to be found, have the same left at his last place of abode; and if the money so due shall not be paid within ten days from the day in which such demand shall have been made, or notice left at his last place of abode as aforesaid, it shall and may be lawful for the President for the time being, or in his absence the three Directors to be quarterly appointed as aforesaid, to write to either of the Clerks of the Court of Common Pleas, or of the Superior Court, in either of the counties in this State, and send

Debts to the Bank, how to be recovered.

to

to the faid Clerk the bond, bill or note due,
with proof of the demand made as aforefaid,
and to order faid Clerk to iffue a writ of execution of *Capias Satisfaciendum Fieri Facias,*
and attachment of real eftate, on which the
debt and coft may be levied, by taking the
property of the delinquents to the amount of
the fum or fums of money mentioned in the
faid bond, bill or note, and cofts ; and fuch
Clerk is hereby required to iffue fuch execution or executions, directed to any Sheriff
or Deputy-Sheriff in the State, which fhall
be made returnable to the Court, whofe
Clerk fhall iffue the fame, which fhall firft
fit after the iffuing thereof, on the fecond
day of fuch Court's fitting, and fhall be as
valid and effectual in law, to all intents and
purpofes, as if the fame had iffued on judgment regularly obtained according to the
common and ordinary courfe of proceeding
in the faid Court. *Provided always,* that
before any execution or executions fhall
iffue as aforefaid, the Prefident of the Bank,
or in his abfence the three Directors aforefaid, fhall make oath or affirmation, afcertaining whether the whole or what part of
the debt mentioned on the faid bond, bill or
note, is due, which faid oath or affirmation
fhall be filed in the office of the Clerk of the
Court from which the execution fhall iffue ;
and if the defendant fhall appear at faid
Court to which fuch execution fhall be made
returnable, on the fecond day thereof, and
difpute the whole or any part of the faid
debt, the Court before whom fuch execution
may be returned as aforefaid fhall order an
iffue to be joined, and trial to be had, at the
fame fitting thereof at which the return fhall be
made, and the juft debt and coft only fhall be
                                              paid

paid on such execution at the same sitting of such Court ; any law, custom or usage, to the contrary hereof in any wise notwithstanding. *And provided also*, that all costs accruing on actions brought upon securities given to the said Bank at common term time, shall be taxed agreeable to the law of the State, as in common actions.

Sec. 5. *And be it further enacted by the* **Penalty for forg-** *authority aforesaid*, That if any person or **ing Bank notes.** persons shall within this State forge or counterfeit any of the notes or checks of or on said Bank, or pay or tender in payment, or offer to pass, any forged or counterfeit note or check, knowing them to be forged or counterfeited, and shall thereof be convicted in any Court of law within this State, he or they shall be adjuged a felon, and suffer such punishment as shall be adjudged by said Court, so as the same do not extend to death, or more than seven years servitude or imprisonment.

A Law, made and passed by the General Assembly, at South-Kingstown, the twenty-eighth Day of October, A. D. 1795.

An Act to incorporate the Stockholders in the Bank of Rhode-Island.

WHEREAS the following plan of a constitution of a Bank in Newport hath been formed and adopted by the Stockholders thereof, to wit :

1. That a subscription be opened at the **Constitution of** State-House in Newport, on Monday the **the Bank** 12th day of October, A. D. 1795, at three o'clock, P. M. for one hundred thousand dollars, in five hundred shares of two hundred

hundred dollars each, to be payable in gold or silver, in the following inftalments, to wit: On each and every fhare, five dollars at the time of fubfcribing; ninety-five dollars on the laft Monday in December next; twenty-five dollars on the laft Monday in March next; twenty-five dollars on the laft Monday in June next; twenty-five dollars on the laft Monday in September next; and twenty-five dollars on the laft Monday in December, A. D. 1796: And that the faid fubfcription be opened under the direction of Mr. Mofes Seixas, who is to receive the five dollars on each fhare at the time of fub-fcribing, to give a certificate thereof to each fubfcriber, and to pay on demand the money fo received by him to the Prefident and Directors, to be appointed as herein after prefcribed

2. That the Prefident and Directors be empowered to receive the other inftalments herein before fpecified; but with authority to fufpend the fifth and fixth inftalments, or either of them, if they fhall confider it for the intereft of the Bank, and to direct the payment or payments on any further pe-riod or periods, giving therefor at leaft ninety days notice.

3. That if any fubfcriber or fubfcrib-ers fhall fail to pay any one of his, her or their inftalments on or before the day of payment, he, fhe or they fhall forfeit the fum or fums of money by him, her or them previoufly paid, and the fhare or fhares, by him, her or them fubfcribed, to and for the ufe of the Bank.

4. The capital of the faid Bank may be increafed from time to time, or at any time hereafter, under fuch regulations, reftric-

M m m   tions

tions and conditions, as a majority of the Stockholders, specially convened for that purpose, shall think proper, to an amount not exceeding five hundred thousand dollars: *Provided*, that such regulations, restrictions and conditions, shall not affect any rights acquired under previous subscriptions.

5. At all general meetings the Stockholders shall be entitled to as many votes as they hold shares respectively; and to vote by themselves, their agents or proxies, duly appointed.

6. The Stockholders shall hold a general meeting at Newport, on the first Monday in January, A. D. 1797, for the election of Directors, and the transaction of such other business as they may deem necessary. And at the same Newport shall hold an annual meeting thereafter, on the first Monday in January in each succeeding year, for the same purposes: But general meetings of the Stockholders may be holden at any other time or times, whenever the President and Directors shall think it expedient, or whenever a number of Stockholders, holding one hundred shares or more, shall require; the time and place of meeting, in Newport, to be fixed and publicly notified by the President and Directors: At which general meetings, all elections and questions shall be determined by a majority of votes.

7. The Stockholders shall choose annually, and at their annual meeting, nine Directors; which Directors, at their first meeting afterwards, shall elect a President from their number; but no person shall be eligible, or continue as President or Director, except such as are actually Stockholders
holders

holders and citizens of the United States, and inhabitants of Newport. And in cafe of vacancy by difqualification, death, refignation or otherwife, the faid vacancy may be filled up by a new election for the remainder of the year, by the Stockholders, in manner as is herein prefcribed, at a meeting fpecially to be convened for that purpofe : *Provided* the Prefident and Directors, or any number of Stockholders, holding one hundred fhares or more, fhall confider it neceffary.

8. The Prefident and Directors fhall hold a meeting on the firft Monday in each month, and at any other time or times they fhall think neceffary : Not lefs than five Directors fhall conftitute a Board for the tranfaction of bufinefs ; of whom the Prefident fhall make one, if prefent, but in cafe of his abfence, one of the Directors fhall prefide for that meeting.

9. The Board of Directors fhall determine the manner of doing bufinefs ; the rules and form to be purfued ; appoint and pay the various officers which they may find neceffary ; make contracts ; difpofe of the money and credit of the Bank, for the intereft and benefit of the Proprietors ; and make, from time to time, at leaft once in every fix months, fuch dividends out of the profits as fhall appear to them advifable : *Provided* they in no inftance do any act contrary to the regulations made by the Stockholders.

10. Three of the Directors fhall, by rotation, monthly, more immediately infpect the bufinefs of the Bank ; and fhall, at leaft once every week, examine into the ftate of the cafh account ; of the notes iffued

and

and received ; and cause the accounts to be regularly stated and balanced, and the balances transferred.

11. A President or Director, as such, shall not be entitled to any compensation or emolument, unless allowed by the Stockholders at a general meeting.

12. The Cashier, and Clerk, or Clerks, before admission to their respective trusts, shall give bond, with two or more sureties, to the satisfaction of the President and Directors; the Cashier in a sum not less than five thousand dollars, and each Clerk in a sum not less than one thousand dollars, conditioned for the faithful discharge of their several duties.

13. The stock or shares of the Bank shall be transferable only at the Bank by the Stockholder or Stockholders, or his, her or their attorney, legally appointed, and in a form to be prescribed by the President and Directors.

14. If any President, Director or officer of the Bank, shall commit any fraud or embezzlement, touching the money, property or securities of the Bank, he shall forfeit all his share or shares, or stock in the Bank, and be prosecuted to the utmost rigour of the law.

15. The Bank shall be opened, and commence business on the first Monday of January, A. D. 1796.

16. All sums of money offered shall be received into the Bank for safe keeping, and delivered out to the order or check of the Proprietor or Proprietors, at his, her or their pleasure, without any charge for receiving, keeping and delivering the same.

17. That the subscribers to the said Bank

convene

convene at the State-House on Tuesday the thirteenth day of October next, at three o'clock, P. M. and elect nine Directors, to continue until the first Monday in January, A. D. 1797; who, at their first meeting, shall appoint one of their number President: That the President and Directors, on being appointed as aforesaid, shall apply to the Legislature of this State for an act to incorporate the subscribers, under the name of *The President, Directors and Company, of the Bank of Rhode-Island*; to grant to them the rights, privileges and security, essential to such a Corporation, and to ratify and establish by law the Constitution of the said Bank, as agreed to by the subscribers; and their acts and doings, under and in conformity to the said Constitution.

And whereas, in pursuance of the first article in said plan, a subscription was opened and filled as therein proposed: And whereas, in pursuance of the seventeenth article of the said plan, *Christopher Champlin, George Champlin, George Gibbs, Peleg Clarke, Caleb Gardner, Thomas Dennis, Simeon Martin, James Robinson,* and *Walter Channing,* were elected Directors of the said Bank, who have elected the said *Christopher Champlin* President thereof: And whereas the said President and Directors have petitioned this General Assembly for an act to incorporate the Stockholders in the said Bank: Therefore,

Sec. 1. *Be it enacted by this General Assembly, and by the authority thereof it is hereby enacted,* That the aforegoing articles are, and shall be, the Constitution of the said Bank. And all acts and doings under, and in conformity to the said Constitution, shall be good and effectual in law.

Constitution established.

Sec.

Sec. 2. *Be it further enacted by the autho-*
rity aforesaid, That the Stockholders in the
said Bank, their succeffors and affigns, fhall
be, and are hereby, created and made a
Corporation and Body politic, by the name
and ftyle of *The Prefident, Directors and*
Company, of the Bank of Rhode-Island : And
by that name fhall be and are hereby made
capable in law to have, purchafe, receive,
pofiefs, enjoy and retain, to them and their
fucceffors, lands, rents, tenements, hereditaments, goods, chattels and effects, of what
kind or nature foever : And the fame to fell,
grant, demife, aliene or difpofe of ; to fue
or be fued; plead and be impleaded ; anfwer and be anfwered ; to defend and be
defended, in Courts of Record, or any
other place whatever : And alfo to make,
have and ufe a common feal, and the fame to
break, alter and renew, at their pleafure : And
alfo to ordain, and eftablifh and put in execution, fuch by-laws, ordinances and regulations, as fhall feem neceffary and convenient for the government of the faid Corporation, not being contrary to law, and the
Conftitution of the faid Bank : And generally to do and execute all and fingular acts,
matters and things, which to them it fhall or
may appertain to do.

Sec. 3. *And be it further enacted by the*
authority aforefaid, That no Stockholder, or
member of the faid Corporation, fhall be anfwerable for any lofs, deficience or failure,
of the capital ftock of the faid Corporation,
for any more or larger fum or fums of money whatever than the amount of the ftock,
or ftocks, or fhares, which fhall appear by
the books of the faid Corporation to belong to him, her or them, at the time or
times

times when fuch lofs or loffes fhall be fuf-
taine'd.

Sec. 4. *And be it further enacted by the* Debts to the
authority aforefaid, That in cafe any perf n Bank, how to be
recovered.
indebted to the faid Bank on any bond, bill
or note, by him duly executed, or indorfed,
with an exprefs confent in writing, that the
fame fhould be negotiable in the faid Bank,
and on any bill of exchange that fhall be accepted, fhall fail of making payment at the
time therein fpecified, the Prefident, or in
his abfence the three Directors to be quarterly appointed, fhall caufe the fame to be
delivered to a Notary-Public, who fhall demand payment thereof; and on refufal, fhall
proteft the fame: And in that cafe it fhall
and may be lawful for the Prefident for
the time being, or in his abfence the three
Directors to be quarterly appointed as
aforefaid, to tranfmit the faid bond, bill,
note, or bill of exchange, to either of the
Clerks of the Courts of Common Pleas, or of
the Superior Court, in either of the counties in this State, together with the faid proteft, and to order the faid Clerk to iffue
a writ of executionof *Capias ad Satisfacien-*
dum, Fieri Facias, and attachment of real
eftate, in the name of *The Prefident, Direct-*
ors and Company, of the Bank of Rhode-
Ifland, on which the debt and all the cofts
may be levied, by taking the property of
the delinquent or delinquents, to the amount
of the fum or fums of money mentioned in
the faid bond, bill, note, or bill of exchange,
and coft: And fuch Clerk is hereby required to iffue execution or executions, directed to any Sheriff or Deputy-Sheriff in
the State; which fhall be made returnable
to the Court whofe Clerk fhall iffue the
fame;

fame, which fhall firft fit after the iffuing thereof, on the fecond day of fuch Court's fitting, and fhall be as valid and effectual in law, to all intents and purpofes, as if the fame had iffued on judgment regularly obtained, according to the common and ordinary courfe of proceedings in faid Court. *Provided always*, that before any execution or executions fhall iffue as aforefaid, the Prefident, or in his abfence the three Directors aforefaid, fhall make oath or affirmation afcertaining whether the whole, or what part, of the debt mentioned in faid bond, bill, note, or bill of exchange, is due, which faid oath or affirmation fhall be filed in the office of the Clerk of the Court from which the execution fhall iffue: And if the defendant fhall appear at faid Court to which faid execution is made returnable on the fecond day thereof, and difpute the whole or any part of faid debt, the Court before whom fuch execution may be returned as aforefaid fhall order an iffue to be joined, and trial to be had, at the fame fitting thereof at which the return fhall be made; and the juft debt and coft fhall be paid on fuch execution, at the fame fitting of fuch Court; any law, cuftom or ufage, to the contrary hereof in any wife notwithftanding: *And provided alfo*, that all coft accruing on actions brought upon fecurity or fecurities, given to the faid Bank at common term time, fhall be taxed agreeably to law.

Penalty for forging Bank notes. Sec. 5. *And be it further enacted by the authority aforefaid*, That if any perfon or perfons fhall forge or counterfeit, or fraudulently utter any of the notes or checks of or on the faid Bank, or pay, or tender in payment, or offer to pafs, any forged or
counterfeit

counterfeit or altered note or check, knowing them to be forged, counterfeited or
altered, and ſhall thereof be convicted before any Court of Law within this State,
he, ſhe or they ſhall be judged a felon or
felons, and ſuffer ſuch puniſhment as ſhall
be adjudged by ſaid Court, ſo as the ſame
do not extend to death, or more than ſeven
years ſervitude or impriſonment.

An Act for quieting Poſſeſſions, and avoiding 1711.
Suits at Law. 1728.
1798.

WHEREAS at the firſt ſettling of this
State, and for ſundry years afterwards, lands were of little or no value, and
ſkilful men in the law were much wanted,
whereby many deeds, grants and conveyances, were weakly made, which may occaſion
great conteſts in law, if not timely prevent-
ed :

Section 1. *Be it enacted by the General* Ancient grants
Aſſembly, and by the authority thereof it is confirmed.
enacted, That all grants, charters and conveyances, heretofore made by the General
Aſſembly of this State, unto any town,
corporation, community or propriety, or
to any other perſon or perſons whatſoever, ſhall be, and they hereby are ratified and confirmed, as good and effectual, to all intents and purpoſes in the law,
for the conveying all ſuch lands, tenements,
rights, privileges and profits, as are therein
mentioned, to the ſaid towns, corporations,
communities, proprieties, perſon or perſons,
and to their reſpective ſucceſſors, heirs
and aſſigns forever.

Sec. 2. *And be it further enacted,* That Twenty year
where any perſon or perſons, or others poſſeſſion to
make a titl.

N n u from

from whom he or they derive their titles, either by themselves, tenants or lessees, shall have been, for the space of twenty years, in the uninterrupted, quiet, peaceable and actual seizin and possession of any lands, tenements or hereditaments, within this State, for and during the said time, claiming the same as his, her or their proper, sole and rightful estate in fee-simple, such actual seizin and possession shall be allowed to give and make a good and rightful title to such person or persons, their heirs and assigns forever; and this act being pleaded in bar to any action, that shall hereafter be brought for such lands, tenements or hereditaments, and such actual seizin and possession being duly proved, shall be allowed to be good, valid and effectual in the law, for barring the same.

The rights of infants, &c. saved.

Provided, that nothing in this act shall be construed, deemed or taken, to extend to prejudice the rights and claims of persons under age, *non compos mentis, feme coverts,* or those imprisoned or beyond seas, they bringing their suit therefor within the space of ten years next after such impediment is removed.

Also those in reversion, &c.

Provided further, that nothing above contained shall extend, or be construed or deemed to extend, to bar any person or persons, having any estate in reversion or remainder, expectant or depending in any lands, tenements or hereditaments, after the end or determination of the estate for years, life or lives, such person or persons pursuing his or their title by due course of law, within ten years after his or their right of action shall accrue; any thing in this act contained to the contrary notwithstanding.

A Law,

A Law, made and passed by the General Assembly, holden at Newport, the third Day of May, A. D. 1682.

An Act confirming the Grants heretofore made by the Inhabitants of the Towns of Newport, Providence, Portsmouth, Warwick and Westerly.

WHEREAS in the fifteenth year of the reign of Charles the Second, there was a Charter granted to this State of Rhode-Island and Providence Plantations, in which were contained many privileges to the free inhabitants thereof, and among others of the said privileges there was granted to the General Assembly of said State full power and authority to make and ordain laws suiting to the nature and constitution of the place, and in particular to direct, rule and order all matters relating to the purchases of land of the native Indians: And whereas the lands of the several towns of Newport, Providence, Portsmouth, Warwick and Westerly, were purchased by the several inhabitants thereof, of the native Indians, chief sachems of the country, before the granting of the said Charter, so that an order or direction from the said Assembly could not be obtained therein; and it being thought necessary and convenient, for the reasons aforesaid, that the lands of the said towns should be by an act of the General Assembly of this State confirmed to the inhabitants thereof, according to their several and respective rights and interest therein :

Sec. 1. *Be it enacted by the General Assembly, and by the authority thereof it is enacted,* Grants confirmed.

That

That all the land lying and being within
the limits of each and every of the aforesaid
towns of Newport, Providence, Portsmouth,
Warwick and Westerly, according to their
several respective purchases thereof, made
and obtained of the Indian sachems, be and
are hereby allowed of, ratified and confirmed to the Proprietors of each of the
aforesaid towns, and to each and every of
the said Proprietors, their several and respective rights and interests therein, by virtue of any such purchase or purchases as
aforesaid. To have and to hold all the
aforesaid lands by virtue of the several
purchases thereof, with all the appurtenances,
privileges and commodities thereunto belonging, or in any wise appertaining, to
them the aforesaid Proprietors, their heirs
and assigns forever, in as full, lawful, large
and ample manner, to all intents, construc-
tions and purposes whatsoever, as if the said
lands, and every part thereof, had been
purchased of the Indian sachems by virtue
of any grants or allowance obtained from
the General Assembly of this State, after the
granting of the aforesaid Charter.   And
whereas there is within several of the towns
within this State considerable of lands lying
yet common or undivided: And for the more
orderly way and manner of the several proprietors, their managing the prudential affairs thereof, and for the more effectual
making of just and equal division or divisions
of the same, so that each and every of the
Proprietors may have their true and equal
part or proportion of land, according to his
or their proportion of right, and that the
exact boundaries of each and every man's
                                   allotments,

allotments, when laid to him, may be kept *in perpetuum:*

Sec. 2. *It is further ordered and enacted by the authority aforesaid,* That it shall and may be lawful for the Proprietors of each and every such town within this State, being convened by a warrant from under the hand and seal of an Assistant or Justice of the Peace in such town, the occasion thereof being specified in the warrant, for them, or the major part of them so met, to choose and appoint a Clerk, and a Surveyor or Surveyors, and such and so many other officers as they shall judge needful and convenient, for the orderly carrying on and management of the whole affairs of such community, and in like manner to proceed from time to time, as often as need shall require.

Commons, how to be divided.

A Law, made and passed by the General Assembly, holden at Providence the 27th Day of January, A. D. 1746.

An Act for quieting Possessions, and establishing Titles of Land within the Towns of Bristol, Tiverton, Little-Compton, Warren and Cumberland.

Section 1. **B**E *it enacted by the General Assembly, and by the authority thereof it is enacted,* That all grants and conveyances of lands heretofore made by the General Assemblies of the late Colony of New-Plymouth, the late Colony of the Massachusetts, or by the Province of the Massachusetts-Bay, or by any commissioners, agents, or persons by them or any of them duly appointed and authorized, or by any other authority derived from them,

Grants, &c. of New-Plymouth, &c. confirmed.

or any of them, lying within any of
the towns aforefaid, fhall be as good, valid
and effectual, to all intents and purpofes
whatfoever, to the grantees, their heirs or
affigns, as if the lands fo granted had really
been fituate in the Colony or Province by
whom, or by whofe authority the fame
were made, and fhall forever hereafter
be fo adjudged and conftrued in all Courts
of Judicature in this State.

Sec. 2. *And be it further enacted,* That

all eftates, both real and perfonal, left by
perfons who have died inteftate before the
publication of this act, and which lie or
are within the bounds of the aforefaid
towns, fhall be diftributed and fettled
among the children or legal reprefentatives
of fuch inteftates, agreeable to the laws of
the Province of the Maffachufetts-Bay in
force at the time of fuch inteftates' death ;
which laws fhall have the fame force and
effect in this State, in the trial of and fettling and diftributing fuch inteftates' eftates,
as if the fame were laws of this State, duly
made, and fhall be fo adjudged, conftrued
and underftood, by all Judges and Minifters
of Juftice in this State : And that the feveral Town-Councils of the above mentioned
towns be and they are hereby fully empowered and required, to complete the
diftribution and fettlement of fuch inteftates'
eftates as aforefaid, which yet remain un-
fettled, in the fame manner, and as fully
and effectually in all refpects, as the fame
could have been by the Courts of Probate,
had the faid towns ftill remained within
the Province of the Maffachufetts-Bay.

Sec. 3. *And be it further enacted,* That

all

all grants, deeds, conveyances, and land evidences whatſoever, that have heretofore been made of any lands within any of the aforeſaid towns, and which were executed and regiſtered according to the laws in force there at the time of making the ſame, ſhall be adjudged and deemed as good, valid and effectual, to all intents and purpoſes whatſoever, as if the ſame had been made, executed and recorded, within and according to the laws of this State : And copies of all ſuch grants, deeds, conveyances and land evidences, produced from and atteſted by ſuch offices and officers, where the ſame are regiſtered, ſhall be received as lawful evidence by all Courts in this State.

An Act for the Limitation of certain perſonal Actions.

1795.
1798.

Section 1. BE it enacted by the General Aſſembly, and by the authority thereof it is enacted, That all actions of treſpaſs, for breaking incloſures or cloſes ; all actions of treſpaſs, detinue, trover or replevin ; all actions of account and upon the caſe, except ſuch accounts as concern trade or merchandize between merchant and merchant, their factors or ſervants ; all actions of debt founded upon any contract without ſpecialty ; all actions of debt for the arrearages of rents ; and all actions of aſſault, menace, battery, wounding and impriſonment, or any of them, which ſhall be ſued or brought at any time after the riſing of this Aſſembly at the preſent ſeſſion, ſhall be commenced and ſued within the time herein after directed, and not after;

that

Perſonal actions, when to be commenced.

that is to fay, the faid actions upon the cafe, excepting actions for flander, and the faid actions of account, and the faid actions for debt, detinue, replevin and trover, fhall be commenced and brought within fix years next after the caufe of the faid actions or fuits hereafter to be commenced, and not after. And where the caufe of fuch fuit hath already happened, and now exifts, then, and in that cafe, fuch fuit fhall be commenced within fix years from the rifing of this Affembly, and not after: The faid actions of trefpafs for breaking inclofures or clofes, and all other actions of trefpafs for affault, battery, wounding and imprifonment, or any of them, fhall be brought within four years next after the caufe of fuch action or fuit, and not after; and the actions upon the cafe for words, within two years next after the words fpoken, and not after.

When to be commenced againft perfons abfent, &c.

Sec. 2. *And be it further enacted,* That if any perfon or perfons againft whom there is or fhall be any caufe of fuit for every and any of the fpecies of actions herein before enumerated, who at the time the fame accrued was without the limits of this State, and did not leave property or eftate therein, that could by the common and ordinary procefs of law be attached, that then, and in fuch cafe, the perfon who is entitled to bring fuch fuit or action, fhall be at liberty to commence the fame within the refpective periods before limited, after fuch perfon's return into this State.

Rights of infants, &c. faved.

Sec. 3. *Provided neverthelefs, and be it further enacted,* That if any perfon or perfons now, or who hereafter fhall be entitled to any fuch action, fhall be at the time

time any such causes of action accrued within the age of twenty-one years, *feme covert*, *non compos mentis*, imprisoned or beyond sea, then and in such case such person or persons shall be at liberty to bring the same within such times as are herein before limited, after their being of full age, discovert, of sane memory, or at large, or returned from beyond sea.

An Act to prevent Frauds and Perjuries.

Section 1. BE it enacted by the General Assembly, and by the authority thereof it is enacted, That no action shall be brought whereby to charge any executor or administrator upon any special promise to answer any debt or damage out of his own estate, or whereby to charge the defendant upon any special promise to answer for the debt, default or miscarriage of another person, or to charge any person upon any agreement made upon consideration of marriage, or upon any contract for the sale of lands, tenements or hereditaments, or the making of any lease thereof for a longer time than one year, or upon any agreement which is not to be performed within the space of one year from the making thereof, unless the promise or agreement upon which such action shall be brought, or some note or memorandum thereof shall be in writing, and signed by the party to be charged therewith, or by some other person by him thereunto lawfully authorized.

Sec. 2. *And be it further enacted,* That every gift, grant or conveyance of lands, tenements, hereditaments, goods or chattels, or of any rent, interest or profit out of the

Marginal notes:
Actions not to be brought in certain cases, unless upon promises in writing, &c.

Fraudulent conveyances, &c. to be void.

O o o   same,

same, by writing or otherwife, and every note, bill, bond, contract, fuit, judgment or execution, had or made and contrived of fraud, covin, collufion or guile, to the intent or purpofe to delay, hinder or defraud creditors of their juft and lawful actions, fuits, debts, accounts, damages or juft demands, of what nature foever, or to deceive or defraud thofe who fhall purchafe, *bona fide*, the fame lands, tenements, hereditaments, goods or chattels, or any rent, intereft or profit out of them, fhall be henceforth deemed and taken, as againft the perfon or perfons, his, her or their heirs, fucceffors, executors, adminiftrators or affigns, and every of them, whofe debts, fuits, demands, eftates, rights or interefts, by fuch guileful and covinous devifes and practices as aforefaid fhall or might be in any wife injured, difturbed, hindred, delayed or defrauded, to be clearly and utterly void; any pretence, colour, feigned confideration, expreffing of ufe, or any other matter or thing to the contrary notwithftanding.

An Act eftablifhing the Rate of legal Intereft, and for preventing exceffive Ufury.

1767.
1795.
1798.
No perfon to contract for more than fix per cent. per annum for the loan of money, &c.

Section 1. BE it enacted by the General *Affembly*, and by the authority thereof it is enacted, That no perfon or perfons whofoever fhall directly or indirectly, by himfelf or themfelves, his or their agent or agents, attorney or attornies, or any other perfon or perfons in his or their behalf, contract for or receive, for loan of any money, wares, goods, or other commodities whatfoever, above the value of fix dollars for the forbearance or giving day

of

of payment of one hundred dollars for one year, and fo after that rate for a greater or leffer fum, or for a longer or fhorter time, or according to that rate and proportion for the loan of any wares, merchandizes, or other commodities.

Sec. 2. *And be it further enacted,* That all bonds, mortgages, fpecialties, agree-ments, contracts, promifes and affurances whatfoever, made prior to the paffing of this act, for the payment of any money, goods, wares or other commodities to be lent on ufury, wherein or whereby there fhall be re-ceived, agreed for or taken, for the for-bearance or giving day of payment, above the rate aforefaid, fhall be utterly void and of none effect.

Such contracts heretofore made to be void.

Sec. 3. *And be it further enacted,* That when any fuit or action fhall be brought on any bond, mortgage, fpecialty, agreement, contract, promife or affurance whatever, made prior to the paffing of this act, for the payment or delivery of money, goods, wares or commodities whatfoever, wherein or whereby any higher or greater intereft has been agreed for or taken, directly or indi-rectly, than the rate aforefaid, the fame being fpecially pleaded and proved, fhall be a fuf-ficient bar to fuch fuit or action.

Actions brought thereon to be barred.

Sec. 4. *And be it further enacted,* That if any action or fuit fhall be commenced on any fuch bond, mortgage, fpecialty, agree-ment, contract, promife or affurance what-ever, and the defendant fhall plead that the fame is ufurious, and that a higher or greater intereft than the rate aforefaid was therein or thereby fecured, agreed for, promifed or taken, and the defendant fhall not have any other proof thereof than his own oath or
affirmation,

Parties may be examined as wit-neffes, in cafe.

affirmation, the Court ſhall and may admit
ſuch defendant as a legal witneſs upon the
iſſue joined before the Jury, to depoſe relative to the nature and circumſtances of ſuch
uſurious agreement ; and ſhall alſo, upon
motion of the plaintiff, admit ſuch plaintiff
as a legal witneſs in like manner ; and if the
ſaid Jury ſhall find ſaid contract to be uſurious in manner ſtated in the defendant's plea,

Judgment in ſuch caſe.
they ſhall nevertheleſs find for the plaintiff
the principal ſum of money, or real value
of the goods or other thing loaned, and the
defendant ſhall recover his coſts.

Forfeiture on uſurious con- tracts.
Sec. 5. *And be it further enacted,* That
a ſum equal to one third part of the principal and all the intereſt of every bond,
mortgage, ſpecialty, agreement, contract,
promiſe or aſſurance whatſoever, which ſhall
be made after the paſſing of this act, for the
payment of money, goods, wares or other
commodities to be lent on uſury, wherein
or whereby there ſhall be received, agreed
for or taken, for the forbearance or giving
day of payment above the rate of intereſt
expreſſed in the firſt ſection of this act, ſhall
be forfeited by the creditor, one half of ſaid
forfeiture for the uſe of the State, and the
other half for the uſe of him, her or them,

How recevered.
who will proſecute for the ſame : That the
ſaid forfeiture ſhall and may be recovered
by information, or action of debt, before
any Court proper to try the ſame : That
in the trial of every ſuch information or
action, the borrower or hirer of the money,
goods, wares or other commodities, on ſuch
uſurious contract, ſhall be admitted a legal
witneſs, if not intereſted in the event of

Proviſo.
ſuch proſecution : *Provided nevertheleſs,* that
all informations and actions for the recovery
of

of such forfeiture, shall be brought and commenced within one year after such forfeiture shall have accrued.

Provided further, That nothing in this act shall extend to the letting of cattle, or other usages of the like nature in practice amongst farmers, or maritime contracts among merchants, as bottomry, insurance, or course of exchange, as hath been heretofore accustomed.

This act not to extend to maritime contracts, &c.

An Act allowing Interest upon Judgments of Courts in certain Cases.

BE it enacted by this General Assembly, and by the authority thereof it is enacted, That upon all judgments of Court which shall hereafter be obtained for debt or damages, to the amount of one hundred dollars or upwards, on which executions shall be issued, and the defendant or defendants shall be committed to gaol, interest on such debt or damages, at the rate of six per cent. per annum, shall be computed, levied and received, from the return day of such executions to the time when such judgments shall be satisfied and discharged.

Interest allowed on judgments, in case.

An Act regulating Marriage and Divorce.

Section 1. BE it enacted by the General Assembly, and by the authority thereof it is enacted, That from and after the passing and publication of this act, no man or woman shall intermarry within the degrees hereafter named ; that is to say,

1749.
1754.
1798.
Degrees of relationship within which marriages are to be void.

No

No man shall marry	No woman shall marry
His mother,	Her father,
Grandmother,	Grandfather,
Daughter,	Son,
Son's daughter,	Son's son,
Daughter's daughter,	Daughter's son,
Step mother,	Step father,
Grandfather's wife,	Grandmother's husband,
Son's wife,	
Son's son's wife,	Daughter's husband,
Daughter's son's wife,	Son's daughter's husband,
Wife's mother,	
Wife's grandmother,	Daughter's daughter's husband,
Wife's daughter,	
Wife's son's daughter,	Husband's father,
Wife's daughter's daughter,	Husband's grandfather,
Sister,	Husband's son,
Brother's daughter,	Husband's son's son,
Sister's daughter,	Husband's daughter's son,
Father's sister,	
Mother's sister.	Brother,
	Brother's son,
	Sister's son,
	Father's brother,
	Mother's brother.

And if any man or woman shall hereafter intermarry within the degrees aforesaid, every such marriage shall be null and void, and the issue of any such marriage hereafter to be had or solemnized shall be deemed and adjudged illegitimate, and be subject to all the disabilities of such issue.

Issue of such marriages to be illegitimate.

Sec. 2. *And be it further enacted*, That all marriages where either of the parties shall have a former wife or husband living at the time of such marriage, or where either of them shall be an idiot or lunatic,

Marriages between parties, either of which has a husband or wife, to be void.

at

at the time of fuch marriage, fhall be abfolutely void; and no dower fhall be affigned
any widow in confequence of fuch marriage;
and the iffue fhall be deemed, taken and adjudged illegitimate, and be fubject to all the
difabilities of fuch iffue.

And the iffue il-
legitimate.

Sec. 3. *And be it further enacted,* That
divorces from the bond of matrimony fhall
be decreed, in cafe any marriage fhall be
hereafter had or folemnized which is declared void as abovefaid. Divorces from
the bond of matrimony fhall alfo be decreed
for impotency, adultery, extreme cruelty,
wilful defertion for five years of either of
the parties, and alfo for neglect or refufal
on the part of the hufband, being of fufficient ability, to provide neceffaries for the
fubfiftence of his wife, and alfo for any other
grofs mifbehaviour and wickednefs in either
of the parties, repugnant to and in viola-
tion of the marriage covenant.

In what cafes
divorces may be
decreed.

Sec. 4. *And be it further enacted,* That
when it fhall appear that the adultery, cruelty, defertion or other caufe of complaint
as aforefaid, is occafioned by the collufion
of the parties, and done or contrived with
an intention to procure a divorce, in fuch
cafe no divorce fhall be decreed.

Adultery, &c. by
collufion not to
be a caufe of
divorce.

Sec. 5. *And be it further enacted,* That
when a divorce fhall be had for the caufes
of affinity, confanguinity, impotency, idiocy
or lunacy of either of the parties, the wife
fhall have reftored to her all her lands, tenements and hereditaments, and a judgment
may be paffed for a reftoration to her of all
or fuch part of the perfonal eftate fpecifical-
ly, or the value thereof, which hath come to
the hufband's hands by virtue of the marriage, as the Juftices of the Supreme Judicial

Divorces de-
creed for affinity,
&c. the wife's
eftate to be re-
ftored.

cial Court, from all the circumſtances of the caſe, ſhall deem equitable. And they may make uſe of ſuch proceſs to carry their judgment into effect, as ſhall be neceſſary ; *For adultery, &c. by the wife, the huſband to hold the eſtate, &c.* and when the divorce ſhall be occaſioned by adultery or other of the cauſes aforeſaid, done or committed on the part of the wife, the huſband ſhall hold the perſonal eſtate forever, and her real eſtate during his natural life, in caſe they have had iſſue born alive of her body, during the marriage, otherwiſe during her natural life only, if he ſhall ſurvive her. *Provided nevertheleſs,* that the Court may allow her for her ſubſiſtence ſo much of ſuch perſonal or real eſtate as they ſhall judge neceſſary.

For adultery, &c. by the huſband, the wife's eſtate to be reſtored, in caſe, &c. Sec. 6. *And be it further enacted,* That when the divorce ſhall be had for the cauſe of adultery, or any other of the aforeſaid cauſes, done or committed on the part of the huſband, the wife, if there be no iſſue living at the time of the divorce, ſhall be reſtored to all her lands, tenements and hereditaments, and be allowed out of his real or perſonal eſtate, or both, ſuch alimony as the Court ſhall think reaſonable, not exceeding the uſe of one moiety of his real eſtate, during the life of the wife ; and the property of one half of his perſonal eſtate, having regard to the perſonal property which came to the huſband by the marriage, and his ability ; but if there be iſſue living at the time of the divorce, then the Court, with regard to ordering reſtoration or granting alimony as aforeſaid, may do as they ſhall judge the circumſtances of the caſe may require ; and upon the application of either party, may from time to time make ſuch alterations therein as may be neceſſary

Sec.

Sec. 7. *And be it further enacted,* That all questions of alimony and divorce shall be heard and tried by the Supreme Judicial Court, and that the decree of the same Court shall be final. *Provided always,* that nothing herein contained shall be construed to extend to, or in any wise affect, any marriage which shall be solemnized among the Jews, within the degrees of affinity or consanguinity allowed of by their religion.

Divorce, &c. to be decreed by the Supreme Court.

Proviso.

An Act to prevent clandestine Marriages.

Section 1. BE it enacted by the General Assembly, and by the authority thereof it is enacted, That all persons within this State, who are desirous of being joined together in the estate of matrimony, shall make their application to an Assistant, Justice of the Peace, or Warden, or to some ordained Minister of the Episcopal church, or to any settled and ordained Minister or Elder of any Presbyterian, Congregational, Independent, Baptist or Methodist church, society or congregation; or to the ordained Minister of any religious denomination in the town or towns wherein such persons respectively dwell, in order that such intention of marriage may be duly published as is herein directed; that is to say, if such application shall be made to an Assistant, Justice of the Peace, or Warden, the officer so applied to shall thereupon make a publication in writing under his hand and seal, declaring such intention of marriage, which shall be in the form following, to wit:

"KNOW all men by these presents, that A. B. of   and C. D. of   have declared unto me their intention of marriage.

1701.
1733.
1749.
1764.
1794.
1798.

Intention of marriage to be published.

Form of a publication by a Justice, &c.

P p p

riage. I do therefore hereby make public the said intention. If any person knows any just cause or impediment why these two persons should not be joined together in marriage, they may declare the same as the law directs. Given under my hand and seal, at   this   day of   ."

Which publication the said Assistant, Justice or Warden shall cause to be affixed in some public place in the town wherein the parties respectively dwell, for the space of fifteen days, to the intent that if any person hath any lawful objection against such persons' being joined in marriage, he may have op-

Penalty for defacing, &c. a publication.
portunity to make the same. And if any person shall deface or pull down any publication posted up in writing as aforesaid, he shall forfeit and pay the sum of two dollars, to and for the use of the town where the offence shall be committed; and if unable to pay the said fine, shall be imprisoned at the discretion of the Justice before whom he may be tried, for a space of time not exceeding fifteen days.

How to be published by Ministers.
Sec. 2. *And be it further enacted,* That if such application be made to any such minister or elder as aforesaid, he shall thereupon openly, and by speaking, publish the bans of marriage between the parties three several Sundays, holidays or other days of public worship, in the meeting in the town where the parties respectively belong.

Parties living in different towns, to be published in both.
Sec. 3. *And be it further enacted,* That when the parties live in different towns, the bans shall be published as aforesaid in both towns where the parties respectively dwell.

Who may join persons in marriage.
Sec. 4. *And be it further enacted,* That any Assistant, Judge of the Supreme Judicial Court, Justice of a Court of Common Pleas,

or

or of the Peace, or Warden, Minifter or
Elder as aforefaid, in this State, is fully empowered and authorized to join perfons together in marriage; provided they may
lawfully enter thereinto, and have been
lawfully publifhed. And the folemnization
of marriage fhall be performed in the pre-
fence of two credible witneffes at the leaft,
befides the officer or Minifter who fhall join
any perfons in marriage, and the fee for
marrying fhall be one dollar.

Sec. 5. *And be it further enacted,* That no perfon, by this act authorized to join perfons in marriage, fhall join in marriage any white perfon with any Negro, Indian or mulatto, on the penalty of two hundred dollars, to be recovered by action of debt, one moiety thereof to be paid to and for the ufe of the State, and the other moiety to and for the ufe of him who fhall profecute for the fame; and all fuch marriages fhall be abfolutely null and void. *No white perfon to be married to a Negro, &c.*

Sec. 6. *And be it further enacted,* That when any perfons belonging to this State fhall apply to be married by any perfon other than him who publifhed the intention of fuch marriage, they fhall produce an authenticated certificate or certificates of both being duly publifhed according to law. *Parties to be married, to pro-duce a certifi-cate.*

Sec. 7. *And be it further enacted,* That if any perfon or perfons fhall come from another State into any town in this State to be married, he, fhe or they fhall produce a certificate under the hand of lawful authori-ty, where fuch perfon or perfons dwell, that he, fhe or they have been duly publifhed ac-cording to the laws of fuch State.

Sec. 8. *And be it further enacted,* That if any perfon fhall have any lawful ob- *Objections to marriages, how to be made.*

jection

jection against any persons' being joined in
marriage, he or she may, with leave and
assent of any Assistant, Judge of the Supreme
Judicial Court, Justice of the Court of
Common Pleas, or of the Peace, or Warden,
living in the same town where such publication is made, make such objection in
writing under his or her hand, therein assign-
ing the impediment, and affix the same under
the publication, if the publication be in
writing; but if the bans were published by
any Minister or Elder as aforesaid, then the
person making such objection in writing
shall, in the presence of two witnesses, deliver such writing to the Minister or Elder
who published the bans; whereupon, and
in such cases, the solemnization of marriage
shall be deferred until such time as the truth
of the objection can be tried.

Person objecting
to enter into re-
cognizance, &c.

Provided always, that the person who hath
any such objection to make, shall, previous
to affixing up the same, or delivering thereof
to such Minister, enter into a recognizance
with two good sureties before any Assistant,
Judge of the Supreme Judicial Court, Justice of a Court of Common Pleas, or of
the Peace, or Warden, living in the town
where such publication is made. to appear
at the next Court of General Sessions of the
Peace for the county where such publication is made, and there make good and
prove his or her allegations and matters
of impediment, set forth in such writing of
objection, and in default thereof to pay
the parties to be married all such damages
as they shall sustain by means of staying their
marriage; which Court of Sessions are hereby fully empowered to have cognizance of
                                        such

fuch matters, and to make order thereupon according to law.

Sec. 9. *And be it further enacted,* That if any Affiftant, Judge of the Supreme Judicial Court, Juftice of a Court of Common Pleas, or of the Peace, or Warden, Minifter or Elder as aforefaid, fhall join perfons together in marriage without due and lawful publication, or when the publication hath been lawfully objected to, and the impediment not removed, the perfon fo offending fhall, upon conviction thereof upon a bill of indictment before the Supreme Judicial Court, forfeit and pay as a fine a fum not exceeding one thoufand dollars, nor lefs than fifty dollars, to be impofed at the difcretion of the faid Court, to be holden in the county where the offence fhall be committed, one moiety of which fine fhall be paid into the general-treafury, and the other moiety to him or them who fhall inform of the faid offence.

Penalty for marrying perfons not publifhed, &c.

Sec. 10. *And be it further enacted,* That if any Affiftant, Judge of the Supreme Judicial Court, Juftice of a Court of Common Pleas, or of the Peace, Warden. Minifter or Elder as aforefaid, fhall prefume to marry any man or woman whom he knows to have a wife or hufband living, or hath had a wife or hufband within his knowledge, and doth not know that fuch wife or hufband is dead in fact or in law, or that the perfon offering to be married hath been lawfully divorced, fuch officer, Minifter or Elder, fo offending, and being thereof lawfully convicted before the aforefaid Court, fhall pay as a fine, to and for the ufe of the State, the fum of five hundred dollars.

Penalty for marrying a perfon having a hufband or wife.

Sec. 11. *And be it further enacted,* That whofoever

Penalty for being married contrary to this act.

whosoever shall presume to be married with-out duly proceeding as by this act is required, shall forfeit and pay the sum of fifty dollars, one moiety thereof for the use of the State, and the other moiety to and for the use of him who shall prosecute for the same.

Quakers and Jews may be married according to their rules.

Sec. 12. *And be it further enacted,* That any marriages which may be had and solemnized among the people called Quakers or Friends, in the manner and form used or practised in their societies, or among persons professing the Jewish religion, according to their rites and ceremonies, shall be good and valid in law, any thing in this act to the contrary notwithstanding.

1701.
1727.
1733.
1798.

An Act for registering Marriages, Births and Burials.

A certificate to be given to persons married.

Section 1. BE it enacted by the General Assembly, and by the authority thereof it is enacted, That all persons, having authority to join persons in marriage, shall, immediately after the solemnization thereof, give a certificate in the following form, to wit:

Form.

" I hereby certify, that A. B. of son of   and C. D. of   daughter of   were lawfully joined together in marriage on the   day of   by me the subscriber."

To be recorded.

Sec. 2. *And be it further enacted,* That the persons married shall, within one month's time after their marriage, have such certificate registered in the Town-Clerk's office of the town where their marriage was performed, on the penalty of forfeiting for eve-ry ry month's neglect afterwards the sum of eight cents per month.

Sec. 3. *And be it further enacted,* That all births and deaths of children shall be registered by the Town-Clerk of the town where they shall happen to be born or die, within two months after the birth or death; and that the parents of such children who shall neglect to have them registered as aforesaid, shall forfeit and pay for every month's neglect afterwards eight cents per month. *Births and deaths to be recorded.*

Sec. 4. *And be it further enacted,* That the Town-Clerks be and they are hereby empowered to recover all the fines and forfeitures contained in this act, that have arisen or shall arise, before a Court of Justices or Wardens, in the town where the fine shall arise, by an action of debt, one moiety thereof to the use of the town, and the other moiety to the use of the said Town-Clerk who shall sue for the same. *Penalty for neglect.*

Provided always, that such suit be brought within two years after such marriage, birth or death. *Provis.*

An Act for destroying Barberry Bushes. 1772.

WHEREAS it is found by experience that barberry bushes are very destructive to English grain:

Section 1. *Be it enacted by the General Assembly, and by the authority thereof it is enacted,* That if any freeholder in this State shall apply to any person having barberry bushes growing in his field or inclosure to destroy them, it shall be the duty of such person forthwith to cause said barberry bushes to be destroyed; and if the owner *Barberry bushes to be destroyed by the owner of the land.*

of

Penalty for neglect.
of the land shall neglect or refuse to cut and destroy them annually, he shall forfeit and pay the sum of thirty dollars, one half to and for the use of the town in which the barberry bushes grow, and the other half to the informer or prosecutor, to be recovered by information before the Court of General Sessions of the Peace, in the county where the land lies, or by action of debt in any Court proper to try the same.

In the highways, &c. to be destroyed by the Town-Treasurer.
Sec. 2. *And be it further enacted,* That if any barberry bushes shall be found in the commons or highways in any town in the State, and any freeholder of any town therein shall make application to the Town-Treasurer of such town to destroy them, it shall be the duty of such Town-Treasurer to cause said barberry bushes to be destroyed at the expence of such town; but if such Town-Treasurer shall refuse or neglect so to do for the space of one year, that then, and in such case, such freeholder may make application to any one of the Justices of the Peace for said town, who is hereby empowered and required to grant his warrant to procure labourers to cut up and destroy the said barberry bushes, the expence whereof shall be paid out of the town-treasury of said town.

1734.
1766.
1773.
1798.

An Act for the Preservation of Oysters within this State.

Penalty for taking oysters with drags, &c.

Section 1. BE it enacted by the General Assembly, and by the authority thereof it is enacted, That if any person or persons shall, in any of the bays, coves, rivers or harbours within this State, take any oysters with drags, or by any
other

other inſtrument or inſtruments, or by any other method which may have a greater tendency to deſtroy the beds of oyſters than by the uſual method of taking them by oyſter-tongs, or ſhall have any drag or drags on board any veſſel or veſſels uſed or employed in taking or catching any oyſters, in any of the bays, coves, rivers or harbours aforeſaid, he or they, or whoſoever elſe ſhall be owner or owners of any ſuch veſſel or veſſels, ſhall forfeit every ſuch veſſel or veſſels ſo employed and found in taking oyſters as aforeſaid, together with all the implements thereto belonging, to be recovered by action, bill, plaint or information, before any of the Courts of Common Pleas or General Seſſions of the Peace within this State, one half whereof to be to and for the uſe of the State, and the other half thereof to ſuch perſon or perſons as ſhall inform and ſue for the ſame.

Sec. 2. *Provided neverthelefs, and be it further enacted,* That this act, or any part thereof, ſhall not extend, or be conſtrued to extend, to the town of Weſterly.

This act not to extend to Weſterly.

Sec. 3. *And be it further enacted,* That no perſon whoſoever ſhall take, by tongs or otherwiſe, any oyſters within any of the bays, waters, rivers, harbours or creeks, within the limits of this State, at any time between the firſt day of May, and the laſt day of September annually; and every perſon who ſhall take any oyſters contrary to this prohibition, ſhall forfeit for each offence ten dollars, to be recovered by an action of debt, or information before any Juſtice of the Peace, one half thereof for the uſe of the State, and the other half

Oyſters not to be taken between May and September.

for

for the ufe of him who fhall inform or fue
for the fame.

1735. *An Act to prevent the Fifh from being hinder-
ed in their Courfes up the feveral frefh
Rivers in this State, in all Cafes and Places
where there is no other and particular
Regulation made by Law.*

A fim way to be
left in all dams,
&c.

Section 1. BE it enacted by the General
Affembly, and by the autho-
rity thereof it is enacted, That no perfon or
perfons within this State fhall erect or make
any mill-dam or other dam or weir acrofs
any frefh river, brook or courfe of water,
where any fifh ufually pafs, nor keep up
any dam or weir already made, acrofs any
fuch river, brook or courfe of water, at any
time between the twenty-firft day of April,
and the firft day of June annually, forever,
except fuch perfon fhall leave and keep
open, all faid time, a good and fufficient
way through fuch dam or weir for the fifh
to pafs and repafs. And if any perfon or

Method of deter-
mining whether
the way be fuffi-
cient

perfons, owning any fuch dam or weir, fhall
not make a fufficient way through fuch his
dam or weir, and keep it open during the
time aforefaid, it fhall and may be lawful
for any freeholder within this State to make
complaint to any Juftice of the Peace within the fame county, that there is not a fufficient way for the fifh to pafs; which faid
Juftice fhall, by a writing under his hand,
fent by a Conftable or Town-Sergeant, notify the perfon owning any fuch dam or weir
that a complaint has been entered againft
him for not opening and keeping a fufficient
way through fuch his dam or weir. And
that at a certain day named in fuch notification

tion (not to be within two days from the date
thereof) he, with fo many other of the Juftices
of the county as fhall fee caufe, will appear at
the place where fuch dam or weir is, in order then and there to judge whether the way
through faid dam be fufficient; and if the
major part of the Juftices fo met fhall adjudge the way through fuch dam to be good
and fufficient, they fhall order the complainant to pay all cofts that have accrued by his
needlefs complaint, and give in their judgment in writing to the owner of fuch dam,
that the way through the fame is fufficient;
but if faid Juftices fo met fhall adjudge the
way through faid dam not to be fufficient,
they fhall order the owner thereof to pay all
cofts and charges that have accrued by
fuch his neglect, and order a fufficient way
to be made through faid dam, which faid
judgment fhall be final. And that the officer by whom the notification fhall be fent,
fhall take a particular view of the dam or
dams againft which complaint is made, and
if it appears that the way is fufficient, but
that it was made fo between the time of
making the complaint and the time of examination made by the Juftices, that then
the perfon againft whom complaint is made
fhall pay all charges. And if the owner or
owners of any fuch dam fhall afterwards
prefume to ftop up the way ordered open by
the faid Juftices, or any part thereof, within the time aforefaid, he or they fo offending fhall forfeit the fum of twenty dollars,
to be levied by a warrant of diftrefs from
under the hand of any Juftice to whom the
truth of the above fact fhall be made out.

Sec. 2. *And be it further enacted,* That No perfon to fifh
all perfons within this State fhall be reftrict- on certain days.
ed

ed from fishing in any river or brook as aforesaid three days, *viz.* Saturday, Sunday and Monday, in each week, during the time aforesaid, saving with an hook and line on Saturday and Monday. And in case any person or persons shall be lawfully convicted of fishing on any of the days aforesaid, he or they shall pay a fine of three dollars upon every conviction. And in case the person convicted shall not pay the money within ten days, then the Justice shall issue a warrant to the Sergeant or Constable of any town in the county, to distrain so much of the goods and chattels of the offender as will satisfy and pay the same, with costs.

Alewives not to be obstructed in coming down rivers. And that all persons within this State shall be wholly restricted from catching or hindering any alewives coming down any such rivers as aforesaid, at all times in the year forever. And in case any person shall be convicted of hindering such fish coming down such rivers, he shall pay a fine of three dollars, to be levied as aforesaid ; and one moiety of all the aforesaid fines shall go to the complainant, or the person who shall prosecute for the same, and the other half shall be put into the town-treasury. where such offence shall be committed, for the use of the town.

1737.

An Act to prevent the drawing of any Net or Seine, for the catching of Fish in the Pond commonly called and known by the Name of Easton's Pond, in Newport.

Penalty for catching fish with nets, &c. in Easton's Pond. BE it enacted by the General Assembly, and by the authority thereof it is enacted, That no person or persons whosoever shall, under any pretence whatsoever, draw any seine or

net

net in the aforesaid pond, or creek adja-
cent, or any of the inlets or rivers belonging thereto, for the catching of any sort of
fish, under the penalty, for every offence,
of forfeiting the sum of eighteen dollars,
to be recovered before any two Justices of
the said town, upon information thereof
made, who are hereby fully empowered to
have cognizance of the same ; the one half
of which fine shall be appropriated to and
for the use of the town, and the other half
to him who shall inform and sue for the
same.

---

*An Act to prevent fishing with Seines in Ke-
kemuit River.* **1755.**

BE it enacted by the General Assembly, and
by the authority thereof it is enacted, That
no seine shall at any time be set or drawn
in Kekemuit River, within half a mile's
distance from the place called and known
by the name of the Narrows, either above
or below said Narrows; and if any person or persons shall at any time presume
to set or draw any seine or seines in said
river, within the limits aforesaid, every
person so offending shall pay as a fine the
sum of fifteen dollars, one half thereof to
and for the use of him who shall inform and
sue for the same, and the other half to the use
of such town where any seine shall be so
set or drawn, to be recovered by action of
debt in any Court proper to try the same.

Penalty for draw-
ing seines in
Kekemuit Ri-
ver.

An

1779.
1792.

*An Act to prevent the Fish from being ob-
structed in their Course into Puncatest, alias
Nomquit Pond, and the Branches of the
River running into said Pond, lying in
Tiverton.*

Penalty for draw-
ing seines, &c.
in Puncatest
Pond.

Section 1. BE it enacted by the General
Assembly, and by the authority
thereof it is enacted, That no person or persons shall haul any net or seine within the
said Puncatest, *alias* Nomquit Pond, or in
the rivers leading into said pond, or in the
breach from said pond into the sea, or within one half mile of said breach, upon the
penalty of ten dollars for each and every
offence ; the which offence shall and may
be enquired into by any three Justices of
the Peace of the county of Newport, who
are hereby fully empowered to hear such
matter, and give judgment thereon: And
on conviction of any offender on the premises before them, to issue a warrant to the
Sheriff, his Deputy, or the Sergeant or
Constable of any town in said county, to
distrain so much of the goods and chattels of
the offender (unless he shall pay the same,
with the costs of conviction) as shall satisfy
and pay the fine aforesaid, and costs ; and that
for want thereof such offender shall be committed to prison until the judgment be satisfied ; and one moiety or half part of such
fines shall go to the complainant, or person
who shall prosecute for the same ; and the
other half shall be paid into the town-
treasury of the town where such offence
shall be committed, to and for the use of said
town.

Sec. 2. *And be it further enacted,* That
no

ho weir, pots or any other contrivances for the Penalty for erecting weirs, &c. obſtructing the courſe of the fiſh, ſhall be made or erected acroſs ſaid pond, or any part thereof, or in any branch of the rivers leading into or out of ſaid pond, in order to hinder or obſtruct the courſe of the fiſh, under the penalty aforeſaid, to be recovered in like manner.

Sec. 3. *And be it further enacted,* That For ſetting nets. no hanging or meſh nets ſhall be ſet in ſaid pond, or the rivers leading into or out of ſaid pond, unleſs from the firſt day of Auguſt until the firſt day of January, under the penalty aforeſaid, to be recovered in like manner.

Provided nevertheleſs, that this act ſhall Proviſo. not be conſtrued to prevent any perſon or perſons from taking or catching fiſh in the pond aforeſaid, or in the rivers or branches thereof, with ſcoop nets, or hooks and lines.

An Act to prevent drawing Seines in a certain 1795. *Part of Warren River.*

BE it enacted by the General Aſſembly, and Penalty for drawing ſeines in Warren River. by the authority thereof it is enacted, That no ſeine ſhall be ſet or drawn in any part of the river running from Warren River, through the town of Barrington, to the dividing line between the ſaid town of Barrington and the town of Rehoboth, upon the penalty of twenty dollars, to be recovered by action of debt in any Court proper to try the ſame; the one moiety thereof to the uſe of the perſon who ſhall inform and ſue for the ſame, and the other moiety to the uſe of the poor of the town where ſuch ſeine ſhall be ſo ſet or drawn.

1787.

An Act to prevent the drawing of Seines in any Part of Providence River which lies to the Northward of Fox-Point, and also that Branch of said River known by the Name of Seacunck River.

Penalty for drawing seines in Seacunck River, &c.

BE it enacted by the General Assembly, and by the authority thereof it is enacted, That no seine shall be drawn in any part of said river, or its branches, within the limits aforesaid, north of Fox-Point, as far as the tide ebbs and flows. And that any person or persons who shall draw any seine in said river, within the limits aforesaid, and thereof shall be lawfully convicted, shall forfeit and pay thirty-five dollars, to be recovered by action of debt before any Court proper to try the same; one moiety thereof to him who shall sue or inform for the same, and the other moiety to and for the use of the State.

1736.
1743.
1798.

An Act to prevent the Fish from being hinder-ed in their Course into Point-Judith Ponds, and Petaquamscutt River.

Penalty for drawing seines, at certain times, in Point-Judith ponds, &c.

Section 1. BE it enacted by the General Assembly, and by the authority thereof it is enacted, That no person or per-sons shall at any time from the tenth day of August to the tenth day of January, in every year, draw or set any net or seine for the catching or hauling of any fish whatever, within half a mile from Point-Judith breach, in the sea, or at the breach or entrance of Petaquamscutt River, nor within one mile thereof; nor, within the said breach as far up as an island in the ponds, commonly called

led Mumford's Island, or the Great Island; nor in the channel at the southwest end thereof; nor within the said Petaquamscutt River, up the same, to the distance of half a mile into the pond, called Petaquamscutt Pond, under the penalty of ten dollars for each person concerned therein, together with the forfeiture of the boat and seine.

Sec. 2. *And be it further enacted,* That no mesh-nets, so called, shall be set in any part of Petaquamscutt River or Pond, or in Point-Judith Pond, from the first day of June to the first day of January in every year, under the penalty of thirty dollars, together with the forfeiture of such net.

For setting nets.

Sec. 3. *And be it further enacted,* That no weirs shall be made or erected across Petaquamscutt River, at any time whatever. Neither shall any standing seine, or any other such contrivances for the catching of fish, be set across or partly across said river, at any time of the year; and any person or persons so offending, and being duly convicted, shall be fined in the sum of thirty dollars, one half to the informer, and the other half to the use of the State.

For erecting weirs, &c.

Sec. 4. *And be it further enacted,* That no standing net or seine shall be set across the channel, nor in Point-Judith Ponds, within the extent of one quarter of a mile's distance of the four following places, to wit: Alder Point, near where Saucatucket River vents itself into the said pond; Wilkinson's Point, so called; Strawberry Hill, on Mumford's or the Great Island, and High Hill, so called, on lands late John Potter's, Esq; upon the penalty of forfeiting the sum of thirty dollars, to be recovered, applied and disposed of in manner and form as hereafter

No seine to be set across the channel, &c.

in this act provided; unless the proprietors of the said several places shall think proper to set such nets and seines, for preventing the fish, after they are in the upper pond, going out; always excepting at Wheatfield Cove, on the lands late George Hazard's, Esq; where the proprietor or his tenants may so do, *provided* the same doth not interfere with the passage of the channel.

Such seines may be destroyed.

Sec. 6. *And be it further enacted,* That it shall and may be lawful to and for the proprietors of the several places aforementioned, to take up and destroy all such nets and seines as they shall discover to be set, contrary to and otherwise than this act doth allow.

How to prosecute for offences against this act.

Sec. 7. *And be it further enacted,* That all offences against this act shall and may be enquired into by any three Justices of the Peace in the county of Washington, who are fully empowered to hear such matter, and give judgment thereon; and on conviction of any offender in the premises before them, to give forth a warrant to the Sergeant or Constable of any town in the said county, to distrain so much of the goods and chattels of the offender (unless he shall pay the same down on conviction) as shall satisfy and pay the same, with costs; and for want thereof, such offender shall be committed to prison, until the judgment be satisfied.

An Act to prevent the Fish being interrupted in their Course up Mill Cove, in Warwick.

Fishing in Mill Cove.

BE it enacted by the General Assembly, and by the authority thereof it is enacted, That no seine or net shall hereafter be drawn

or

or set any where in the cove in Warwick, called the Mill Cove, nor from the mouth thereof to the pond of fresh water into which the fish pass in going up the said cove, under the same restrictions and penalties as are provided with regard to setting and drawing seines in Pawtuxet River.

An Act for regulating the Fishery and removing Obstructions in Pawcatuck River.

Section 1. **B**E it enacted by the General Assembly, and by the authority thereof it is enacted, That no weir, or other obstruction, shall be erected, set, or continued in any part of Pawcatuck river, dividing this State from the State of Connecticut, upon the penalty of twenty-six dollars and sixty-seven cents for erecting or setting the same; and thirteen dollars and thirty-four cents for every twenty-four hours any such weir, or other obstructions, shall be continued in said river.

Sec. 2. *And be it further enacted,* That no person or persons, citizens of this State, be permitted to set or draw any seine or seines in said Pawcatuck river, from the twentieth day of March to the first day of June annually, excepting between sun-rising on Thursday morning and sun-rising on Saturday morning in each week, upon the penalty of thirteen dollars and thirty-four cents for each and every time such seine shall be set or drawn, otherwise than as aforesaid: That in setting and drawing any seine as aforesaid, at any time from the said twentieth day of March to the first day of June annually, no person or persons shall be permitted to drive the fish in said river, by thrashing,

No weir, &c. to be erected in Pawcatuck River.

When to fish in said river.

thrashing, beating, or in any other way by
founds, upon the penalty of six dollars and
sixty-seven cents for each and every offence.

Sec. 3. *And be it further enacted*, That
no person or persons be permitted to fish
in said river, except on the days aforesaid,
and such other days as shall be appointed by
the State of Connecticut, for the benefit of
the citizens of that State, except with hooks
and lines, upon the penalty of six dollars
and sixty-seven cents for each and every
offence.

And to the end that the fish may more
freely pass to the various sources of the said
river :

Sec. 4. *Be, it further enacted*, That
yearly and every year, from the twentieth
day of March to the first day of June, there
be a passage opened in the mill-dam below
Pawcatuck bridge, and in all the other
dams in said river, ten feet in length, from
the middle of said river easterly : And the
owner or owners, occupier or occupiers of
any of the dams aforesaid, who shall neglect
or refuse to open a passage or passages as
aforesaid, on or before the said twentieth day
of March annually, shall forfeit the sum of
thirteen dollars and thirty-four cents, for
every such refusal or neglect ; and for every
succeeding day's refusal or neglect to open
a passage as aforesaid, from the said twentieth
day of March to the first day of June annually, the offender or offenders shall forfeit the sum of six dollars and sixty-seven
cents. The one half of all the penalties im-
posed by this act shall be to him or them
who shall sue for and prosecute to effect,
and the other half to the town-treasury of
the town of Westerly or Hopkinton, to be
determined

Except, &c.

*Dams in said ri-
ver when to be
opened.*

Penalty.

determined by the refidence of the complainant; and if he fhall not refide in either
Wefterly or Hopkinton, one fourth part of
faid penalties fhall be paid into the town-
treafury of each of faid towns; but if the
profecutions are brought by indictment,
the whole penalty fhall be paid into the general-treafury.

Sec. 5. *And be it further enacted*, That no fuit in law or equity fhall be inftituted or maintained by the citizens of this State againft the citizens of the State of Connecticut, for or on account of the difturbances, riots and breaches of the peace, that have heretofore taken place between them, relative to the fifhery in faid Pawcatuck River; and all fuits that may have been inftituted as aforefaid, in the matters aforefaid, fhall ceafe and determine.

Difputes, &c. between citizens of this State and Connecticut, relative to, &c. to ceafe.

An Act regulating the Fifhery in Pawtuxet River, its Branches, and below the Falls thereof. 1767.

Section 1. BE it enacted by the General Affembly, and by the authority thereof it is enacted, That all perfons whofoever fhall be reftricted, and they hereby are prohibited, from fetting or drawing any feine or net in any cove or part of Pawtuxet River below the falls called Pawtuxet Falls, to the end of the Long Neck, fo called, from a ftraight line drawn weftward to the oppofite fhore, and fo up ftream from faid falls, in any branch or fmall ftream, leading into any pond or ponds, to the uttermoft extent of all and every other branch of faid river, where the fifh called alewives have heretofore been known to pafs, from the twenty-

No feine to be drawn on certain days in Pawtuxet River, &c.

twenty-fifth day of March to the fifteenth day of June annually; saving and excepting only on the following days in each week during the time aforesaid, to wit, Tuesday, Wednesday and Thursday; but that on all Fridays, Saturdays, Sundays and Mondays, during said time, no seining, netting or obstruction whatever to the passing of said fish in said river, or its branches, shall be permitted : *Provided nevertheless*, that any person may fish with hooks and lines.

Nor weirs to be erected, &c. Sec. 2. *And be it further enacted*, That no person shall make any weir or weirs, or keep any standing seine at any time across said Pawtuxet River, or any branch thereof, so as to obstruct or hinder the fish in their free course up the said river and its branches, under the penalty of fifty dollars, to be sued for and recovered before any Court proper to try the same; one half thereof to and for the use of the town where such offence shall be committed, and the other half to and for the use of the person or persons who shall inform and sue for the same.

Regulations and penalties. Sec. 3. *And be it further enacted*, That all the regulations contained and specified in a certain act of the Legislature of the late Colony, now State of Rhode-Island and Providence Plantations, passed in the year 1735, entitled, " An act to prevent the fish from being hindered in their courses up the several fresh rivers in this State, in all cases and places where there is no other and particular regulation made by law," be and the same hereby are extended to the said river of Pawtuxet and its branches; and where the word dam or dams is mentioned in said act, it shall be construed as meaning and extending to any mill-dams and other

dams

dams whatever, on the said river or the branches thereof : That the first fine mentioned as a penalty therein, be increased to thirty dollars ; and that the two last fines mentioned in said act, be increased to fifty dollars ; any law, custom or usage, to the contrary hereof notwithstanding.

Sec. 4. *And be it further enacted,* That the fish-ways upon the north branch of said Pawtuxet River, in the dams across the said river, shall be twelve feet wide : *Provided nevertheless,* that the owners of the Furnace Hope shall not be obliged to open any fish-way through their dam, nor shall any fish-way be required to be opened above said dam. Fish-ways in dams.

Provided further, that nothing herein contained, relative to dams or opening of fish-ways, shall be construed to extend to the fouth branch of said Pawtuxet River, or any part of said branch.

An Act to prevent the purloining of Fish caught in any Pots, Weirs or Nets.

1723. 1763. Penalty for drawing fish-pots, &c.

BE it enacted by the General Assembly, and by the authority thereof it is enacted, That if any person or persons shall be found robbing or drawing any fish-pots, weirs or nets, belonging to any other person, they shall be liable to be sued by the owner or owners of such pots, weirs or nets ; and upon due proof thereof, shall pay to the owners of such pots, weirs or nets, the sum of seven dollars and costs, to be recovered before any two Justices of the Peace or Wardens of each respective town where the offence shall be committed.

An

An Act for regulating Water-Mills.

1798.
Owners of mills
permitted to
continue their
ponds, &c.

Section 1. BE it enacted by the General Assembly, and by the authority thereof it is enacted, That where any person or persons have already, or shall hereafter, set up any water-mill or mills upon his or their own lands, or upon any other lands, with the consent of the proprietors thereof, that then the owner or owners of such mill or mills shall have free liberty to continue and improve the pond or ponds in such land for their best advantage, without any molestation. And if the lands of

Remedy for persons injured by such ponds.

any person or persons shall be injured, by being overflowed by the owners or occupants of such mills' stopping or raising the water, that in every such case, the party so aggrieved may make application for relief to the Court of General Sessions of the Peace in the county where such mills or ponds are ; which Court is hereby empowered to issue a warrant, directed to the Sheriff of the said county, to summon and impannel a Jury of twelve or more good and lawful men, at the cost and charge of the owner or owners of such mill or mills ; and the said Jury shall be sworn by a Justice of the Peace to a faithful and indifferent appraisal of the yearly damage done to the lands of the person complaining as aforesaid.

And the Jurors' verdict being returned by the hand of the Sheriff to the next Court of General Sessions of the Peace for the county where such mill or pond is, and being allowed and recorded, shall be a sufficient bar against any action to be brought for any damages occasioned by the flowing of such lands

lands as aforesaid, save only an action of debt, which the complainant may bring for the recovery of such yearly sum or sums of money from the owner or occupant of such mill assessed as aforesaid, during the time of such flowing. But if the Jury find no damage for the complainant, then he or they shall be at the cost of the Jury, to be allowed by the Justices of said Court.

Action of debt may be brought for the yearly damages.

Sec. 2. *And be it further enacted,* That where any persons have or shall erect or build any mill or mills in partnership, and where each of the partners has a property in the place where said mill or mills are or shall be erected or built, and any controversy or dispute hath arisen, or shall arise, between the owners of said mills, whereby said mills shall go to ruin and become useless, that then and in such case it shall and may be lawful for the partner or partners who are desirous said mill or mills should be kept in repair, to take with him or them two good and credible freeholders of the neighbourhood, and with them to go to the owner or partners who neglect to maintain, repair and rebuild his or their part of said mill or mills, and request or demand of him or them to repair or rebuild his or their part of said mills, as the case may require; and if the said owner or partners still refuse or neglect to repair or rebuild as aforesaid, that then and in such case the owner or partner thereby aggrieved, may make his or their application to the Court of General Sessions of the Peace within the county where such difference arises; which Court, upon proof of his or their proceedings as is above required, is hereby fully empowered to grant forth a license to

Disputes between part owners of mills, how determined.

the

the partners or owners fo complaining, to repair and maintain faid mill or mills fo gone to ruin, and the fame to improve to their beſt advantage : Always upon condition, that he or they fhall pay or caufe to be paid to the other owners or partners, fuch and fo much yearly rents for his or their parts of lands, waters and privileges, as are of neceſſity to be made ufe of for faid mills, as the faid partners or owners agree upon. But in cafe it fhall fo happen that the faid own-ers cannot agree upon the yearly rents afore-faid, that then and in fuch cafe the owner or partners who have neglected to repair his or their parts as aforefaid, may make applica-tion to the Court of General Seſſions of the Peace, which is hereby empowered to fend a Jury, in the manner as abovefaid, to value the yearly rents of faid lands, waters and pri-vileges ; and the owner or partners who occupy faid mills and privileges are to pay the rents yearly, according to the value fet by the faid Jury.

Sec. 3. *And be it further enacted,* That if the owners or partners of faid mills, who have neglected to maintain his or their parts as aforefaid, after faid mill is repaired or rebuilt by the other partners as aforefaid, fhall again defire to have his or their parts, and improve them themfelves, that then and in fuch cafe the owners or partners who have repaired or rebuilt faid mills, fhall render true and perfect accounts of the coſts and charges of repairing and rebuild-ing as aforefaid, to the other partner or partners who have neglected as aforefaid, who, upon the payment of his or their pro-portionable part of faid charges, fhall and may re-enter into fuch his part or propor-tion

Part owners who have neglected to repair, may re-enter, &c.

tion of said mills, saving where there is or shall be any contract to the contrary.

Sec. 4. And to the end that rivers and streams of water may be improved and made as useful to the public as possible,

Be it further enacted, That all and every person or persons, owning any dam or mill in this State, shall at all times from the twenty-sixth day of June to the twenty-sixth day of October annually, forever, maintain a waste-gate in their said dam, sufficient to vent so much water as naturally runs in said river; and, after the water shall have risen to the height of three feet perpendicular on his or their flumes which convey the water to his or their water-wheel, keep the same open from six of the clock in the morning until nine of the clock at night of each day during the time abovesaid, if the same be desired by any persons owning any mill within one mile below such mill on the same stream; except when said upper mill is going, at which time the waste-gate of said upper mill may be kept shut down.

Waste-gates to be kept open at certain times.

Sec. 5. *And be it further enacted,* That if at any time or times hereafter any person or persons whosoever, owning any such dam or mill, shall refuse or neglect to keep said waste-gate open as aforesaid, and be thereof duly convicted before any two or more of the Justices of the Peace within the town where the offence shall be committed, such person shall forfeit the sum of seven dollars, the one half thereof to the informer and prosecutor, and the other half to and for the use of the said town.

Penalty for neglect.

An

1726.　　　*An Act regulating Millers in their taking Toll.*

Section 1. **B**E *it enacted by the General Assembly, and by the authority*
Millers to take a sixteenth part for toll.　*thereof it is enacted,* That no miller, or person taking corn or grain to grind, shall, upon any pretence whatsoever, take more toll for grinding the same than a sixteenth part, or two quarts, for grinding a bushel, and so proportionably for a greater or lesser quantity, upon the penalty of forfeiting a fine of one dollar for each offence, the one half there-
Penalty for taking more.　of to the informer, and the other half to the use of the town where such offence shall be committed ; the offender to be tried before any one Justice of the Peace or Warden of such town where such offence shall be committed : And the party offending shall be liable to pay the party aggrieved his lawful
Except.　damages ; excepting where any miller or person erecting a mill shall for some reason make a particular contract with any town or person, for greater toll, then such miller or person tending such mill shall not be liable to such penalty, except he or they exceed the toll contracted for.

　　Sec. 2. *And be it further enacted,* That
Duty of millers.　all millers, and persons tending mills, shall make good meal according to custom, and grind for each person bringing corn or grain to be ground in his turn, without distinction, upon the penalty aforesaid, to be recovered in manner aforesaid, and applied one half to the informer, and the other half to and for the use of the town where such offence shall be committed.

　　　　　　　　　　　　　　　　An

An Act regulating the Inspection of Beef, 1731.
Pork, pickled Fish and Tobacco, ascer- 1784.
taining the Assize of Casks, and for other 1790.
Purposes therein mentioned. 1798.

Section 1. **BE** *it enacted by the General* Beef, &c. to be
Assembly, and by the authority packed by sword
thereof it is enacted, That in every town in packers.
this State where beef, pork or pickled fish
are packed up for sale, the sworn packers
of such town where they shall be put up
for sale or shipped, shall previously thereto
see that they are properly repacked and
pickled, that the casks are in good shipping
order, and that there is good salt in each
cask, sufficient to preserve such beef, pork
and fish from damage, to any foreign port.

Sec. 2. *And be it further enacted,* That How many
every barrel of beef, salted for sale or ex- pounds to the
portation, shall contain, at the least, two barrel, and how
hundred pounds weight of beef, and every branded.
half barrel one hundred pounds weight of
beef; that beef of the first quality, packed
in barrels or half barrels, consisting of the
best pieces, being free of necks and shanks,
be denominated mess beef: That beef of a
good quality, packed in barrels or half barrels, consisting of a due proportion of the
best as well as the poorest part of each quarter respectively, without having any part
culled out, nor more than half the neck,
and two shanks, in each barrel, be denominated prime beef: That the same be packed in good sound white oak casks, and full
bound: That every barrel of pork, salted for
sale or exportation, shall contain at least
two hundred weight of pork; and that pork
of the first quality, packed in barrels or half
barrels,

barrels, confifting of the beft pieces, being
free from legs, fhoulders and heads, fhall be
denominated mefs pork : That pork of a
good quality, confifting of a due proportion
of the beft as well as the pooreft part of each
hog, without having any part culled out, and
not having more than three half heads and
fix legs, be denominated prime pork : That
all fuch other beef and pork as the packer
fhall find wholefome and ufeful, although
upon account of the inferior quality it be
not merchantable, he fhall caufe to be well
packed and falted, and the barrel containing
the fame to be well filled, and the fame fhall
be denominated refufe beef or pork, as the
cafe may be, and the packer fhall brand the
head of the barrel or half barrel, viz. of mefs
beef and pork, with the words " mefs beef,"
or " mefs pork," as the cafe may be ; prime
ditto, with the words " prime beef," or
" prime pork," as the cafe may be, and refufe, with the letter " R. beef," or " R.
pork" only, as the cafe may be, without
any other brand ; and that the letters of the
brand be three quarters of an inch long.
And it fhall be the duty of the fworn packers, in the refpective towns where beef or
pork fhall be put up for fale, or fhipped, to
fee that the fame be packed in the manner
above directed.

Sec. 3. *And be it further enacted,* That
if any perfon fhall offer for fale, or fell any
cafk of falted beef or pork, not being of
the quality, containing the quantity, and
packed in the manner, directed in this act,
he fhall forfeit for every cafk of falted beef
or pork he fhall fo offer for fale or fell, the
fum of ten dollars, to be recovered by action
or information in any Court proper to try
the

*Penalty for fel-
ling beef, &c. not
packed accord-
ing to this act.*

the fame, one moiety thereof to the ufe of the perfon profecuting for the fame, and the other moiety to the ufe of the poor of the town wherein the offence fhall be committed.

Sec. 4. *And be it further enacted,* That all pickled fifh fhall be packed, all of one kind, in cafks well feafoned, bound with twelve hoops, and containing not lefs than twenty-eight gallons : That the cafks be full, and the fifh found and well feafoned ; and that every cafk of beef, pork, and pickled fifh, being firft fearched, examined and approved, it fhall be the duty of the fworn packers of the town in which the fame may be put up for fale, or fhipped, previoufly thereto, to brand or imprint thereon with a burning-iron the following brands or marks, R. H. O. D. and R. P. D. with the initial letter of his Chriftian name, and his furname at length, and the letter P. at the end thereof, to denote that the fame is merchantable, and in good order for exportation : That if any beef, pork or fifh, be offered for fale without having been approved by a fworn packer, and the cafks containing them have not fuch packer's ftamp, mark or brand upon them, the offender or offenders fhall incur the penalty of thirty dollars for each cafk of beef and pork, and ten dollars for each barrel of fifh, fo offered for fale, to be fued for and recovered in any Court of Record proper to try the fame ; and that all fuch beef, pork and fifh, fhall be forfeited, unlefs the fame fhall appear to have been infpected agreeably to the laws of fome other State.

Sec. 5. *And be it further enacted,* That if any cooper, packer, or other perfon, fhall fhift any flefh or fifh, either on board any fhip or veffel, or on fhore, after the fame hath

Pickled fifh how to be packed, &c.

Beef, &c. how to be branded.

Penalty.

Penalty for fhifting beef, &c.

hath been fo branded, ftamped, or marked by the packer, and fhip and export the fame, and brand, ftamp or mark anew the cafk whereinto fuch provifions are fhifted, all perfons acting, ordering or affifting therein, and being thereof convicted, fhall forfeit and pay a fum not exceeding one hundred and fixty dollars, nor lefs than thirty dollars, and pay a fine for each cafk fo fhifted, of thirty dollars; and that every perfon, other than a sworn packer, who fhall prefume to mark, ftamp or brand, any cafk of beef, pork or fifh, with the ftamping or branding inftruments belonging to a fworn packer, or with another inftrument made in imitation thereof, fhall upon conviction forfeit and pay a fum not lefs than thirty dollars, nor more than one hundred and fixty dollars for each cafk fo marked, ftamped or branded, to be recovered by action or information in any Court proper to try the fame.

Penalty for branding by any perfon other than a packer.

Sec. 6. *And be it further enacted,* That no tobacco fhall be fhipped or exported from this State, but fuch only as fhall be infpected and found to be well cured and fit for a foreign market, and packed in ftraight cafks, which fhall be four feet four inches in length, and two feet feven inches diameter at the head, containing not lefs than nine hundred nor more than fourteen hundred pounds weight each; or if packed in half cafks, to contain not lefs than four hundred nor more than fix hundred pounds weight in each, unlefs fuch cafks of tobacco fhall appear to have been infpected and marked agreeably to the law of fome other State.

Tobacco to be infpected, &c.

Sec. 7. *And be it further enacted,* That the General Affembly annually appoint, in fuch towns as there fhall be occafion,

Infpectors to be appointed by the General Affembly.

.one

one or more skilful and disinterested person or persons, to be inspectors of tobacco that shall be exported from this State, who shall be sworn to the due and impartial execution of their trust; that it shall be their duty to inspect all tobacco that shall be intended to be laden on board any vessel for foreign exportation, or that shall be intended to be transported to either of the United States; that every such inspector be and he is hereby required and authorized to open the casks containing tobacco, intended for exportation as aforesaid, and to inspect in four divisions, that is to say, he shall take the cask from the tobacco, and with an iron bar, or other instrument, lift one quarter, and then go through the whole, until it shall be examined in four different parts, and see that it be properly dry, well cured, and not rotten or damaged; and that it be of the weight, and packed in such casks as is above directed; that such part as shall appear to be damaged or rotten, or unfit for exportation, shall be burned; and that on every cask containing such quantity as aforesaid, which by inspection, according to the inspector's best judgment, appears to be well cured, and fit for exportation, he shall mark or impress, with a burning-iron, the letters A. P. with the name of the town where it shall be approved, and such inspector's name at large, and the letter I. at the end thereof, denoting that the same hath been inspected and approved.

Their duty.

Sec. 8. *And be it further enacted,* That if the owner of any tobacco, or any other person employed by him, shall presume to lade or put on board any vessel, bound to any port without this State, any tobacco,

Penalty for exporting tobacco not inspected.

T t t   other

other than such as shall have been approved by an inspector, and contained in casks not having the aforesaid marks, stamps or brands, or if any master of a ship or other vessel, or other officer or mariner, shall receive on board any such, the offender or offenders shall incur the penalty of thirty dollars for each cask of tobacco so shipped, to be sued for and recovered by action or information, in any Court proper to try the same; and all such tobacco so laden or received on board shall be forfeited.

Penalty for shifting tobacco inspected.

Sec. 9. *And be it further enacted,* That if after any cask of tobacco shall have been approved and marked with the inspector's marks, stamps or brands as aforesaid, any cooper or other person shall presume to shift the contents of such casks, and put therein any tobacco that hath not been duly inspected, proved and approved as aforesaid, such cooper, or other person so offending, shall forfeit and pay the sum of sixteen dollars for every cask of tobacco so shifted, to be recovered in manner as aforesaid.

Penalty for fraud in packers, &c.

Sec. 10. *And be it further enacted,* That in case any packer or inspector, appointed and sworn as aforesaid, shall be guilty of any fraud or neglect in packing any beef, pork or fish, or inspecting any tobacco, contrary to the true intent and meaning of this act, or shall mark with his brand or stamp any cask containing beef, pork, fish or tobacco, which he has not actually and thoroughly packed or inspected, and which may be intended for exportation out of this State, he shall forfeit and pay the sum of sixteen dollars

lars for every such neglect, or for every cask so falsely marked, to be recovered as aforesaid ; and that if any person or persons, not appointed and sworn as aforesaid, shall presume to mark or brand any cask of beef, pork, fish or tobacco, as above described, he shall incur the aforesaid penalty of sixteen dollars for every cask so marked or branded, to be recovered as aforesaid.

Sec. 11. *And be it further enacted,* That each cask, before any tobacco be packed therein, shall be weighed by the owner of such tobacco, who shall with a marking-iron mark on one of the heads thereof the full weight of the cask, and the initial letters of his name ; and in case he shall falsely mark the same, such owner, upon conviction thereof, shall forfeit and pay the sum of ten dollars for each cask so falsely marked.

Tobacco casks to be weighed and marked.

Penalty.

Sec. 12. *And be it further enacted,* That the packers of beef, pork and fish, shall be paid by the owners at the rate of sixteen cents per barrel for beef and pork, and twelve and an half cents per barrel for fish, for a compensation for unheading, repacking, heading up, pickling, branding, and a certificate of the same ; and that the inspectors shall be paid by the owner, for every cask of tobacco they shall inspect and prove as before directed, twenty-five cents, provided the number do not exceed four, and seventeen cents for each cask exceeding that number.

Packers' fees.

Sec. 13. *And be it further enacted,* That prior to the clearing out of any of the aforesaid commodities, directed to be packed and inspected by this act, there shall be produced to the collector, or other officer of the customs

Beef, &c. not to be cleared out, unless a certificate thereof be produced to the collector.

toms of the United States, a certificate under the hand of a sworn packer or inspector, that such commodities respectively have been packed, inspected and proved, agreeably to this act : *Provided nevertheless*, that nothing in this act shall extend to any of the aforesaid commodities brought into this State from any other of the United States, and which shall have been inspected and branded agreeably to the laws of the State from whence the same shall have been brought.

Proviso.

Sec. 14. *And be it further enacted*, That every fish-barrel containing pickled fish, which shall be exposed for sale in this State, shall contain twenty-eight gallons ; that all barrels containing cider, beer, or other liquid commodity, shall contain thirty-one gallons and an half; every half barrel containing any liquid commodity, shall contain fifteen gallons and three quarts, and be made of good sound and well seasoned stuff ; and that every cooper, making any barrel or half barrel, shall set his brand-mark thereon, with the initial or two first letters of his name.

Assize of casks.

Sec. 15. *And be it further enacted*, That all barrels and half barrels, the assize whereof is prescribed by the last preceding section, which shall be more than a gallon under the assize aforesaid, shall be forfeited, one half to him or her who shall sue or inform for the same, and the other moiety to the use of the poor of the town where the same shall be seized, to be paid into the town-treasury, and to be recovered before any Court proper to try the same.

Casks under the assize to be forfeited.

Sec. 16. *And be it further enacted*, That in case any cider, beer or other liquid commodity,

Cider, &c. offered for sale in casks under the assize to be forfeited.

modity, be expofed to fale in this State, in
any barrels or half barrels that are not of
the affize aforefaid, the fame fhall be forfeited, the one half to him who will inform
or fue for the fame, and the other half to the
ufe of the State, to be recovered before any
Court proper to try the fame; and that it
fhall and may be lawful for any Juftice of the
Peace in the feveral counties, on complaint
or information to him made, to iffue his warrant for feizing and fecuring any barrels,
half barrels, or other article declared to be
forfeit by this act.

An Act regulating the Affize of Lime-Cafks, 1792.
and the Infpection of Lime. 1798.

Section 1. **B**E *it enacted by the General
Affembly, and by the authori-* Stone lime to be
ty thereof it is enacted, That all ftone lime infpected, &c
in cafks, which fhall be offered or expofed
to fale in this State, fhall be put up in cafks
of the following dimenfions, to wit: Hogfheads, which fhall be thirty-five inches long
within the heads, and the heads twenty-fix
inches and an half in diameter, and which
fhall contain one hundred gallons; half
hogfheads, which fhall be thirty inches in
length between the heads, and the heads
twenty inches and an half in diameter, and
of fufficient bulge to contain fifty gallons,
which fhall be well filled with good merchantable lime, with twelve good hoops to
each hogfhead, and ten good hoops to each
half hogfhead, and fhall be infpected and
branded with the initial letter of the infpector's Chriftian name, and his furname at
large, with the word *Infpected.*

Sec. 2. *And be it further enacted,* That
it

it shall be the duty of each town in this State, in which stone lime is or may be burnt, to appoint annually, at the usual time of electing town officers, as many persons fillers and inspectors of lime as there are lime-kilns in such town, by whom all the lime offered or exposed to sale as aforesaid shall be filled and branded; that the said inspectors shall be allowed and paid by the burners of lime, for filling and branding every hogshead, six cents, and for every half hogshead four cents; and that each inspector shall take an oath or affirmation for the faithful execution of his trust, before he shall enter upon the execution thereof.

Sec. 3. *And be it further enacted,* That all casks of lime offered for sale or exportation in this State, not branded in manner as aforesaid, shall be forfeited, one moiety thereof to and for the use of the poor of the town wherein the same shall be offered for sale, and the other moiety to the complainant or informer, to be recovered in any Court of Record proper to try the same, in the county where the same shall be offered for sale or exportation.

Sec. 4. *And be it further enacted,* That every inspector of lime, who shall brand any cask or casks of lime in manner aforesaid, contrary to the true intent and meaning of this act. and be thereof convicted, on any bill of indictment, or other due process, before any Court of Record before described, shall forfeit double the value of the lime so proved to be branded, one moiety thereof to the prosecutor, and the other moiety to the poor of the town, as aforesaid.

Sec. 5. *And be it further enacted,* That every person who shall counterfeit the brand
of

of any inſpector appointed as aforeſaid, or
ſhall imprint any caſk or caſks of lime with
his brand without his conſent or approbation, or ſhall fill any caſk or caſks a ſecond
time which have been before filled and branded, without firſt cauſing the former brand to
be cut out, ſhall forfeit double the value
of the lime ſo filled or branded, by counterfeiting, or without leave or approbation, or without firſt cutting out the former brand, to be recovered in manner
as aforeſaid, one moiety to and for the uſe
of the proſecutor, and the other to and for
the uſe of the inſpector whoſe brand ſhall
be ſo counterfeited or imprinted without
leave, or whoſe brands ſhall be upon the
caſks filled a ſecond time as aforeſaid, and
not cut out.

Sec. 6. *And be it further enacted,* That
it ſhall be the duty of every perſon exporting ſtone lime, previous to the exportation thereof, to make and produce his certificate to the collector of the diſtrict in
which it ſhall be exported, that the ſame
hath been inſpected and branded agreeably
to law. And all Magiſtrates, Judges, Juſtices of the Peace and Grand Jurors within
this State, are enjoined to take notice of all
breaches of this act that ſhall come to their
knowledge.

Exporters of lime to produce to the collector a certificate of inſpection.

---

*An Act for the Inſpection of Gun-Powder
manufactured within this State.* 1776.

Section 1. BE *it enacted by the General
Aſſembly, and by the autho-
rity thereof it is enacted,* That if any perſon or perſons within this State ſhall vend
or expoſe to ſale any gun-powder manufactured

*Penalty for ſel-
ling powder not
inſpected, &c*

factured within the fame, unlefs faid gun‑
powder be packed in a good dry cafk,
marked with the two firft letters of the
manufacturer's name, and hath been exam‑
ined and approved by the infpector of gun‑
powder for faid State, and be marked with
the letters U. S. A. and fuch other marks as
are neceffary to diftinguifh the feveral forts
of gun-powder, the perfon or perfons fo of‑
fending fhall forfeit and pay twenty dollars
for every cafk fo expofed to fale, to be re‑
covered by action of debt before any Court
proper to try the fame, which forfeiture
fhall, one moiety thereof, be given to the
perfon who fhall inform and fue for the fame,
and the other moiety be paid into the ge‑
neral-treafury of this Stase.

Infpector's fees.　Sec. 2. *And be it further enacted,* That
the faid infpector be paid, by the owner of
the powder infpected, twelve cents for every
cafk fo marked and infpected by him.

1770.
1798.

An Act to prevent Frauds in the Tare of But‑
ter-Firkins or Tubs.

Butter-firkins to
be branded, &c.　Section 1. BE it enacted by the General
　　　　　　Affembly, and by the au‑
thority thereof it is enacted, That each and
every cooper or other perfon who fhall
make any butter-firkins or tubs, or fhall
purchafe any butter-firkins or tubs which
are made out of this State, fhall, before they
expofe the fame to fale, caufe each firkin and
tub to be branded or marked with the two
firft letters of his or her name, and alfo with
the neat weight of faid firkin and tub;
which brand and weight fhall be fo made as to
remain and appear plainly to be feen.

　　Sec. 2. *And be it further enacted,* That
if

if any person or persons in this State shall offer for sale any butter by the firkin or tub, without the same being first branded or marked as aforesaid, the person or persons so offering such firkins or tubs of butter for sale, shall forfeit and pay as a fine the sum of one dollar, to be recovered by action of debt, before any one Justice of the Peace in the town where such offence shall be committed, upon complaint of any person to whom such butter shall be offered for sale. And upon the facts being proved before said Justice, the person offering the butter for sale shall pay all costs, and the judgment shall be final.

Sec. 3. *And be it further enacted,* That when any person or persons shall purchase a firkin or firkins, tub or tubs of butter, he or they shall have liberty, if there be any appearance of fraud in the tare marked upon the firkins or tubs, to cause such firkins or tubs to be justly weighed, and if it shall be found that the firkins or tubs weigh more than shall be marked upon them, allowing two pounds for each firkin or tub with the butter therein weighing under sixty pounds, and three pounds for each firkin or tub with the butter therein weighing above sixty pounds, on account of the brine the firkins or tubs may have absorbed, then for whatever such firkins or tubs shall weigh more than shall be marked upon them, the seller shall return the money to the buyer for as many pounds as shall be found wanting, and upon his refusing so to do, the buyer shall, in presence of one or two persons of good reputation, weigh such firkins or tubs, and shall, within twenty-four hours thereafter, have his action against the

U u u offender,

[marginal notes:]
Penalty for selling butter in firkins not branded.

Firkins overmarked, seller to return the money, &c.

offender, to be tried by one Justice of the Peace in the town where the offence shall be committed, who shall hear the parties, give judgment, and award execution, which shall be final.

Sec. 4. *And be it further enacted,* That when any firkin or tub shall be found to weigh more than the same shall be marked, with the aforementioned allowance, and the seller is obliged to make good the deficiency, he shall be entitled to an action against the cooper, or other person in this State of whom he purchased such firkin or tub, for his damages. And the conviction of the seller of the butter shall be sufficient evidence against the person of whom he shall have purchased the firkin or tub.

An Act regulating the Assize of Clapboards and Shingles, and the measuring of Boards, Plank, Timber and Slit-Work.

Section 1. BE it enacted by the General Assembly, and by the authority thereof it is enacted, That in each town within this State, where boards, plank, shingles, clapboards and slit-work are usually imported or brought for sale, or exported beyond sea, there be two or more honest persons, who are skilful, annually elected by such town, at the time of the choice of their town-officers, to be surveyors and measurers of boards, plank, timber, slit-work, shingles and clapboards, who shall be sworn or affirmed, as other officers are, to the faithful performance of their office.

And all boards, plank, timber and slit-work, imported or brought for sale, before their delivery, shall be viewed, surveyed and measured, by one of the said officers,
where

where he fhall have any doubt of the meafure; and he fhall maik the juft contents
thereof, making reafonable allowance for
the drying and fhrinking, and for rots, fplits
and wanes.

And the buyer fhall pay the officer fix Surveyor's fees.
cents per thoufand for viewing only, and
ten cents per thoufand for meafuring and
marking, and in like proportion for a lefs
quantity than a thoufand feet.   And no
boards, plank, timber, flit-work, fhingles or
clapboards, fhall be delivered upon fale, or
exported beyond fea, before they have been
viewed and furveyed, and alfo meafured, if
neceffary, and marked anew by one of faid
furveyors, on penalty of being forfeited, or
the value thereof, by the feller or fhipper, to
the ufe of the poor of the town where they
are fold or fhipped.

Sec. 2. *And be it further enacted,* That Shingles and
clapboards to be
forfeited, in
cafe.
all fhingles and clapboards expofed to fale
by quantities in bundles, that do not hold
out the number they are marked for, unlefs
it appears that fome have been drawn or
fhaken out of the bundles after packing,
fhall be forfeited to the ufe of the poor of
the town where they are expofed to fale, the
charge of fearching and telling them to
be firft deducted.   And every bundle of Their fize.
fhingles and clapboards, which, according
to the found judgment of the furveyor will
hold out, one with another, four inches and
an half in breadth, fhall be accounted merchantable, *provided* the fhingles are eighteen
inches in length; and the clapboards not
lefs than four feet and an half long, and the
leaft to be four inches or more in breadth,
and one half of an inch or more in thick-
nefs, and all that are otherwife, to be culled
                                    and

and burnt, and so many more, if need be, until what are left of said bundles will bear four inches and an half, according to the judgment of the surveyor, who shall have for his services three cents for every thousand surveyed, and three cents for every thousand for telling, to be paid by the buyer; where there is no forfeiture for want of tale, to satisfy the charge; and for every thousand he culls and binds up again, ten cents per thousand, and proportionably for less quantities, to be paid by the owner and seller of said shingles and clapboards, returning the remainder to the owner, if any there be, after the charge is deducted; any law, custom or usage, to the contrary hereof notwithstanding.

An Act to prevent Frauds and Abuses in the Sale of Hoops.

1766.
1798.

Assize of hoops.

Section 1. BE it enacted by the General Assembly, and by the authority thereof it is enacted, That all hoops made or brought into any town in this State, and offered for sale as hogshead hoops, shall be at least one half thereof eleven feet and an half in length; and the other half not less than ten feet in length; and that all those offered for barrel hoops shall hold out, one with another, at least seven feet and an half in length, and that they be of such size and substance as shall be sufficient for locking at the small end, and be otherwise suitable for immediate working.

Viewers of hoops to be chosen.

Sec. 2. *And be it further enacted,* That each town in this State, where hoops are usually sold or exported, shall annually choose two or more honest men, of good judgment, as viewers of hoops, who shall be under oath

for

for the faithful performance of their truft, and whofe bufinefs and duty it fhall be, to view and examine all hoops that may be offered for fale in or exported from this State; and whenever they fhall view and find any hoops fo offered for fale, or to be exported, fall fhort in the length aforefaid, or not of fuch fize and fubftance as by this act is required, they fhall be condemned and fold at auction by the officer who fhall view the fame, within twenty-four hours after giving notice to the owner or owners thereof; and one quarter part of the money arifing from the fale fhall be applied to and for the ufe of the town where they fhall be fold, and the remainder, after paying thereout unto the viewer of fuch hoops his fees, fhall be returned to the owner or owners.

Hoops not of a fufficient fize, &c. to be forfeited.

Sec. 3. *And be it further enacted,* That all hoops fhall be put up either thirty or forty in each bundle; and that when the officer viewing fhall find any fraud in the bundles, by their not containing the full number they were offered for, every fuch bundle fhall be condemned as forfeited, to be fold by the viewer in manner as aforefaid; and that the money, after paying the viewer his fees, fhall be by him lodged in the town-treafury of the town where they are fold, for the ufe of the poor of fuch town.

How many to be in a bundle.

Sec. 4. *And be it further enacted,* That if any perfon fhall fhip for exportation any hoops but fuch as have been duly furveyed and allowed to be merchantable, agreeably to the true intent and meaning of this act, he fhall pay as a fine three dollars and thirty-three cents for every thoufand fo fhipped, to be recovered by fuch officer appointed as aforefaid,

Penalty for fhipping hoops not furveyed, &c.

aforefaid, by profecution againft the offend-er, before any Juftice of the Peace in the town where the offence fhall be committed, for the ufe of the poor of the town.

Viewer's fees.

Sec. 5. *And be it further enacted,* That the perfons appointed as viewers of hoops, fhall receive at and after the rate of twenty-five cents for every thoufand they fhall view and examine, and if the hoops fhall be ad-judged good and merchantable, the buyer fhall pay the fame.

1784

An Act afcertaining the Weight of a Bufhel of Indian Meal.

Weight of a bufhel of meal, &c.

WHEREAS Indian meal is fold by weight, eftimating fifty pounds to one bufhel, the price whereof is regulated by that of corn; and whereas a bufhel of found corn, when ground into meal, after deduct-ing the toll, will weigh fifty-four pounds at the leaft:

Wherefore be it enacted by the General Af-fembly, and by the authority thereof it is en-acted, That in the fale of Indian meal by weight, the fame fhall be eftimated at and after the rate of fifty-four pounds weight per bufhel; and if any perfon fhall fell a lefs number of pounds of Indian meal for a bufhel, he or fhe fhall forfeit feventeen cents for every pound weight that is deficient of the aforefaid weight of fifty-four pounds, to be recovered upon complaint thereof be-fore any Juftice or Warden within this State, the one half thereof to and for the ufe of the poor of the town in which the fame fhall be fold, and the other half to the in-former or complainant.

An

An Act regulating the Weight of Onions, sold 1785.
by the Rope or Bunch.

Section 1. BE it enacted by the General
Assembly, and by the autho-
rity thereof it is enacted, That each and every
rope or bunch of onions, which shall be offered for sale in this State, shall weigh three
pounds: That every rope or bunch of
onions which shall be offered for sale,
weighing less than three pounds, shall be
forfeited to and for the use of the person
who will give information thereof before
any Justice of the Peace or Warden, who is
hereby authorized to receive such information, and thereupon cause all such ropes or
bunches of onions to be immediately seized,
and on such information being duly proved,
to cause the same to be declared forfeit as
aforesaid.

Weight of a rope of onions.

Sec. 2. *And be it further enacted,* That
every person who shall offer for sale any
bunch or rope of onions, short of the weight
hereby prescribed, shall also forfeit the sum
of twenty dollars, to be recovered by information or action before any one Justice of
the Peace or Warden.

*Penalty for sel-
ling under
weight.*

An Act establishing Pounds. 1669.
1798.

BE it enacted by the General Assembly, and
by the authority thereof it is enacted,
That each respective town in this State shall
erect and maintain, at their own charge,
one public pound, for the impounding of
horses, mules, neat cattle, sheep, goats, hogs
and asses, for securing such animals agreeably to law in some convenient place in such
town,

*Towns to erect
pounds.*

town, on the penalty of forfeiting the sum of thirty dollars for such neglect, to and for the use of the State, by every town which shall neglect the same.

2745.
1798.

An Act for impounding Cattle, Sheep, Horses and Hogs, and for recovering Damages that shall be done by them.

Cattle, &c. doing damage, may be impounded.

Section 1. BE it enacted by the General Assembly, and by the authority thereof it is enacted, That if any cattle, horses, sheep or hogs, shall break through a lawful fence, into the grounds of any person, the person aggrieved shall have the liberty either to recover his damages by an action against the owner or owners thereof, or to impound the said cattle, horses, sheep or hogs, in the public town pound, until the damage and charge of impounding be paid by the owner or owners. And the party aggrieved, in order to entitle him to recover damages, either by action or impounding, shall, within four days after such creatures break into his ground, get two freeholders of the town wherein the trespass is committed to appraise the damage, and give the same under their hands, and lodge the same with the pound-keeper.

May be sold, unless, &c.

Sec. 2. *And be it further enacted,* That in case the owner or owners of such cattle, sheep, horses or hogs, impounded as aforesaid, shall not, within ten days after the impounding thereof, pay and satisfy the damages appraised as aforesaid, and the charge of impounding and feeding said creatures, or replevy the same, in manner as is hereafter in this act directed, that then so many of said creatures shall be sold by public auction by the

the pound-keeper, as will pay and fatisfy
the damages and charges as aforefaid : And
the pound-keeper fhall be allowed the fame
fees for fuch fale as are ftated for the auctioneers in this State ; and the overplus, if
any there be, fhall be paid to the owner
or owners of fuch creatures.

Sec. 3. *And be it further enacted*, That
the pound-keeper fhall feed fuch cattle,
horfes, fheep or hogs, fo impounded, at the
charge of the owner or owners thereof, and
fhall alfo be allowed as his fee for impounding, for each neat beaft or horfe four cents,
and for each hog or fheep two cents, which
fhall be paid him before faid creatures are
releafed from the pound.

Duty and fee of the pound-keep-er.

Sec. 4. *Provided always, and be it further
enacted*, That in cafe the owner or owners of
fuch cattle, horfes, fheep or hogs, fhall fee
caufe, they may replevy the fame, giving
fufficient bond to the Juftice or Warden
who fhall grant fuch writ of replevin, in
double the damages appraifed, to profecute the fame with effect, if the damages
exceed not the fum of twenty dollars, before two or more Juftices or Wardens of
the town where fuch creatures are impounded ; and if the damages be above twenty
dollars, then to be profecuted at the next
fucceeding Court of Common Pleas to be
holden for the county where the damage was
fuftained. And the Juftices or Wardens,
who fhall grant fuch writ of replevin, fhall
return the fame, with the bond by them
taken (if triable at the Court of Common
Pleas) into the Clerk's office of faid Court,
five days before the fitting of fuch Court,
and the party diftraining fhall, before trial,
put in his avowry or juftification of im-

Method of re-plevying.

X x x pounding,

pounding; and in cafe the replevin be triable before the Juftices or Wardens of the
town as aforefaid, that then the fame fhall
be profecuted and determined by them,
within five days after fuch writ of replevin
fhall be ferved, and not after.

Hogs not to run
at large, unlefs,
&c.

Sec. 5. *And be it further enacted,* That
no hog or hogs in any town in this State,
from the twelfth day of February to the
twenty-fixth day of October, annually, fhall
go at large, without being yoked and rung,
unlefs by act of any town it be ordered
otherwife. And it fhall and may be lawful
for any perfon to impound any hog or hogs
running loofe contrary to this act ; and the
owner of fuch hog or hogs fhall pay the fees
and expences of impounding the fame, before they be difcharged from the pound.

Form of the Writ of Replevin.
To the Town-Sergeant of the Town of   or
    to any of the Conftables of faid Town,
    greeting.

Writ of replevin.

YOU are hereby, in the name of the State
of Rhode-Ifland and Providence Plantations, required to replevy   belonging to   of   in the county of   now
diftrained or impounded by   of
in the county abovefaid, and deliver the faid
            unto the faid   he having
given bond to me in the fum of   dollars, to profecute his replevin at the next
Court of Common Pleas to be holden for
faid county, on the   Monday in
next, and to pay fuch cofts and damages as
the faid   fhall then and there recover
againft him.   Hereof fail not, and make
true return to me of this writ, with your
doings thereon.   Given under my hand and
feal, in   aforefaid, in the year
                                                    The

The fame form of writs of replevin to be obferved when cognizable before the Juftices and Wardens, *mutatis mutandis.*

An Act to prevent Horfes from going at large in the Town of Newport.

Section 1. BE it enacted by the General Affembly, and by the authority thereof it is enacted, That if any horfe fhall at any time be found going at large within the limits of the town of Newport, it fhall be lawful for any inhabitant of faid town to take up and impound fuch horfe, and the owner fhall not receive fuch horfe again until he pay a fine of forty cents into the town-treafury, with the coft of impounding and keeping fuch horfe, one half of which fine fhall be for the ufe of faid town, and the other half to him who fhall impound the fame. And the pound-keeper fhall not releafe any horfe fo impounded, without a certificate from the Town-Treafurer that fuch fine is paid.

Horfes going at large in Newport, may be impounded, &c.

Sec. 2. *And be it further enacted,* That when any horfe fo taken up fhall have continued in the pound forty-eight hours, the pound-keeper fhall fet up a notification in three public places in each of the towns of Newport, Middletown and Portfmouth, defcribing the marks of fuch horfe ; and if no owner fhall appear within twenty days from the date of faid notification, and pay the fine, and all cofts and charges, then the Town-Treafurer fhall caufe fuch horfe to be fold at public auction, and out of the money raifed by the fale fhall pay the coft of impounding, keeping, and all other incidental charges, and the refidue (if any there

Pound-keeper's duty, &c.

there be) shall be put into the town-treasury.

Provifo.

Provided nevertheless, and it is the true intent and meaning hereof, That this act shall not extend unto any horse belonging to any person living without the bounds of the town of Newport, that may stray away from the owner or keeper by mere accident and casualty, without any default or neglect of such owner or keeper.

1757.
1759.
1789.

An Act to prevent Sheep and Horses from going at large in the Towns of Providence and North-Providence, and Goats and Kids in the Town of Providence.

Horfes, &c. going at large in Providence, &c. to be impounded,

Section 1. BE it enacted by the General Assembly, and by the authority thereof it is enacted, That if any sheep or horse be found going at large in the towns of Providence or North-Providence, it shall be lawful for any of the inhabitants of said towns to take up and impound the same; and the owner fined. and the owner of such sheep or horse shall not have them again until he shall have paid as a fine, into the town-treasury where such sheep or horse shall be so found and impounded, five cents for every sheep, and forty cents for every horse so taken up and impounded, together with all costs and charges of impounding and keeping such sheep or horse: And the pound-keeper shall not discharge any such sheep or horse from the pound, until he shall have produced a certificate, under the hand of the Town-Treasurer of such town, that the fine is paid, agreeably to this act.

Pound-keeper to fet up notifications.

Sec. 2. *And be it further enacted,* That when any sheep or horse shall have continued
ed

ed in the pound forty-eight hours, the pound-keeper fhall fet up a notification in three public places in each of the towns of Providence, North-Providence and Johnfton, defcribing the marks of any fheep or horfe fo impounded; and if no owner fhall appear within twenty days after the date of fuch notification, and pay the fine, together with the charges, then the Town-Treafurer fhall caufe fuch fheep or horfe to be fold at public auction, and out of the money arifing from the fale fhall pay the cofts and charges ; and the refidue thereof fhall be put into the treafury of the town, for the ufe thereof. *Horfes, &c. to be fold, in cafe.*

Provided neverthelefs, and it is the true intent and meaning of this act, That it fhall not extend unto any fheep or horfe belonging to any perfon living without the bounds of faid towns, that may ftray away from the owner or keeper by mere accident and cafualty, without any default or neglect of fuch owner or keeper. *Provifo.*

Sec. 3. *And be it further enacted,* That no perfon dwelling in the town of Providence fhall permit any goat or kid to run at large in any of the ftreets, highways or commons, in the faid town, upon the pain and penalty of forfeiting every fuch goat or kid fo running at large; and it fhall and may be lawful for any perfon, being a freeman of faid town, upon finding any goat or kid going at large within the bounds of the faid town, to flay, feize and take up every fuch goat or kid, belonging to any inhabitant of the faid town, fo going at large, and to convert it to his own ufe, without being anfwerable or accountable in any fort or manner whatfoever for the fame. *Goats, &c. not to run at large in Providence.*

An

Hogs not to run at large in Providence, &c.

May be feized, &c.

An Act to prevent Hogs going at large in the Places therein mentioned.

Section 1. BE it enacted by the General Assembly, and by the authority thereof it is enacted, That no perfon shall permit any hog or swine to go at large in the streets, highways or commons, within the town of Providence or North-Providence; or within the compact part of the town of Newport; or in that part of the town of Cranston called Pawtuxet; or within one mile of Pawtuxet Falls, in the town of Warwick or Cranston; or in the town of Bristol, within one mile of the court-house in said town; or in the town of East-Greenwich, within half a mile of the court-house in said town; or within the compact part of the town of Warren. And that all hogs or swine, which shall be found at large in the streets, highways or commons, within the limits aforesaid, shall be liable to be feized by any freeholder inhabiting within said limits, who, upon feizing the fame, shall set up a notification in the office of the Town-Clerk, and in one or more public houses within the limits within which such hogs or swine shall be fo feized; and unless the owner of said hog or swine shall, within forty-eight hours next after the notification shall be fo posted up as aforesaid, pay to the Treasurer of the town where the fame shall be feized, as a fine, to and for the use of said town, one dollar for every hog or swine fo feized, and one dollar to the perfon feizing the fame, such hog or swine may be disposed of by the perfon feizing the fame to his own use.

Sec.

Sec. 2. *And be it further enacted*, That the compact part of the town of Newport shall, in and by this act, be understood to be within a line drawn from the southwest corner of land late belonging to Samuel Dyer, to the southeast corner of said land; from thence to the house commonly known by the name of Richard Long's; from thence to the east end of Taylor's Lane; from thence west to the harbour, or salt water; from thence, along shore, to the first mentioned bound. And that the compact part of the town of Warren shall, in and by this act, be understood to be within the following bounds, to wit: Beginning at Childs' Bridge, and from thence running south to the line dividing Bristol from Warren; from thence westerly, to the salt water or shore; and thence, by the same, to the first bound.

Compact part of Newport.

Of Warren.

Sec. 3. *And be it further enacted*, That if any hog or swine, belonging to any person or persons inhabiting within any of the limits aforesaid, shall be found at large without the limits aforesaid, such hog or swine shall be liable to be seized by any freeholder inhabiting within this State, who, upon seizing the same, shall set up a notification in the office of the Town-Clerk of the town to which the owner or owners of such hog or swine shall belong, and in one or more public places in such town; and unless the owner of such hog or swine shall, within forty-eight hours after such notification shall be so posted up as aforesaid, pay to the Treasurer of the town where the same hog or swine shall be seized, as a fine, one dollar to and for the use of such town, and one dollar to the person seizing the same; such hog

Hogs at large, without the town of Providence, &c. may be seized, &c.

hog or fwine may be difpofed of by the perfon feizing the fame, to his own ufe.

---

*An Act to prevent Sheep and Lambs from run-
ning at large in the Highways and Commons within the Towns of Cumberland and
Tiverton, and alfo Goats in the faid Town
of Tiverton.*

Penalty for per-
mitting fheep,
&c. to run at
large in Cum-
berland, &c.

BE it enacted by the General Affembly, and
by the authority thereof it is enacted, That
whoever, inhabiting or refiding within the
faid towns of Cumberland and Tiverton,
fhall willingly and knowingly fuffer his, her
or their fheep or lambs to run at large in
the highways or commons, within the faid
towns of Cumberland and Tiverton, or
their goats in the faid town of Tiverton, at
any time between the tenth day of April and
the tenth day of November, in any year, and
be thereof lawfully convicted before any
one or more Juftice or Juftices of the
Peace in either of the faid towns in which
the offence fhall be committed, on the complaint or information of any freeman thereof, he, fhe or they, fo offending, fhall forfeit and pay as a fine, for each and every
offence, the fum of four cents for each and
every fheep or lamb fo fuffered to run at
large as aforefaid, and twelve cents for every goat fo fuffered to run at large as aforefaid, in the faid town of Tiverton, one half
thereof to and for the ufe of the town where
the offence fhall be committed, and the other
half to the ufe of him who fhall complain
and profecute for the fame. And moreover
the offender or offenders fhall pay cofts of
profecution and conviction.

An

An Act to prevent exceſſive Riding in any of 1666.
the Places therein mentioned. 1730.
1759.

Section 1. BE it enacted by the General 1766.
Aſſembly, and by the autho- 1798.
rity thereof it is enacted, That if any per- Penalty for ex-
ſon ſhall ride faſter than a common travel- ceſſive riding in
Newport, &c.
ling pace, in any of the ſtreets of the towns
of Newport or Providence; or in ſuch part
of the towns of Warwick and Eaſt-Greenwich as is hereafter deſcribed; or in
the compact part of Briſtol or Warren;
or that part of North-Providence called Pawtucket; or that part of South-
Kingſtown called Little-Reſt; or that part
of Warwick called Opponaug; or that part
of Warwick and Cranſton called Pawtuxet;
ſuch perſon ſhall pay as a fine the ſum of
two dollars for every offence; one half
thereof to the informer, and the other half to
and for the uſe of the poor of the town where
ſuch offence ſhall be committed, to be recovered upon complaint thereof made before any one Juſtice of the Peace in the town
where the offence ſhall be committed, with
coſts, unleſs juſtifiable cauſe for ſuch riding
ſhall be made to appear before ſuch Juſtice
of the Peace who ſhall try the ſame; which
trial and judgment thereon ſhall be final.

Sec. 2. *And be it further enacted,* That Part of War-
the part of the towns of Eaſt-Greenwich and wick and E.
Warwick firſt mentioned, where ſuch exceſ- Greenwich.
ſive riding is by this act prohibited, ſhall be
deemed and underſtood to be, and hereby is
declared to extend from the houſe of the late
Rufus Green, Eſq; in ſaid Eaſt-Greenwich,
unto the houſe of the late Gideon Caſey, in
Warwick.

Y y y *An*

*An Act to prevent Sheep and Cattle from be-
ing worried and torn by Dogs.*

1698.
1729.
1761.
1794.
1798.
Remedy againſt
owners of dogs
killing ſheep,
&c.

Section 1. **B**E it enacted by the General
Aſſembly, and by the au-
thority thereof it is enacted, That when any
perſon ſhall have any ſheep or cattle worried, torn or killed, by any dog or dogs, in
ſuch caſe the owner of ſuch ſheep or cattle
ſhall recover his damages againſt the owner of ſuch dog or dogs, by action of the
caſe, with coſt of ſuit; and if afterwards
any further damage be done by ſuch dog
or dogs to any ſheep or cattle, the owner of
ſuch dog or dogs ſhall pay to the party aggrieved thereby, double damages, to be recovered in like manner as aforeſaid, with
coſts; and that an order be made by the
Court before whom ſuch recovery ſhall be
had for killing ſuch dog or dogs, and that
the ſame be done accordingly by the officer
who ſhall be charged therewith.

Town-Councils
may tax owners
of dogs, &c.

Sec. 2. *And be it further enacted,* That
the Town-Councils of the ſeveral towns in
this State be and they are hereby authorized and empowered, to impoſe ſuch tax or
taxes upon every perſon within their reſpective towns, who ſhall own or keep any dog
or dogs, as they may think proper; and alſo to make ſuch orders, by-laws and regulations, to prevent damage being done to
flocks of ſheep and cattle, by dogs, as they
may deem neceſſary.

An

*An Act to prevent Frauds and Abuſes in driv-
ing Flocks of Sheep.*

1767.
1798.

Purchaſers of
ſheep to take a
certificate of
their marks, &c.

Section 1.   BE it enacted by the General
Aſſembly, and by the authori-
ty thereof it is enacted, That every perſon
who ſhall purchaſe ſheep to be driven out
of or through this State, or from or out of
any town therein, ſhall demand and receive
from the perſon they are purchaſed of, a
certificate of the number purchaſed, and the
ear-marks, and other artificial marks, and
ſhall alſo red them acroſs their backs before
they are driven away, which ſhall be between
ſunriſe and ſunſet; and upon no pretence
whatever ſhall ſheep at any other time be
driven through this State, or any town
therein.

Penalty for ne-
glect.

Sec. 2. *And be it further enacted,* That
if any perſon whoſoever ſhall come into this
State, or paſs through the ſame, or from or
out of any town therein, with a flock or
drove of ſheep, without the proper certificate or certificates, or without having ſuch
ſheep marked, as by this act is required,
ſuch perſon ſhall for each offence forfeit and
pay the ſum of fifty dollars, one half to the
informer who ſhall ſue for the ſame, and the
other half to and for the uſe of the State, to
be recovered in any Court of Record in
this State competent to try the ſame.

---

*An Act for the Crying of Horſes, neat Cat-
tle, Sheep and Hogs.*

1734.
1798.

Eſtrays, how to
be proceeded
with.

Section 1.   BE it enacted by the General
Aſſembly, and by the authori-
ty thereof it is enacted, That it ſhall and may
be

be lawful for any perſon within this State, who ſhall find any horſes, neat cattle, ſheep or hogs, damage feaſant within his own land in this State, not knowing to whom the ſame belong, to take any creature ſo found as an eſtray, and within ten days next after ſuch taking up of any ſuch creature, to repair to the Town-Clerk of the town in which the ſame may be taken up, and give notice thereof; and the ſaid Town-Clerk ſhall thereupon cauſe to be made three notifications, atteſted under his hand, ſetting forth the natural and artificial marks of ſuch creature, one of which notifications ſhall be ſet up in the ſame town, and the other two in ſome public places in the two next towns in this State. And any creature ſo ſtrayed and taken up, ſhall be kept by the perſon who took it up one year and a day, (and if it be a horſe, to have a withe kept about his neck the whole of ſaid time) and any perſon laying juſt claim to ſuch creature may, at any time within the year and day, have the ſame again, upon paying the juſt and reaſonable charges of keeping and crying; but in caſe any difference ſhall happen to ariſe between the ſaid parties about the claim or charge of keeping ſuch creature, the ſame ſhall be referred to the two or three next Juſtices of the Peace or Wardens within ſaid town, who are hereby directed and empowered to hear and determine the ſame, according to juſtice and equity, and to tax coſt as in other caſes, which judgment ſhall be final. And in caſe no owner ſhall appear within ſaid limited time, the perſon who took up ſaid creature ſhall repair to the Town-Clerk, taking with him two good freeholders of the neighbourhood,

hood, who ſhall be by the Town-Clerk engaged to make a faithful and true appraiſal
of ſaid creature, and the perſon who took
up ſuch creature ſhall pay one half of the
ſum ſaid creature ſhall be appraiſed at (after
all juſt charges are deducted) into the hands
of the Town-Clerk, who ſhall give the ſaid
perſon a certificate from under his hand that
he hath proceeded according to law with
ſaid creature; and upon the receipt thereof,
the perſon who took up ſaid creature may
convert the ſame to his own uſe ; and any
perſon taking up any creature, and not proceeding as is by this act required, ſhall forfeit the ſum of five dollars, to be recovered before any two Juſtices or Wardens in
the town where the offence ſhall be committed, by action of debt, one half thereof to
and for the poor of ſaid town, and the other
half to and for the uſe of him who will ſue
for the ſame.

Sec. 2. *And be it further enacted,* That
each Town-Clerk ſhall keep a fair record of
all his proceedings according to this act,
and ſhall return all money by him received
for any creature ſtrayed, and for which no
owner appears, into the town-treaſury, immediately on receipt thereof. And the
Town-Clerk ſhall be paid for every creature
ſo cried, and for every advertiſement poſted
up as aforeſaid, twelve cents ; and if no
owner appear, and it be appraiſed, and he
give a certificate as aforeſaid, he ſhall have
twenty-five cents therefor.

Town-Clerk to
keep a record,
&c.

An

1760.

*An Act to prevent laying Veffels to, and lad-
ing and unlading Wood, or heavy Wares, or
Merchandize, upon the Bridge over Opponaug River.*

Penalty for lay-
ing veffels at
Opponaug
Bridge, &c.

BE it enacted by the General Affembly, and
by the authority thereof it is enacted,
That no perfon, on any pretence whatfoever, fhall lay or bring any floop or other
veffel unto the bridge aforefaid, or there
lade or unlade wood, or other heavy wares
or merchandize, upon the penalty of four
dollars for every fuch offence, to be recovered of the perfon fo offending, before any
two Juftices of the Peace in the town of
Warwick ; one half thereof to the ufe of
him who fhall inform and fue for the fame,
and the other half to and for the ufe of the
poor of the faid town of Warwick.

1757.
1798.

*An Act to prevent Canoes and Boats being
made faft to the Abutments, or any Part
of the Bridge at Pawtuxet Falls.*

Penalty for mak-
ing faft boats to
Pawtuxet
Bridge, &c.

Section 1. BE it enacted by the General
Affembly, and by the authority
thereof it is enacted, That no perfon fhall
make faft any canoe or boat to either of the
abutments, or any part of the bridge at
Pawtuxet Falls, or throw any ftones off from
the fame, on the penalty of forfeiting and
paying as a fine the fum of five dollars, to
be recovered by an action of debt before
any one Juftice of the Peace of either of the
towns of Warwick or Cranfton, to whom
complaint fhall be made, one half thereof to
and for the ufe of the complainant, and the
other half to and for the ufe of the poor of the
town where fuch complaint fhall be made.

Sec.

Sec. 2. *And be it further enacted,* That the towns of Warwick and Cranston respect-ively shall be empowered to appoint each one suitable person to take care of said bridge, and to prevent damage or inju-ry being done thereto; that each of the said persons so appointed shall have power, and it shall be their especial duty, to prosecute for any penalties incurred under this act: *Provided nevertheless,* that nothing in this act contained shall be construed to subject or render the State, in any manner what-ever, liable to maintain said bridge, or to keep the same in repair.

Persons to be appointed to take care of the bridge.

An Act to prevent Damage being done to Weybosset Bridge, in Providence, by fastening Vessels to the same.

1757.

B E it enacted by the General Assembly, and by the authority thereof it is enacted, That whoever shall fasten any vessel to any part of Weybosset Bridge, above the piers, shall forfeit and pay as a fine the sum of two dol-lars for every offence, to be recovered by the Town-Treasurer of Providence for the time being, by an action of debt, at a Court of Justices; and that all fines so recovered be appropriated towards keeping the said bridge in repair.

Penalty for fast-ening vessels to Weybosset Bridge.

An Act apportioning the Expence of repairing Hunt's Bridge among the Towns of North-Kingstown, Warwick and East-Greenwich.

1783.

W HEREAS doubts and disputes have arisen respecting the building and re-pairing of the bridge commonly called Hunt's Bridge, which divides the towns of East-

East-Greenwich, Warwick and North-Kingstown, by reason whereof the said bridge is frequently impassable:

Expence of repairing, &c. how apportioned.

Be it enacted by the General Assembly, and by the authority thereof it is enacted, That whenever the said bridge shall not be in repair, the same shall be repaired, or a new bridge erected. by the said towns of North-Kingstown, Warwick and East-Greenwich, in the following proportion, to wit : That the one half part of all the expences in repairing or rebuilding the said bridge, shall be paid by the said town of North-Kingstown; one fourth part by the said town of Warwick ; and one fourth part by the said town of East-Greenwich.

1666.
1725.
1728.
1753.
1797.
1798.

Lawful fences.

An Act for regulating Fences.

Section 1. BE it enacted by the General Assembly, and by the authority thereof it is enacted, That the fences herein after described are and shall be adjudged lawful fences, to wit : A hedge with a ditch shall be three feet high, upon the bank of the ditch, well staked, at the distance of two feet and a half, bound together at the top, and sufficiently filled to prevent small stock from creeping through, and the bank of the ditch shall not be less than one foot above the surface of the ground. A hedge without a ditch shall be four feet high, staked, bound and filled, as a hedge with a ditch. Post and rail fence on the bank of a ditch shall be four rails high, each well set in posts, and not less than four feet and a half high. A stone wall fence shall be four feet high, with a flat stone hanging over the top thereof, or a good rail or pole thereon,

thereon, well ſtaked or ſecured with crotches or poſts; and a ſtone wall, without ſuch flat ſtones, rails or poſts on the top, ſhall be four feet and a half high; and all other kinds of fences not herein particularly deſcribed, ſhall be four feet and a half high.

Sec. 2. *And be it further enacted,* That all partition fences between lands under improvement, ſhall be made and maintained in equal halves, in length and quality, by the proprietors or poſſeſſors of ſuch lands reſpectively; and in caſe any proprietor of land ſhall improve his land (the land adjoining being unimproved) and ſhall make the whole partition fence, in ſuch caſe the proprietor or poſſeſſor of the land adjoining and unimproved ſhall, upon improvement thereof, pay for one half of ſuch partition fence according to the value thereof at that time, and ſhall keep up and maintain the ſame ever afterwards, whether he ſhall continue to improve ſuch land or not; and all partition fences ſhall be kept up and maintained in good order through the year, except the parties concerned ſhall otherwiſe agree;

Partition fences to be maintained equally by the parties.

Sec. 3. *And be it further enacted,* That when any proprietor or poſſeſſor of land ſhall neglect or refuſe to ſupport the one half part of any diviſional fence, or ſhall withdraw his fence from any diviſional line, upon complaint thereof to any one fence-viewer of the town in which ſuch cauſe of complaint ſhall ariſe by the party aggrieved, and upon requeſt to him to view ſuch inſufficient or defective fence, ſuch fence-viewer ſhall attend and cauſe the ſame to be immediately erected or repaired, as the caſe may be; which fence-viewer may apply to any Juſtice of the Peace or Warden, in the

On refuſal, application to be made to a fence-viewer.

Z z z   town

town where the land lies, for a warrant to
imprefs workmen and teams for the more
fpeedy erecting or repairing of fuch fence,
who is hereby empowered to grant the fame;
and the proprietor or poffeffor of faid defective fence fhall pay double the accuftomed rates for fuch workmen and teams, and
double the lawful fees to the fence-viewer
for his time in viewing the fame, to be recovered by the party aggrieved, if not above
twenty dollars, before any two Juftices of
the Peace or Wardens of the town; and if
the charges and damages exceed twenty dollars, then at the Court of Common Pleas in
the county.

Water-fences,
how maintained.
    Sec. 4. *And be it further enacted,* That
whenever any two perfons' lands fhall lie
together, adjoining the water, and each under improvement, the proprietors or poffeffors of fuch adjoining lands fhall make and
maintain a fufficient water-fence, to prevent
trefpaffes of each other's cattle, to be made
and maintained in the fame manner as other
partition fences are directed to be made by
this act.

Partition fences
by agreement,
&c.
    Sec. 5. *Provided neverthelefs, and be it
further enacted,* That in all cafes where partition fences are erected as the half part of
the dividing line between proprietors or
poffeffors of adjoining lands, or where the
fame may be hereafter erected by the agreement of the parties in intereft or other lawful means, the proprietor or proprietors of
the fences in either of the faid cafes erected,
his or their heirs or affigns, fhall hold and
improve the fame without moleftation, and
fhall be forever excufed from making
other half fence on fuch dividing line, in all
cafes whatever, except by the fpecial agreement

ment of fuch parties to the contrary: Agreements to be recorded. And that all agreements which fhall be made hereafter relating to fuch partition fences, be regiftered in the Town-Clerk's office in the town where fuch lands fhall lie.

Sec. 6. *And be it further enacted,* That where the whole, or more than one half of any dividing line, hath been or fhall be made by the proprietor or poffeffor of the land on one fide of the line, the proprietor or poffeffor of the land adjoining fhall pay to the proprietor or poffeffor who made fuch fence, where he improves the land adjoining, the value of fo much of the fence, erected as aforefaid, as the fame may exceed one half of the fence on the whole line; and in cafe of his refufal fo to do, the value fhall be afcertained by any one fence-viewer of the town where fuch land is fituated. on application to him for that purpofe, which fence-viewer, upon fuch application, fhall forth-with cite the parties in intereft on fuch dividing line, at a convenient time, view the fence, afcertain the value of the whole, and award the one half of fuch fum againft the proprietor or poffeffor fo refufing, with coft, and divide the whole fence between fuch parties, and make report into the Town-Clerk's office, which divifion fhall be permanent. And if any perfon or perfons, againft whom report fhall be made as aforefaid, fhall refufe to pay the fum fo reported, that faid fum, with coft, fhall be recovered againft fuch perfon or perfons by action of debt, before any Court proper to try the fame.

One party making more than his fhare of the fence, &c.

Sec. 7. *And be it further enacted,* That whenever it fhall become the duty of any fence-viewer to make or repair the fence of

Fence-viewers may purchafe materials for fences.

any

any perfon againſt whom legal complaint ſhall have been made, and there ſhall be a deficiency of rails or other materials for making or repairing ſaid fence, it ſhall be lawful for the fence-viewer to take from the land or poſſeſſion of the perſon ſo refuſing, ſo many rails or other materials as ſhall be neceſſary to complete ſuch fence ; and in caſe the perſon ſo refuſing hath not, in the opinion of the fence-viewer, ſuitable ſtuff for ſaid uſe, that the ſaid fence-viewer ſhall purchaſe the ſaid ſtuff, and the perſon ſo refuſing ſhall pay the expence thereof, to be recovered in the ſame manner as is by this act provided in other caſes.

Penalty on fence-viewers refuſing to do their duty.

Sec. 8. *And be it further enacted,* That if any fence-viewer, to whom complaint ſhall be made againſt any perſon for a breach of this act, ſhall neglect or refuſe to do the duty by this act enjoined on him to do, ſuch fence-viewer, ſo refuſing, ſhall forfeit and pay five dollars for every ſuch neglect, to be recovered by any perſon who ſhall ſue for the ſame, before any Court of Record in the county where ſuch fence-viewer ſhall live.

Fence-viewers' fees.

Sec. 9. *And be it further enacted,* That every fence-viewer ſhall be allowed one dollar per day, and in proportion for half a day, and ten cents an hour for any leſs time, for viewing any fence, on complaint made to him for that purpoſe ; which fees ſhall be paid by the owner of the fence, in caſe there ſhall appear to be good cauſe of complaint; but if the perſon complaining hath no juſt cauſe of complaint, then the perſon ſo complaining ſhall pay the expence, to be recovered before any Court proper to try the ſame.

A2

An Act for preventing Trespasses. 1743.

Section 1. BE it enacted by the General Assembly, and by the authority thereof it is enacted, That no person or persons shall cut, fell, destroy or carry away, any tree or trees, timber, wood or underwood whatever, standing, lying or growing, on the land of any other person or persons, without leave from the owner or owners of such land, whereon such trees, timber, wood or underwood was standing, lying or growing, on pain that every person so cutting, felling, destroying or carrying away the same, or who shall be aiding or assisting therein, shall, for every such trespass, forfeit and pay to the party or parties injured or trespassed upon, the sum of sixty-six cents, for every tree of one foot over; and for all trees of greater dimensions, three times the value thereof, besides sixty-six cents as aforesaid; and thirty-three cents for every tree or pole under the dimensions of one foot diameter; and for the wood or underwood, treble the value thereof; which several penalties, forfeitures and damages, shall and may be recovered by action, bill, plaint or information, on conviction of the trespasser or trespassers, as is hereafter especially provided and enacted, before any Court of Justices of the Peace in the county. if the penalty or damage exceed not the sum of twenty dollars; but if it be above that value, then before the Court of Common Pleas in the same county.

Sec. 2. *And be it further enacted,* That in case any dispute shall arise, upon any action, bill, plaint or information, brought

[marginal note: No person to cut wood, &c. without leave.]

[marginal note: Method of convicting offenders.]

as aforefaid, where the plaintiff, complainant or informer, fhall charge the defendant
in trefpafs, for cutting, felling, deftroying
or carrying away, any particular tree or
trees, parcels of timber, wood or underwood, off or from any fuch land as aforefaid,
or of being aiding or affifting therein, then
and in fuch cafe, if the plaintiff, complainant or informer, or his agent or attorney,
fhall make oath or affirmation, that there
hath been cut, felled, deftroyed or carried
away, fuch and fo many trees, parcels of
wood or underwood, as mentioned in the
writ, and that he fufpects the defendant to
have committed the faid trefpafs, although
the plaintiff, complainant or informer, or
his agent or attorney, may not be able to
produce any other evidence thereof than
fuch circumftances as render it highly probable in the judgment of the Court of Juftices, or fuch other Court before whom the
trial is, then and in fuch cafe, unlefs the
defendant fhall acquit himfelf upon oath or
affirmation, to be adminiftered to him by
the Court or Juftices who fhall try the caufe,
the plaintiff fhall recover againft the defendant damages and cofts; but if the defendant
fhall acquit himfelf upon oath or affirmation
as aforefaid, the Court or Juftices, before
whom the trial is, may and fhall enter up
judgment for the defendant to recover
againft the plaintiff double his cofts, occafioned by fuch profecution.

1793.

*An Act granting to the United States of Ame-
rica the public Light-Houfe within this State.*

Light-houfe
granted to the
United States.

Section 1.   *B*E *it enacted by the General
Affembly, and by the authority
thereof it is enacted,* That there be and hereby is
granted

granted unto the United States of America, the light-houfe, fituate in Jameftown, being the property of this State, together with all the right, title and claim of the State, to the lands and tenements thereto adjoining, with the jurifdiction of the fame.

Sec. 2. *Provided neverthelefs, and be it fur-ther enacted,* That if the United States fhall at any time hereafter neglect to keep lighted and in repair the light-houfe aforefaid, that then the grant of the faid light-houfe fhall be void and of no effect.

Provido.

Provided alfo, That all civil and criminal proceffes iffued under the authority of this State, or any officer thereof, may be exe-cuted on the faid land, or in the faid light-houfe or tenements, in the fame way and-manner as if the jurifdiction had not been ceded as aforefaid.

And provided further, That if the United States fhall at any time hereafter make any compenfation to any one of the United States for the ceffion of any light-houfe heretofore made, or which may be hereafter made to the United States, that then the like compenfation be made to this State by the United States, for the ceffion of the light-houfe, lands and tenements aforefaid, in proportion to their value refpectively.

An Act empowering the United States to hold Lands for Fortifications.

1794.

WHEREAS the Congrefs of the United States have paffed an act for fortify-ing the port and harbour of Newport, and empowered the Prefident of the United States to receive from any State (in behalf

Preamble.

of

of the United States) a ceffion of the land on which any fortification may ftand, or where fuch ceffion fhall not be made, to purchafe fuch land in behalf of the United States; *provided* that no fuch purchafe fhall be made where fuch land is the property of a State:

Section 1. *Be it therefore enacted by the General Affembly, and by the authority thereof it is enacted,* That there be and is hereby granted unto the United States of America, all the right, title and claim of this State, to the lands on which the fortifications on Goat-Ifland, in the townfhip of Newport, ftand, together with the circumjacent lands which have been heretofore improved by the State, for the purpofes of defence.

Fort on Goat-Ifland ceded to the United States.

Sec. 2. *And be it further enacted,* That it fhall and may be lawful for the town of Newport, or any other town in this State, or any individual perfon in the State, by and with the confent of his Excellency the Governor, to fell and difpofe of to the Prefident of the United States, for the ufe of the United States, all fuch lands as fhall be deemed neceffary to erect fortifications upon, for the defence of the port and harbour of Newport, and to execute deeds thereof in due form of law; and if the town of Newport, or any other town, or any individual, fhall not agree with the perfon or perfons who may be appointed by the Prefident of the United States to purchafe fuch lands, on the value thereof, then and in fuch cafes his Excellency the Governor is hereby empowered to appoint three fuitable perfons to appraife the faid lands, and upon payment of the value thereof at fuch appraifement, or upon the tender thereof being refufed,

Towns, &c. may fell lands for fortifications.

refused, the fee and property of such lands shall vest in the United States.

Sec. 3. *Provided nevertheless, and be it further enacted,* That all civil and criminal processes issued under the authority of this State, or any officer thereof, may be executed on the lands which may be so ceded, and within the fortifications which may be thereon erected, in the same way and manner as if such lands had not been ceded as aforesaid.

Processes may be executed thereon.

An Act for the Preservation of Stakes and Buoys in Providence River.

1794.

WHEREAS the channel from Kinnimicut to Providence hath been staked, and one or more buoys placed therein, at the expence of the United States, which are of great public utility ; and whereas inconsiderate people have made fast scows and boats to the stakes, whereby some have already been injured :

Preamble.

Be it therefore enacted by the General Assembly, and by the authority thereof it is enacted, That every person who shall hereafter make fast any scow, boat or canoe, to any of the said stakes, or shall remove such buoy or buoys, or in any way injure the said stakes or buoys, he or they, so offending, shall forfeit and pay, as a fine, a sum not exceeding ten dollars, nor less than three dollars, to be recovered before any Justice of the Peace in the counties of Providence or Kent ; two thirds to be paid to the Collector of the Customs for the district of Providence, for the use of the United States, in order to replace such stakes and buoys,

Penalty for injuring stakes, &c. in Providence River.

A a a a 　　　　　and

and the other third to the informer, who
shall prosecute for the same.

An Act establishing Auctioneers.

Towns to appoint auctioneers.

Section 1. BE it enacted by the General
Assembly, and by the autho-
rity thereof it is enacted, That every town in
this State shall annually, at their election
of town officers, appoint an auctioneer,
who shall give bond to the Town-Treasurer
of such town, with one good surety in the
sum of two thousand dollars, and shall be
sworn or affirmed as other town officers are
for the faithful discharge of his office, which
auctioneers shall sell within their respective
towns all real and personal estate which shall
be sold at public auction, always excepting
such sales at auction as shall be made by the
Marshal of this district, any Sheriff or other
officer, in virtue of any writ or execution,
or by any executor or administrator of the
estates or effects of their testators or in-
testates.

Sales at auction.

Sec. 2. *And be it further enacted,* That
the auctioneer, before the exposing of any
real or personal estate to public sale, shall
make out in writing and sign and publicly
read the conditions of sale.

Auctioneer's fees.

Sec. 3. *And be it further enacted,* That
where the whole amount of sales at any public auction doth not exceed four hundred
dollars, the auctioneer shall have two and
an half per cent. commissions; but if the
amount exceeds that sum, he shall have only
one and an half per cent.

Penalty for others selling.

Sec. 4. *And be it further enacted,* That
in case any person shall hereafter assume or
take upon himself the exercise of such office,
without

without being legally chofen by the town where he lives, and be duly qualified, he fhall pay as a fine the fum of five hundred dollars, to be recovered by the Town-Treafurer to and for the ufe of fuch town, by action of debt, always excepting fuch perfons as are by law allowed to fell real and perfonal eftate at public auction as aforefaid.

Sec. 5. *Provided neverthelefs, and be it further enacted,* That the towns of Newport and Providence fhall have power to appoint as many auctioneers, and to eftablifh fuch regulations for the conducting of fales at auction in their refpective towns, as they may think neceffary ; and alfo to afcertain the commiffions to be received by auctioneers for the fale of perfonal eftate at auction, any thing in this act to the contrary notwithftanding.

Newport, &c. may regulate their fales at auction, &c.

An Act eftablifhing a juft and equal Method of Gauging, in and throughout this State.

1751.
1798.

Section 1. BE it enacted by the General Affembly, and by the authority thereof it is enacted, That no rum, molaffes, wine, cider, beer, brandy, or any other liquid whatfoever, ufually fold by meafure in cafks, or any other commodities fold by the gallon, fhall be gauged in any other way or method than that which is commonly called gauging by gunter ; for which purpofe proper perfons fhall be chofen gaugers in each town in the State, where there fhall be occafion for it, who fhall be under oath for the faithful performance of their truft : And that the fees for gauging a fingle cafk fhall be fix cents ; and for gauging any number of cafks not exceeding ten,

Liquors, how to be gauged.

Gaugers to be chofen.

Their fees,

ten, three cents for each cafk; and for any number above ten, two cents for each cafk: And that the gauger, who fhall gauge any cafk, fhall fairly mark the initial letters of his name, and the quantity of the gauge or contents of fuch cafk, with branding or marking-irons, on the head or bulge of each cafk.

Rule to find the mean diameter. Sec. 2. *And be it further enacted,* That the rule and method to be ufed in and throughout this State to find the mean diameter of any cafk, in order to give the true gauge thereof, fhall be by multiplying the difference between the head and bung diameter, with 0, 65, and adding the product to the head diameter, or, which is the fame otherwife expreffed, by adding fix tenths and an half of the difference between the diameter at bung and head, to the diameter at the head.

Penalty for felling by any other gauge. Sec. 3. *And be it further enacted,* That whofoever in this State fhall fell any commodities, which by this act ought to be gauged, in the manner afore defcribed, or any other commodity whatfoever, in cafk, by gauge, gauged in any other manner than is herein d rect d, every perfon fo offending fhall forfeit the value of all the commodities fo fold, to be recovered againft him by action, or bill of indictment, in any Court of Record proper to try the fame; one half of which forfeiture fhall accrue to him who fhall inform or profecute for the fame, and the other half to the ufe of the town where the goods fhall be fo unlawfully gauged.

An Act for fuppreffing private Lotteries.

1732.
1798.
Penalty for putting forth lotteries,

Section 1. **B**E it enacted by the General Affembly, and by the authority thereof it is enacted, That if any perfon or perfons

perfons whofoever, directly or indirectly,
fet up or put forth any lottery, by whatever
name the fame may be called, without
the leave of the General Affembly firft had
and obtained, he or they fhall forfeit and
pay, as a fine, a fum not exceeding one
thoufand dollars, nor lefs than fifty dollars,
to and for the ufe of the State, to be recovered by the General-Treafurer, by action of
debt, in any Court of Record.

Sec. 2. *And be it further enacted,* That
if any perfon fhall purchafe any ticket or and purchafing tickets therein.
tickets in any fuch lottery, fo fet up or
put forth, he fhall forfeit the fum of feven
dollars for every ticket fo purchafed, to be
recovered and appropriated in manner as
aforefaid.

---

*An Act providing in cafe of Fire breaking
out in the Town of Newport, and for other* 1750.
Purpofes therein mentioned. 1762.
1798.

Section 1. **B**E *it enacted by the General* Fire-wards, &c. their power in pulling down houfes.
Affembly, and by the authority
thereof it is enacted, That when any fire
fhall happen to break out in the town of
Newport, the Governor, Lieutenant-Governor and Affiftants, for the time being, and
the fire-wards of the town or the major
part of fuch officers as aforefaid prefent
at any fire, fhall and may, and are hereby
empowered, to give directions for pulling
down, or blowing up, any houfe or houfes
as fhall be by them prefent adjudged meet
and neceffary to be pulled down or blown
up, for ftopping and preventing the further
fpreading of the fame. And if it fhall happen that the pulling down or blowing up of
any houfe or houfes fhall be the occafion of
ftopping

stopping the progress of such fire, or that the fire stop before it comes to the same,

Owners thereof to be paid. then all and every owner of such house or houses shall receive reasonable satisfaction, and be paid for the same by the rest of the inhabitants of said town, whose houses shall not be burnt, who are hereby empowered to make a tax for levying and raising such sum or sums of money as shall, by the Court of General Sessions of the Peace for the county of Newport, be thought sufficient for that end, which Court is hereby fully empowered and authorized, on application to them in this behalf made, to determine and make

Proviso. order thereon. *Provided always*, that if the house or houses where the fire shall first begin and break out, shall be adjudged fit to be pulled down or blown up, to hinder and prevent the spreading of the fire, that then the owner or owners of such house or houses shall receive no manner of satisfaction for the same, any thing in this act contained to the contrary notwithstanding.

Fire-wards to be chosen. Sec. 2. *And be it further enacted*, That the freemen of said town of Newport shall, on their days for electing town officers, choose and appoint such a number of prudent persons of known fidelity in the several parts of the town, as they may think fit, who shall be denominated and called fire-wards, and have a proper badge assigned to distin-

Their power. guish them in their offices, to wit; a speaking-trumpet painted red, and at the times of the breaking forth of fire and during the continuance thereof, they shall have full power and authority to command and require assistance for the extinction and putting out of the same, and for removing household furniture, goods and merchandize, out

of

of any dwelling-houfe, ftore or other building actually on fire or in danger thereof, and
to appoint proper guards to take care of
and fecure the fame ; as alfo to require and
command affiftance for the pulling down or
blowing up of any houfe or houfes, and
performing all and every fervice relating
thereto, to ftop and prevent the further
fpreading of the fire, and to fupprefs all tumults and diforders.   And the faid fire-
wards, from time to time appointed as aforefaid, are required, upon notice of the breaking forth of fire, to take each one his badge,
and repair immediately to the place, and vigoroufly exert their authority for obtaining
affiftance, and to ufe their utmoft endeavours
to extinguifh or prevent the fpreading of
the fire, and to preferve and fecure the
eftates of the inhabitants : And due obedi-
ence is required to be yielded to them and
each of them accordingly in faid fervice.
And all difobedience, neglect or refufal, in Perfons difobey-
any perfon, fhall be informed of to fome of ing, to be fined.
the Juftices of the Peace of faid town, with-
in two days next after; and the offender, upon conviction thereof by the oath of one or
more of the fire-wards, or other due proof
made before any two of faid Juftices, fhall
forfeit and pay as a fine the fum of fix dollars and fixty-fix cents, to be levied by a warrant of diftrefs, and when collected to be
diftributed at the difcretion of the Town-
Council of Newport, among fuch poor perfons as were moft diftreffed by the fire. And
in cafe fuch offender or offenders fhall be
unable to pay the fame, they fhall be committed to gaol, there to remain ten days.

    Sec. 3. *And be it further enacted,* That Stealing, &c. in
if any evil-minded wicked perfons fhall take time of fire.

advantage

advantage of such calamity to rob, plunder, purloin, embezzle, convey away or conceal any goods, merchandize or effects of the diftreffed inhabitants whofe houfes were on fire, or endangered thereby, and put upon removing their goods, and fhall not reftore the fame to the owner (if known) or bring the fame to fuch public place as fhall be affigned by the Governor, Lieutenant-Governor, or either of the Affiftants, within two days next after proclamation made for that purpofe, the perfon or perfons fo offending fhall, on conviction thereof, be deemed thieves, and fhall fuffer the fevereft pains and penalties by law provided againft fuch crimes.

Town to be furnifhed with fire-hooks, &c.

Sec. 4. *And be it further enacted,* That there fhall be kept, for the ufe and at the charge of the town of Newport, fix firehooks, fuitable for pulling down houfes and other buildings, and the fame number of ladders of a convenient length, one half of which fire-hooks and ladders fhall be always kept at the lower market-houfe, and the other half at the market-houfe near the town fchool-houfe, or at fuch other places as the town of Newport fhall direct : And that the fame be made ufe of at the breaking out of any fire in faid town, and upon no other occafion whatever.

Perfons to be chofen to take care of them.

Their duty, &c.

Sec. 5. *And be it further enacted,* That eight perfons be annually chofen by faid town to have the care of the faid fire-hooks and ladders, and upon the breaking out of any fire, they are immediately to repair to the faid fire-hooks and ladders, and caufe them to be carried where they fhall be moft wanted, and after the fire fhall be over, to caufe them to be returned again to the

places

places from whence they were brought: That the said persons, and each of them, shall have full power to command any persons to assist them in transporting the said ladders and fire-hooks; and that whosoever shall refuse to assist, upon being commanded as aforesaid, shall pay as a fine into the town-treasury the sum of two dollars for every offence; and that such persons, during the time for which they shall be appointed to the office aforesaid, shall be exempted from all such town duties as the fire-men chosen to take care of the engines are by law exempted from.

Sec. 6. *And be it further enacted,* That every house in the said town of Newport shall be furnished with two good leather buckets, with the owner's name painted at large thereon, and with a ladder that shall reach from the ground to the top of said house, or with a trap-door or scuttle in the roof of said house, with stairs or a ladder to go out of the garret upon the top of the house: And that for every dwelling-house in said town of Newport which shall not be furnished with two leather buckets, and a ladder to reach from the ground to the top of the house, or in the room of such ladder a trap-door or scuttle in the roof of said house, and stairs or a ladder to go out of the garret upon the top of the house, the owner of said house shall pay as a fine into the town-treasury the sum of two dollars for every six months neglect; but if the owner of the house doth not live in the town of Newport, the tenant or tenants shall pay such fines, and the same shall and may be deducted out of the rent of the house.

Sec. 7. *And be it further enacted,* That three persons shall be annually chosen by

Every house to be provided with buckets, &c.

Penalty for neglect.

Examiners to be chosen.

Bbbb   the

the said town of Newport, to examine every house in said town twice a year, and make report of all delinquents unto the Town-Council, who are hereby directed and empowered to cause every delinquent to be prosecuted.

Penalty for refusing to use buckets, &c.

Sec. 8. *And be it further enacted,* That every person in possession of a bucket, who shall neglect or refuse to make use of the same himself, or deliver it to some other person to make use of, at any fire which shall break out in said town, or put his buckets to any other use but to extinguish fire, shall pay as a fine into the town-treasury aforesaid the sum of one dollar for every offence.

Buckets lost to be paid for.

Sec. 9. *And be it further enacted,* That every bucket that shall be lost or damaged at any fire, upon satisfactory proof thereof being made before the Town-Council, an order by them shall be given to the owner of such bucket on the Town-Treasurer for as much money as will make good the loss or damage.

Powder to be conveyed to the powder-house.

Sec. 10. *And be it further enacted,* That every person who shall import gun-powder into the said town of Newport, shall cause the same to be conveyed immediately to the powder-house at the north-easterly part of the town, before the vessel in which such powder shall be imported be brought to any wharf, upon the penalty of paying into the town-treasury of the said town of Newport a fine of two dollars, for every cask which shall not be conveyed to the powder-house as aforesaid: That every other person who shall have gun-powder in his possession, and shall neglect or refuse to cause the whole of the same to be conveyed to the said powder-house immediately, excepting twenty-

twenty-five pounds, which fhall be kept in a tin powder-flafk, fhall pay as a fine into the town-treafury aforefaid the fum of two dollars, for every cafk which he fhall neglect or refufe to caufe to be conveyed to the powder-houfe as aforefaid, and in proportion for any lefs quantity: That no veffel of war or other veffel fhall take on board any powder, before fuch veffel fhall have departed from the wharf, upon the penalty of the mafter's paying a fine of two dollars for every cafk fo taken on board. And that the keeper of the powder-houfe be allowed the fame fees as heretofore have been allowed by law for delivering out every hundred weight of powder, and in proportion for a greater or lefs quantity.

Sec. 11. *And be it further enacted,* That no perfon whofoever fhall fire a gun or other fire-works within one hundred yards of the faid powder-houfe, upon the penalty of two dollars for every fuch offence, to be recovered by the Town-Treafurer, for the ufe of faid town. *Guns, &c. not to be fired near the powder-houfe.*

Sec. 12. *And be it further enacted,* That no fhip or veffel, having more than five barrels of gun-powder on board, fhall come to anchor in the harbour of Newport, any where to the eaftward of Goat-Ifland, and lie there more than twenty-four hours, after notice and warning fhall be given by the Prefident of the Town-Council of the faid town, upon the penalty of two dollars per barrel for every barrel of gun-powder on board fuch fhip or veffel, coming to and remaining at anchor contrary to this act, to be recovered of the mafter, fupercargo, or owner of fuch fhip or veffel, by the Town-Treafurer of the faid town, to and for the ufe of faid town. *Veffels with powder not to anchor within the harbour.*

Sec.

Fines, how to be
recovered.
Sec. 13. *And be it further enacted,* That
all the fines that shall accrue by this act, shall
be recovered by the Town-Treasurer before
any two Justices of said town by action of
debt, except where it is otherwise directed
in this act.

---

*An Act providing in case of Fire breaking out
in the Town of Providence.*

1754.
1759.
1798.
Every house-
keeper to keep
two buckets.
Section 1. BE it enacted by the General
Assembly, and by the authority
thereof it is enacted, That every house-
keeper in the town of Providence shall provide and keep two good leather buckets,
under the penalty of forfeiting the sum of
two dollars, to be recovered by the Town-
Treasurer, to and for the use of the poor of
said town, before any two Justices of the
Peace of said town, by action of debt.

Presidents of
fire-wards to be
chosen.
Sec. 2. *And be it further enacted,* That
from time to time, at the yearly meeting for
the election of town-officers, the freemen
of said town shall annually choose and appoint three or more persons, on whose fidelity, judgment and impartiality they can rely,
Their power.
to be called Presidents of the fire-wards;
and that they, the said Presidents, or any
one of them, who shall be present when any
fire shall happen to break out in the said
town, shall and may, and they are hereby
empowered to give directions for the pulling down or blowing up of any such house
or houses as shall be by them judged meet
and necessary to be pulled down, or blown
up, for preventing the further spreading of
the fire. And if it shall happen that the
Owners of hous-
es pulled down,
to be paid.
pulling down or blowing up of any such
house or houses, by direction as aforesaid,
                                          shall

shall be the occasion of stopping the progress of such fire, or that the fire stop before it comes to the same, that then all and every the owner or owners of such house or houses shall be reasonably paid therefor by the rest of the inhabitants of said town, whose houses shall not be burnt; and they are hereby authorized, and fully empowered, to make a tax or taxes for levying and raising such a sum of money as shall be by the Court of General Sessions of the Peace for the county of Providence thought sufficient for that end; which Court are hereby fully empowered and authorized, on application to them in this behalf made, to determine and make order thereon. *Provided always,* that Proviso. if the house or houses where the fire shall first begin and break out shall be judged fit to be pulled down or blown up, to hinder the further spreading of the flames, then the owner or owners of such house or houses shall receive no manner of satisfaction for the same, any thing in this act contained to the contrary notwithstanding.

Sec. 3. *And be it further enacted,* That Fire-wards to be it shall and may be lawful for the freemen of chosen. said town, at their aforesaid annual meetings, to appoint such a number of prudent persons, of known fidelity, in the several parts of the town, as they may think proper, who shall be denominated and called firewards, and have a proper badge assigned to distinguish them in their offices, to wit: A speaking-trumpet painted red; and at the Their power, times of breaking forth of fire, and during &c. the continuance thereof, they shall be, and are hereby authorized, and fully empowered, to require and command assistance for suppressing and extinguishing the fire; for removing

moving houfehold ftuff and furniture, goods
and merchandize, out of any dwelling-houfes, ftore-houfes, or other buildings actually
on fire, or in danger thereof, and to appoint
proper guards for taking care of and fecuring the fame ; as alfo to require and command affiftance for the pulling down or
blowing up of any houfe or houfes, and
performing all and every fervice and fervices relative thereto, by the directions of
the Prefidents aforefaid, or any one of
them, to prevent and ftop the further fpreading of the fire, and to fupprefs all tumults
and diforders. And the faid fire-wards,
from time to time appointed as aforefaid,
are required, upon notice of the breaking
forth of fire, to take each one his badge,
and repair immediately to the place, and
vigoroufly exert their authority for obtaining affiftance, and ufe their utmoft endeavours to extinguifh or prevent the fpreading of the fire, and to preferve and fecure
the eftates of the inhabitants. Due obedi-
ence is hereby required to be yielded to
them, and each of them, in the faid fervice ;
and all difobedience, neglect or refufal, in
any perfon or perfons, fhall be informed of
to fome of the Juftices of the Peace of the
faid town, within two days next after. And
if any perfon or perfons fhall offend, contrary to the true intent and meaning of this
act, he or they, upon conviction thereof
before any two Juftices of the Peace, fhall
forfeit and pay, as a fine, the fum of four
dollars each, to be levied and diftributed
at the difcretion of the Town-Council of
faid town of Providence, among fuch poor
perfons as fhall be moft diftreffed by the
fire. And in cafe any offender fhall be unable

Difobedience,
how punifhed.

able to pay such fine, he shall suffer ten days imprisonment.

Sec. 4. *And be it further enacted,* That if any evil-minded person or persons shall take advantage of such calamity, either by robbing, plundering, purloining, embezzling, conveying away or concealing any goods, wares, merchandize, effects or things whatsoever, belonging to any inhabitant or inhabitants of the said town of Providence, whose house or houses is or are on fire or endangered thereby, so as to put such person or persons upon removing his or their goods or effects, and shall not restore or give notice thereof unto the owner or owners (if known) or bring them to such public place or places as shall be assigned by the Presidents of the fire-wards, or any one of them, within the space of two days next after proclamation made for that purpose, the person or persons so offending shall, on conviction thereof, be deemed thieves, and suffer the utmost severities of the law.

Stealing in time of fire.

An Act for enforcing the several Town Acts relating to the Fire-Engines.

BE it enacted by the General Assembly, and by the authority thereof it is enacted, That any two Justices of the Peace of any town in this State, are fully empowered to take cognizance of any breach of any town acts that are already or shall hereafter be enacted, relating to the management of the fire-engines in the respective towns where such Justices live, and to make up judgment pursuant to the same, and to award execution for the penalties incurred thereby : And that any person who shall think himself

1737.
Two Justices may take cognizance of breaches of town acts, &c.

Appeal

himself aggrieved at any such judgment, may appeal to the next Court of General Sessions of the Peace in the county, observing the same rules as in other cases of appeal.

1731.
1737.
17 8.
1798.
Penalty for firing guns, &c. in roads, &c.

An Act to prevent unnecessary firing of Guns, Pistols, Squibs, or other Fire-Works.

Section 1. BE it enacted by the General Assembly, and by the authority thereof it is enacted, That if any person shall fire any gun, pistol, rocket, squib, or other fire-works, in any road, street, lane or tavern, or other public house, after sun-setting and before sun-rising, he shall, upon complaint and conviction thereof before any one Justice of the Peace or Warden, pay as a fine the sum of five dollars for the first offence, and seven dollars for every subsequent offence, one half thereof to the informer, and the other half to the State.

For making bonfires.

Sec. 2. *And be it further enacted,* That if any person shall make a bonfire in any public street, road, square or lane, without permission from the Town-Council of the town in which the same shall be made, he shall, upon conviction as aforesaid, forfeit a sum not exceeding ten dollars, to be appropriated in manner aforesaid.

For firing guns loaded with bullets, &c.

Sec. 3. *And be it further enacted,* That if any person shall fire any gun, musket, blunderbuss or pistol, loaded with a bullet or shot, in or across any road, street, square or lane, he shall, upon conviction as aforesaid, forfeit and pay as a fine a sum not less than three dollars, nor more than ten dollars, to be appropriated in manner as aforesaid.

An

An Act for preventing Damage by firing 1750.
Woods. 1798.

Section 1. BE it enacted by the General
Affembly, and by the authority
thereof it is enacted, That no perfon or perfons whofoever, by him or themfelves, or
by his or their means or procurement, fhall
fet, or fuffer to be fet, any fire, or caufe
any fire to be fet in the woods, in any
part of this State, to run and fpread at large,
at any time of the year, under any pretence
whatfoever; and that whofoever fhall be
lawfully convicted, upon complaint or bill
of indictment, of doing the fame, in any
Court in the county proper to try the fame,
either by his or their confeffion, or by evidence of one fufficient and credible witnefs,
upon oath or affirmation, fhall forfeit the
fum of twenty dollars, and for the fecond offence forty dollars; one half thereof to the
informer, and the other half to the ufe of
the poor of fuch town where the offence
fhall be committed: And if the perfon or
perfons fo convicted fhall refufe to pay the
fame, that then the Court where fuch offender
fhall be convicted, fhall grant forth a warrant of diftrefs to any Conftable of faid town,
or to the Town-Sergeant, to diftrain fo
much of the goods and chattels of the offender or offenders, as will fatisfy and pay
the fame, to the ufe and ufes aforefaid, and
all incident charges thereon accruing; and
for want of fufficient goods and chattels,
then to apprehend the body or bodies of the
offender or offenders, and to fecure him or
them in the State's gaol in the county wherein the offence fhall be committed, there to

C c c c be

be kept until he or they ſhall ſatisfy and pay ſuch fine and coſt, or be, by order of the Court, ſold for the payment thereof.

Perſons damaged may have an action.

Sec. 2. *And be it further enacted*, That whoſoever ſhall ſuffer any damage, by reaſon of ſuch offence as aforeſaid, ſhall and may have an action of treſpaſs upon the caſe againſt the offender, and ſhall recover damages and coſts.

An Act to prevent the breaking of Lamps and Lanterns in Newport and Providence.

Penalty for breaking lamps, &c.

Section 1. BE it enacted by the General Aſſembly, and by the authority thereof it is enacted, That every perſon who ſhall be convicted before a Juſtice's Court, or the Court of General Seſſions of the Peace, of wilfully breaking any lamp or lantern which is already ſet up, or hereafter ſhall be ſet up, in either of the towns of Newport or Providence, ſhall, for every ſuch lamp or lantern ſo broken, forfeit and pay a ſum not exceeding twenty dollars, one moiety thereof for the uſe of the town in which ſuch lamp or lantern ſhall be broken, and the other moiety for the uſe of him or her who ſhall ſue for the ſame; and ſhall moreover, on conviction as aforeſaid, pay double damages to the proprietor or owner of ſuch lamp or lantern, and all coſts of proſecution and conviction.

Broken by apprentices, &c. to be paid for by the maſter.

Sec. 2. *And be it further enacted*, That if ſuch lamp or lantern ſhall be broken by any ſervant or apprentice who ſhall not be able to pay ſuch fine, damages and coſts, and ſuch ſervant or apprentice ſhall be convicted thereof as aforeſaid, the maſter of ſuch ſervant or apprentice ſhall be obliged

to

to pay the fine, damages and cofts; and the Court, before whom fuch conviction fhall be had, fhall render fentence, and grant a warrant of diftrefs accordingly.

An Act regulating Ferries.

Section 1. BE it enacted by the General Affembly, and by the authority thereof it is enacted, That the refpective proprietors (on each fide) of the two ferries kept between Newport and Jameftown; of that between Jameftown and South-Kingftown, called the South Ferry; of that between Briftol and Portfmouth; of that between Portfmouth and Tiverton, called Howland's Ferry (until the bridge at the latter ferry, belonging to the Rhode-Ifland Bridge Company, fhall be completed) of that between Portfmouth and Tiverton, called Fogland Ferry (if the proprietors thereof fhall think fit to re-eftablifh faid ferry within one year) and of that between Warren and Barrington, be and they are hereby vefted with the exclufive right and privilege of conveying and tranfporting paffengers, horfes, neat cattle, and all other freight, acrofs their refpective ferries, for the feveral rates of ferriage herein after prefcribed, and fubject to the regulations and penalties in this act provided and enacted.

Exclufive right vefted in the proprietors of ferries.

Sec. 2. And be it further enacted, That the faid proprietors refpectively fhall conftantly keep and maintain, at each of their faid ferries, and on each fide thereof, one good boat, with proper and fufficient tackle and apparel, together with two good oars,

Proprietors to keep boats in readinefs, &c.

and

and one boat-hook, which fhall at all times
be kept afloat, and in conftant readinefs,
and fhall, on the application of any perfon or
perfons whomfoever, for the conveyance or
tranfportation of themfelves or freight
acrofs faid ferries, and on paying or tendering the lawful ferriage therefor, be put
off, and fhall proceed acrofs faid ferries,
wind and weather permitting.

Times of paffing
at Briftol and
Howland's fer-
ries.

Sec. 3. *And be it further enacted,* That
paffengers and freight at Briftol and Howland's ferries fhall and may, on payment or
tender of fingle ferriage, be conveyed acrofs
faid ferries, at all times between fun-rifing
and nine of the clock in the evening, between
the firft days of April and October; and
between fun-rifing and fix of the clock in the
evening, between the firft days of October
and April, in each year.

At Warren ferry.

Sec. 4. *And be it further enacted,* That
at the ferry between Warren and Barrington, paffengers and freight fhall be ferried
acrofs at all times for fingle ferriage; and

Free for foldiers,
&c.

that officers and foldiers, with their horfes
and accoutrements, croffing faid laft mentioned ferry, to attend the trainings or muf-
ters of their feveral corps, fhall be tranfport-
ed free from charge of ferriage; and that
the inhabitants of Barrington and Warren
fhall and may be permitted to tranfport
freight acrofs faid ferry in their own boats.

At other fer-
ries.

Sec. 5. *And be it further enacted,* That at
the faid other ferries, paffengers and freight
fhall and may, on payment or tender of
fingle ferriage, be conveyed acrofs faid
ferries, at all times between fun-rifing and
fun-fetting.

Paffengers may
be conveyed at
all times for dou-
ble ferriage.

Sec. 6. *And be it further enacted,* That
at all times, other than as before provided,
and

and on Sundays, thankſgiving days, and faſt days, paſſengers and freight ſhall and may, on payment or tender of double ſerriage, be conveyed acroſs ſaid ferries : *Provided neverthelefs*, that all phyſicians, ſurgeons, midwives, and perſons going for them, ſhall at all times be conveyed for ſingle ferriage.

Sec. 7. *And be it further enacted,* That if any ferryman ſhall refuſe or neglect to keep his boat afloat, and in readineſs as aforeſaid, or ſhall refuſe or neglect to convey or tranſport any perſon applying for paſſage or conveyance of freight, and tendering or paying lawful ferriage therefor, according to the proviſions aforeſaid, the proprietor of ſuch ferry where ſuch refuſal or neglect ſhall happen. ſhall forfeit and pay, for each neglect or refuſal, the ſum of ten dollars, one moiety thereof to the State, and the other moiety to the perſon who ſhall ſue for the ſame.

Provifo.

Penalty for neglect in ferrymen.

Sec. 8. *And be it further enacted,* That it ſhall be the duty of the ferrymen, at each of ſaid ferries, to put off the boat whenever it ſhall appear that the boat from the other ſide is on her paſſage, or nearly arriving on that ſide where the boat is at the wharf, under the penalty of one dollar, to be recovered by an action of debt, in any Court proper to try the ſame.

Boat when to be put off, &c.

Sec. 9. *And be it further enacted,* That no proprietor or keeper of ſaid ferries ſhall cauſe or ſuffer his ferry-boat to be abſent from the ſaid ferry, on any pretence whatever (excepting for neceſſary repairs) under the penalty of thirty dollars for every three hours abſence thereſrom, to be recovered by an action of debt in any Court of

Penalty for permitting a boat to be abfent.

of Record proper to try the fame, one half thereof to the ufe of the State, and the other half to the ufe of him who fhall fue for the fame.

Ferry-wharves to be kept in repair. Sec. 10. *And be it further enacted,* That the proprietors of each of faid ferries fhall keep their refpective ferry-wharves in good repair, fo that at common low water their refpective boats can receive on board freight and paffengers afloat, and come to fail, and proceed acrofs faid ferries, weather permitting.

Penalty for neglect. Sec. 11. *And be it further enacted,* That if faid proprietors, or either of them, fhall neglect to have their refpective wharves in fuitable repair, on or before the firft day of October, A. D. 1798, the proprietor or proprietors fo neglecting, fhall pay to and for the ufe of the State one hundred dollars, and for every month afterwards, ten dollars per month, until completed; fuch **To be afcertained by a committee annually appointed.** neglect to be afcertained by a committee to be annually appointed in May, as other State officers are, whofe duty it fhall be to report, at the May and October feffions of the General Affembly; and all fuch penalties as they fhall report to have become forfeit to the ufe of the State, fhall be profecuted, fued for and recovered, by an action of debt by the General-Treafurer.

No perfon but the proprietor to convey paffengers. Sec. 12. *And be it further enacted,* That no perfon fhall tranfport paffengers or freight acrofs either of the faid ferries, except the proprietors thereof, or their agents, or take off or land the fame at or from either of the faid ferry-wharves, except as before provided, under the penalty of fifty dollars, one half thereof to the ufe of the State, and the other half to the ufe of the perfon who

fhall

shall profecute and fue for the fame, to be recovered in an action of debt, in any Court proper to try the fame.

Sec. 13. *And be it further enacted*, That Rates of ferriage. the proprietors or keepers of faid ferries are and fhall be entitled to receive the following rates of ferriage, and no more, to wit:

	Newport & S. Fer.	Fogland Ferry.	Briftol Ferry.	Warren Ferry.	Howland's Ferry.
	Cts.	Cts.	Cts.	Cts.	Cts.
For each and every footman,	10	8	8	4	6
For ditto, who puts off a boat,	20	16	16	6	12
For a man and horfe,	25	16	16	6	12
For each and every drift horfe,	18	16	16	6	12
For ditto neat beaft, two years old and upwards,	20	18	18	6	14
For each and every yearling beaft,	13	10	10	4	8
For each and every calf,	5	4	4	2	3
For ditto hog,	6	5	5	2	4
For ditto fheep or lamb,	3	2	2	1	1
For every horfe and carriage, with the perfons in it,	85	50	50	12	33
For all heavy goods per cwt.	6	5	5	2	4

An Act eftablishing the Rates of Toll, demandable at the feveral Toll-Bridges in this State.

Section 1. BE it enacted by the General Rates of toll. Affembly, and by the authority thereof it is enacted, That the following rates of toll, and no higher, fhall be demanded or received at the bridge over Seacunck River, belonging to Mofes Brown and others, called the Central Bridge; at the bridge over Seacunck River, belonging to John Brown, Efq; called India Bridge; and at the bridge over Palmer's River, belonging to Mr. Duncan Kelly, called Kelly's Bridge, to wit:

For

	D. C.
For every carriage or sleigh with four horses,	0 31¼
Ditto, two horses,	0 18¾
Ditto, one horse,	0 12½
Every load of hay,	0 16¾
Ditto, wood, timber or stone,	0 8¼
Ditto of other description,	0 12½

And in all cases where there are more than four cattle in a loaded team, three cents for each creature to be added.

Every empty cart or sleigh, with more or less cattle,	0 8¼
Every loaded horse-cart, with one horse,	0 7
Ditto, empty,	0 6¼
Every man and horse,	0 5½
Every drift horse or neat beast,	0 4¼
Every yearling,	0 3
Every calf, hog, sheep or lamb,	0 2
Every foot passenger,	0 3
Every wheelbarrow or hand-cart, with the driver,	0 5½

Horses, cattle, sheep and lambs, by the dozen, half the above prices.

Militia exempted from payment of toll at Kelly's Bridge.

Sec. 2. *And be it further enacted,* That the said bridge over Palmer's River shall be free on training days, for all persons belonging to the militia, with their horses and military accoutrements, who shall be exempted from the payment of toll on said days, either passing or repassing said bridge, to or from training.

An

An Act prohibiting Sports and Labour on the first Day of the Week.

1679.
1750.
1784.
1798.

Section 1. BE it enacted by the General Assembly, and by the authority thereof it is enacted, That no person in this State shall do or exercise any labour or business or work of his ordinary calling, or use any game, sport, play or recreation, on the first day of the week, or suffer the same to be done by his children, servants or apprentices (works of necessity and charity only excepted) on the penalty of one dollar for the first offence, and two dollars for the second offence, for the use of the poor of the town where the offence shall be committed, to be recovered on conviction thereof before any Justice of the Peace or Warden of such town, and to be levied by warrant of distress from such Justice or Warden, which shall be levied upon the goods and chattels of such offender; and for want of his goods and chattels sufficient to satisfy and pay said fine and costs, such offender shall be committed to the gaol in the county wherein such offence shall happen, for the space of ten days.

Penalty for labouring, &c. on the first day of the week.

Sec. 2. *And be it further enacted,* That whosoever shall employ, improve, set to work, or encourage, any other person's servant to commit the aforesaid offence, and be convicted thereof, shall suffer the like punishment. And if any person shall think him or herself aggrieved at any such judgment or sentence as aforesaid, he or she may have an appeal therefrom, to the next Court of General Sessions of the Peace in such county, by paying down the costs of such Court, and

For employing others.

Appeal.

entering

entering into recognizance, with furety, for his perfonal appearance, before the faid Court of Seffions appealed to, and then and there to profecute his faid appeal with ef-fect.

Sec. 3. *And be it further enacted,* That all complaints againft the offender, for of-fences expreffed in this act, fhall be made within ten days after the committing there-of, and not afterwards.

Sec. 4. *Provided neverthelefs, and be it further enacted,* That all the profeffors of the Sabbatarian faith, or Jewifh religion, throughout this State, and fuch others as fhall be owned and acknowledged by any other church or fociety of faid refpective profef-fions, as members of, or belonging to, fuch church or fociety, fhall be permitted to la-bour in their refpective profeffions or vo-cations on the firft day of the week ; and that they fhall have liberty quietly and peaceably to pafs and repafs on foot or horfeback about their ordinary bufinefs, any thing herein to the contrary notwithftanding.

Provided always, That this act fhall not extend to grant any liberty of opening fhops or ftores on the faid day, for the purpofe of trade and merchandize, nor to the lading, unlading or fitting out of veffels, nor to the working at the fmith's bufinefs, or any other mechanical trade, in any compact place, except the compact villages in Wefterly and Hopkinton, nor to the drawing of feines, or fifhing or fowling, in any manner, in public places, and out of their own poffeffions. And in cafe any difpute fhall arife refpecting the perfons entitled to the benefit of this act, and who fhall be exempted thereby,

Sec. 5. *Be it further enacted,* That in all
fuch

such cases a certificate from a regular pastor A certificate from the pastor to be conclusive. or priest of any of the aforesaid churches or societies, or from any three of the standing members of such church or society, declaring the person or persons claiming the exemptions aforesaid to be a member or members of, or owned by, or belonging to such church or society, shall be received as full and conclusive evidence of the fact.

An Act to prevent unlawful Gaming.

1749.
1753.
1777.
1798.
Penalty for playing at cards, &c.

Section 1. BE it enacted by the General Assembly, and by the authority thereof it is enacted, That if any person or persons in this State shall play or game at cards, dice, tables, bowls, wheel of fortune, shuffle-boards, raffling, cock-fighting, or any other game of chance other than billiards, for money or any other valuable consideration, the person losing at any such game or games, shall forfeit as a penalty or fine four dollars for the first offence; and for the second offence, eight dollars; and for the third offence, sixteen dollars : And the winner at any such game or games shall pay as a fine four dollars, and the sum or sums won, for the first offence; and for the second offence, eight dollars, and the sum or sums won; and for the third offence, sixteen dollars, and the sum or sums won.

Sec. 2. *And be it further enacted,* That At billiards. if any person shall play or game at billiards, for money, or other valuable consideration, the person losing at such game shall forfeit as a penalty or fine twenty dollars for the first offence; and for the second offence, fifty dollars; and for the third offence, one hundred dollars : And the winner

at

at such game shall pay as a fine twenty dollars, and the sum or sums won, for the first offence; and for the second offence, fifty dollars, and the sum or sums won; and for the third offence, one hundred dollars, and the sum or sums won.

For tavern-keepers, &c. permitting games to be played.

Sec. 3. *And be it further enacted,* That if any tavern-keeper, innholder, retailer, coffee-house keeper, tea-house keeper, or keeper of any other house of public resort, within this State, shall suffer any person or persons whomsoever to use or play at any of the said games in his or her house, out-house, yard, garden or other place or places in his or her possession or improvement, he or she shall, for every such offence, forfeit and pay as a fine or penalty the sum of thirty dollars, for the first offence; and for the second offence, fifty dollars; and upon conviction thereof, if the offender be a retailer, tavern-keeper or innholder, or keeper of any other of the public houses aforementioned, his or her license shall be declared null and void by the Court where he or she shall be convicted.

For betting.

Sec. 4. *And be it further enacted,* That all persons betting at any of the aforesaid games, shall be liable to the same fines and penalties as persons playing at any of the said games are by this act.

Securities for money, &c. won, void.

Sec. 5. *And be it further enacted,* That all bills, bonds, notes, judgments, mortgages, deeds, or other securities, given for money or lands, houses, or other things, won by playing at any of the aforesaid games, or by betting on either side of such as play at any of the aforesaid games, or for repayment of any money lent, knowingly for such gaming or betting, shall be utterly void: And

Town-Councils to take bonds of tavern-keepers, &c.

that the Town-Councils in this State be and

and they are hereby required and commanded to take good fecurity of all perfons they
fhall grant licenfe to for tavern-keeping,
inn-holding, or retailing ftrong drink, to
comply with this act in all refpects, as far as
poffible, according to its true intent and
meaning.

Sec. 6. *And be it further enacted,* That Penalties, how.
all the fines and penalties in this act expreffed recovered.
may be profecuted for and recovered in
any Court proper to try the fame, by action of debt. or bill of indictment ; one moiety of faid fines or penalties fhall be paid
to him who fhall inform and profecute for
the fame, and the other moiety to and for
the ufe of the town where fuch offence or
offences fhall be committed. But if there be
no informer or private profecutor, then the
whole fine or penalty fhall be to and for
the ufe of faid town.

Sec. 7. *And be it further enacted,* That Penalty for bet-
any perfon or perfons whofoever, that fhall ting on horfe-
races.
hereafter make any bet or lay any wager of
any kind upon any horfe, mare or gelding,
to ftart or run therefor, fhall forfeit and pay
the fum of one hundred dollars, one half to
him or her who will fue for the fame, and
the other half to the State, to be recovered
by action of debt or information, before any
Court proper to try the fame.

Sec. 8. *And be it further enacted,* That Horfes forfeited.
if any perfon or perfons fhall knowingly
fuffer or permit any horfe, mare or gelding,
belonging to him or them, to ftart or run
for any bet or wager. he, fhe or they, fo offending, fhall forfeit his, her or their horfe,
mare or gelding, ftarting or running as
aforefaid, to and for the ufe of the town
where fuch offence fhall be committed, to be
recovered

recovered by information before any Court proper to try the fame.

An Act to prevent Routs, Riots and tumult-uous Affemblies, and the evil Confequences thereof.

Juftice, &c. to make proclama-tion to rioters, &c.

Section 1. BE it enacted by the General Affembly, and by the authori-ty thereof it is enacted, That fiom and after the publication of this act, if any perfons, to the number of twelve or more, being armed with clubs or other weapons; or if any number of perfons, confifting of thirty or more, fhall be unlawfully, routoufly, ri-otoufly or tumultuoufly affembled, any Juf-tice of the Peace, Sheriff, Deputy-Sheriff, Town-Sergeant or Conftable, fhail, among the rioters, or as near to them as he can fafely come, command filence, while procla-mation is making, and fhall openly make proclamation in the like words:

Form.

State of Rhode-Ifland and Providence Planta-tions.

BY virtue of an act of this State, made and paffed in the year of our Lord one thou-fand feven hundred and ninety-eight, en-titled, " An act to prevent routs, riots and tumultuous affemblies, and the evil confe-quences thereof," I am directed to charge and command; and I do accordingly charge and command, all perfons being here af-fembled, immediately to difperfe themfelves, and peaceably to depart to their habitations, or to their lawful bufinefs, upon the pains inflicted by the faid act.   God fave the State.

And if fuch perfons affembled as aforefaid fhall

shall not disperse themselves within one hour after proclamation is made, or attempted to be made as aforesaid, it shall be lawful for every such officer to command sufficient aid, and he shall seize every such person, who shall be had before a Justice of the Peace; and the aforesaid Justice of the Peace, Sheriff or Deputy-Sheriff, is hereby further empowered to require the aid of a sufficient number of persons in arms, if any of the persons assembled are in arms; and if any such person or persons shall be killed or wounded, by reason of his or their resisting the persons endeavouring to disperse or seize them, the said Justice, Sheriff, Deputy-Sheriff, Town-Sergeant, Constable, and their assistants, shall be indemnified, and held guiltless. *Refusing to disperse, to be apprehended, &c.*

Sec. 2. *And be it further enacted,* That if any person, being commanded by such Justice, Sheriff, Deputy-Sheriff, Town-Sergeant, or Constable as aforesaid, shall refuse or neglect to afford the assistance required, and shall be convicted thereof upon the oath of either of the said officers so commanding, or other legal evidence, he shall forfeit and pay a sum not less than seven dollars, nor exceeding thirty dollars, to be recovered on conviction thereof before the Supreme Judicial Court, or any Court of General Sessions of the Peace, according to the aggravation of the offence, to be paid into the general-treasury for the use of the State. *Penalty for refusing to aid the Sheriff, &c.*

Sec. 3. *And be it further enacted,* That all persons, who for the space of one hour after proclamation made, or attempted to be made as aforesaid, shall unlawfully, routously, riotously and tumultuously continue together, *For obstructing him, &c.*

gether, or shall wilfully obstruct or hinder any such officer who shall be known, or shall openly declare himself to be such from making such proclamation, shall on conviction thereof forfeit a sum not exceeding one thousand dollars, and shall suffer imprisonment not more than twelve months; and if any such person or persons, so riotously assembled, shall demolish or pull down, or begin to demolish or pull down, any dwelling-house or other house, or parcel thereof, any house built for public uses, any barn, mill, malt-house, store-house, shop or ship, he or they shall be fined and imprisoned as abovesaid.

An Act to reform the penal Laws.

Preamble.

WHEREAS all punishments ought to be proportionate to the offences for which they are inflicted : And whereas the punishments of offences, as now prescribed by law, are in many instances severe and sanguinary : And whereas a more mild and lenient system of penal laws will probably tend, with equal if not greater effect, to promote the great object of all public punishments, the prevention of crimes :

Murder of the first degree.

Section 1. *Be it therefore enacted by the General Assembly, and by the authority thereof it is enacted,* That all murder which shall be perpetrated by means of poison, or by lying in wait, or by any other kind of wilful and premeditated killing, or which shall be committed in the perpetration of, or attempt to perpetrate, any arson, rape, robbery or burglary, shall be deemed murder of the first degree ; and all other kinds of

Second degree. murder shall be deemed murder of the second

cond degree; and the Jury, before whom any person indicted for murder shall be tried, shall, if they find such person guilty thereof, ascertain in their verdict whether it be murder of the first or second degree; but if such person shall be convicted by confession, the Court shall proceed, by the examination of witnesses, to determine the degree of the crime, and to give sentence accordingly.

Sec. 2. *And be it further enacted,* That every person who shall be convicted of murder of the first degree, his or her aiders, abettors and counsellors, shall suffer death.

Punishment for murder of the first degree.

Sec. 3. *And be it further enacted,* That every person liable to be prosecuted for petit treason, shall in future be indicted, proceeded against, and if found guilty punished, as is directed in other cases of murder.

Petit treason.

Sec. 4. *And be it further enacted,* That every person who shall be convicted of murder of the second degree, shall be fined not exceeding four thousand dollars, and be imprisoned not exceeding six years, at the discretion of the Court.

Punishment for murder of the second degree.

Sec. 5. *And be it further enacted,* That every person who shall be duly convicted of the crime of arson, or of being accessary thereto before the fact, shall suffer death.

Arson.

Sec. 6. *And be it further enacted,* That every person who shall be convicted of the crime of rape, or of being accessary thereto before the fact, shall suffer death.

Rape.

Sec. 7. *And be it further enacted,* That every person who shall be convicted of robbery or burglary, or of being accessary to said crimes, or either of them, before the fact, shall suffer death.

Robbery and burglary.

E e e e

Sec.

Sodomy.

Sec. 8. *And be it further enacted,* That every perfon who fhall be convicted of fodomy, or of being acceffary thereto before the fact, fhall, for the firft offence, be carried to the gallows in a cart, and fet upon the faid gallows, for a fpace of time not exceeding four hours, and thence to the common gaol, there to be confined for a term not exceeding three years, and fhall be grievoufly fined at the difcretion of the Court; and for the fecond offence fhall fuffer death.

Forgery of coin and bank notes.

Sec. 9. *And be it further enacted,* That every perfon who fhall be convicted of having falfely forged and counterfeited any gold or filver coin of the United States, or any other gold or filver coin, which is or fhall be current within this State, or of having falfely uttered, paid, or tendered in payment, any fuch counterfeited and forged gold or filver coin, knowing the fame to be forged and counterfeit, or of having aided, abetted or commanded the perpetration of any of faid crimes, or fhall be concerned in printing, figning or paffing any counterfeit notes of the bank of the United States, of the Providence bank, the bank of Rhode-Ifland, or any other bank, which is or may be legally incorporated and eftablifhed within the United States, knowing fuch notes to be counterfeit, or fhall engrave any plate, or make any inftrument to be ufed for any of the purpofes aforefaid, or fhall be concerned in fraudulently altering any genuine note or notes of faid banks, or of any of them, fhall be placed in the pillory, in fome public place in the county town of the county in which he fhall be convicted; fhall be cropped while in faid pillory, by having a piece of each of his ears cut off; fhall be branded

while

while in said pillory, with the brand of the letter C. shall be imprisoned for a term of time not exceeding six years, and shall be fined in a sum not exceeding four thousand dollars, or shall be subjected to any or all of said punishments, at the discretion of the Court.

Sec. 10. *And be it further enacted*, That if any person shall steal, take away, alter, falsify, or otherwise avoid any record, writ, process or other proceedings in any Court of this State, by means whereof any Judgment shall be reversed, made void, or not take effect, or if any person shall acknowledge, or procure to be acknowledged in any of said Courts, any recognizance, bail or judgment, in the name or names of any other person or persons, not privy or consenting to the same, or shall forge, make or alter, or willingly or deceitfully cause or procure, aid, abet or command the forging, making or altering of any matter of record, or any other matter of a public nature, or any false deed, last will and testament, obligation, or writing sealed, or any promissory note, bill of exchange, acceptance, assignment or indorsement upon them, acquittance or receipt for money or goods, or any warrant, order, or request for the payment of money or delivery of goods or chattels of any kind, any certificate or accountable receipt for money or other things, any lottery ticket, or any assurance of money or other property whatsoever, with intent to defraud any person, or who shall utter or publish, or cause, procure or abet to be uttered or published as true, any of the above false, forged or altered matter, as above specified and described, knowing the same to be false,
altered

Forgery, &c. of records, &c.

altered and forged, with intent to deceive and defraud any person, shall be pilloried, cropped, branded, imprisoned and fined, in manner herein in the next preceding section provided, or shall suffer any or all of said punishments, at the discretion of the Court.

Sec. 11. *And be it further enacted,* That every person who shall be convicted of wilful and corrupt perjury, or subornation of perjury, by procuring another person to commit wilful and corrupt perjury, shall be fined in a sum not exceeding one thousand dollars, be placed in the pillory not exceeding four hours, and be cropped and branded as aforesaid, and shall be imprisoned for a term not exceeding three years, or shall suffer all or any of said punishments, at the discretion of the Court.

Perjury and subornation of perjury.

Sec. 12. *And be it further enacted,* That every person who shall wilfully and corruptly endeavour to incite or procure another person to commit wilful and corrupt perjury, and the person so incited do not commit such perjury, shall be fined not exceeding five hundred dollars, and shall be imprisoned for a term not exceeding one year.

Inciting to perjury.

Sec. 13. *And be it further enacted,* That if any person shall, directly or indirectly, give any sum or sums of money, or any other bribe, present or reward, or any promise, contract or obligation, or security for the payment or delivery of any money, present or reward, or any other thing, to obtain or procure the opinion, judgment, verdict or sentence of any Judge, Justice or Juror, in any controversy, matter or cause, depending before him or them, the said person, and the Judge, or Justice or Juror, who shall in any wise accept, receive or agree for the

Bribery.

the fame, fhall be fined not exceeding two
thoufand dollars, and be imprifoned for a
term not exceeding two years, and fhall
forever thereafter be d fqualified from holding any office of honour, truft or profit, under this State.

Sec. 14. *And be it further enacted,* That
every perfon who fhall commit voluntary Manflaughter.
manflaughter, fhall be fined not exceeding
one thoufand dollars, and fhall be imprifoned for a term not lefs than fix months, nor
more than two years, according to the nature and enormity of the offence, and fhall
find fecurity for his good behaviour during
life.

Sec. 15. *And be it further enacted,* That
whenfoever any perfon fhall be charged with May be profecut-
involuntary manflaughter, happening in con- ed as for a mif-
fequence of any unlawful act, it fhall and may demeanor.
be lawful for the Attorney-General, or
other perfon profecuting in behalf of the
State, with leave of the Court, to wave the
felony, and proceed againft and charge fuch
perfon with a mifdemeanor, or the faid
Attorney-General, or other perfon profecuting for the State, may charge both offences in the fame indictment; in which cafe the
Jury may acquit the party of one, and find
him or her guilty of the other.

Sec. 16. *And be it further enacted,* That
if any perfon on purpofe, and of malice Cutting out
aforethought, fhall unlawfully cut out or tongues, &c.
difable the tongue, put out an eye, flit the
nofe, cut off the nofe, ear or lip, or cut off
or difable any limb or member of another,
with intention to maim or disfigure fuch perfon, or fhall voluntarily, malicioufly and of
purpofe, pull out or put out an eye, while
fighting or otherwife, every fuch offender,

his or her aiders, abettors and counfellors, fhall be fined not lefs than fifty nor more than two thoufand dollars, three fourth parts thereof to the party injured, and one fourth to the State, and fhall be imprifoned for a term not exceeding two years.

Duelling.

Sec. 17. *And be it further enacted,* That every perfon who fhall voluntarily and from malice, difpleafure fury or revenge, engage in a duel with fword or piftol, or other dangerous weapon, to the hazard of life, although death doth not enfue thereby, fhall be carried publicly in a cart to the gallows, with a rope about his neck, and fet thereon for the fpace of one hour, with a rope about his neck as aforefaid, and be imprifoned for a term not exceeding one year, or fhall fuffer either or both faid penalties, at the difcretion of the Court.

Horfe-ftealing.

Sec. 18. *And be it further enacted,* That every perfon convicted of horfe-ftealing, or of being acceffary thereto before the fact, fhall reftore the horfe, mare or gelding ftolen, to the owner or owners thereof, and fhall pay to him, her or them, the value thereof ; and in cafe the fame fhall not be reftored, fhall pay two fold fuch value, fhall be fined not exceeding one thoufand dollars, and be imprifoned not exceeding three years, and whipped not exceeding one hundred ftripes.

Acceffaries before the fact.

Sec. 19. *And be it further enacted,* That every perfon who fhall aid, affift, abet, counfel, hire, command or procure any perfon to commit the crime of murder, either in the firft or fecond degree, or rape, fodomy, arfon, robbery or burglary, is and fhall be confidered an acceffary before the fact to the principal offender or offenders, and fhall fuffer the like punifhment as is by law affigned

ed to the crime, to the commiffion of which he fhall be fo acceffary.

Sec. 20. *And be it further enacted,* That every perfon who fhall knowingly receive, harbour, conceal, maintain, affift or relieve any perfon or perfons who have committed any of the crimes aforefaid, or hereafter mentioned, although the principal offender cannot be taken fo as to be profecuted, is and fhall be confidered an acceffary after the fact, and fhall be fined not exceeding five hundred dollars, and be imprifoned not exceeding two years.

Acceffaries after the fact.

Sec. 21. *And be it further enacted,* That every perfon who fhall, by force, fet at liberty, or refcue, any perfon convict of murder of the firft degree, or charged therewith, fhall be fined not exceeding two thoufand dollars, and be imprifoned for a term not exceeding five years.

Refcuing convicts of murder.

Sec. 22. *Provided always, and be it further enacted,* That no perfon accufed of any of the aforefaid crimes fhall be admitted to bail but by the Judges of the Supreme Judicial Court, or fome or one of them, nor fhall he or fhe be tried but by the Supreme Judicial Court, holden in and for the county wherein the offence fhall have been committed; and that peremptory challenges fhall be allowed in all cafes wherein they have heretofore been allowed by law.

Bail.

Peremptory challenges

Sec. 23. *And be it further enacted,* That every perfon who fhall felonioufly fteal any money, goods or chattels; any note of the Treafurer of this State for the payment of money; any note or certificate of any bank or any public office, fecuring the payment of money to any perfon, or certifying the fame as due; any order entitling any perfon to money;

Stealing

money ; any bill of exchange, bond, warrant,
obligation, bill, or promiffory note for the
payment of money, or any valuable property; any record or other papers belonging to
any public office ; any book of account, re-
ceipts for money, or other article paid or
delivered, or adjuftments or documents of
any kind, relating to the payment of money or
other article; any indenture of apprentice-
fhip, deed, covenant, indenture of affurance
whatever, refpecting any property real or
perfonal, or fhall be acceffary thereto before
the fact ; fhall reftore the money, goods, chattels or other article fo ftolen to the owner
or owners thereof, and fhall pay to him,
her or them, the full value thereof ; and in
cafe fuch reftoration fhall not take place,
fhall pay two fold the value of fuch money,
goods, chattels or other articles ftolen, to the
faid owner or owners, and fhall moreover be
fined not exceeding one thoufand dollars,
be imprifoned not exceeding two years, and
be whipped not exceeding fifty ftripes ; or
fhall fuffer any or all of the faid punifhments
of fine, imprifonment and whipping, at the
difcretion of the Court.

Sec. 24. *And be it further enacted,* That
Receiving ftolen every perfon who fhall receive fuch ftolen
goods. money, goods, chattels or other articles,
knowing them to be ftolen, fhall be fubject
to the like penalties and punifhments as are
herein prefcribed for ftealing the fame.

Sec. 25. *And be it further enacted,* That
Juftices jurifdic- it fhall and may be lawful for any two or
tion, in cafes of more Juftices of the Peace or Wardens, to
theft. try any perfon or perfons charged with theft,
in their refpective counties, when the money
or article or articles ftolen fhall not exceed
in value the fum of twenty dollars ; and on
fufficient

sufficient proof, to convict the person so charged, and to sentence such convict to a fine not exceeding twenty dollars, to restoration of the money or other thing or things stolen, and the value thereof; or in default of restoration, two fold the value thereof to the owner or owners; or in default of the payment of said fine, and the restoration, and payment of the value as aforesaid, to sentence such convict to be whipped not exceeding twenty stripes, or to be imprisoned not exceeding one month.

Provided always, That in case such convict or convicts shall be afterwards charged again with theft, the trial shall be either before the Court of General Sessions of the Peace, or the Supreme Judicial Court, who shall, upon conviction of the offender, pass sentence against him or her, as is prescribed in the last preceding section.

Proviso.

Sec. 26. *And be it further enacted,* That every person who shall be convicted of conspiracy, or champerty, or maintenance, or common barratry, or embracery, shall be fined not exceeding five hundred dollars, and be imprisoned not exceeding six months.

Embracery, &c.

Sec. 27. *And be it further enacted,* That every person who shall challenge another, by word, message, or any other way, to fight a duel, or who shall accept a challenge, though no duel be fought, or shall any way abet, prompt, encourage or seduce any person to fight a duel, or to challenge another to fight, shall be fined not exceeding five hundred dollars, and be imprisoned not exceeding six months.

Challenging to a duel.

Sec. 28. *And be it further enacted,* That if any officer of this State shall exact or extort any more or greater fees than by law

Extortion.

are

are stated or allowed, or under colour of his office shall levy, or demand and receive, any more or greater sum of money than by any judgment, execution, order, decree or warrant, he shall be authorized to levy, or demand and receive, he shall be fined not exceeding five hundred dollars, and be imprisoned not exceeding two years; and shall also forfeit to the party aggrieved two fold damages, to be recovered by an action of the case.

Exercising an office without authority.

Sec. 29. *And be it further enacted,* That every person who shall exercise or officiate in any office, without being thereunto lawfully appointed and authorized, shall be fined not exceeding two hundred dollars, and be imprisoned not exceeding one year.

Obstructing officers.

Sec. 30. *And be it further enacted,* That every person who shall menace, threaten, obstruct, strike, insult or assault, or in any other manner abuse any officer, civil or military, while in the execution of his office, shall be fined not exceeding two hundred dollars, and be imprisoned not exceeding one year, or shall suffer either or both of said punishments, at the discretion of the Court.

Adultery.

Sec. 31. *And be it further enacted,* That every person who shall commit the crime of adultery, shall be fined not exceeding two hundred dollars, and be imprisoned not exceeding six months.

Fornication.

Sec. 32. *And be it further enacted,* That every man or woman who shall commit fornication, and be thereof convicted, before any two or more Justices of the Peace in the county where such offence shall be committed, shall be fined not exceeding five dollars, and be imprisoned not exceeding five days.

Sec.

Sec. 33. *And be it further enacted,* That Blasphemy.
every person who shall commit the crime of
blasphemy, shall be fined not exceeding one
hundred dollars, and be imprisoned not exceeding two months.

Sec. 34. *And be it further enacted,* That Profane swear-
every person who shall be guilty of the crime ing.
of profane cursing and swearing, and shall
be thereof convicted before any one or more
Justices of the Peace or Wardens, shall, for
the first offence, be fined, for the use of the
poor of the town in which the offence shall be
committed, in a sum not exceeding one dollar, nor less than fifty cents; and for the second, or any further offence of the like nature, shall be fined not exceeding two dollars, nor less than one dollar and fifty cents,
to be appropriated in like manner; and in
case such offender shall not pay such fine or
fines, he shall be imprisoned not exceeding
ten days; and it shall be lawful for any Justice of the Peace or Warden, in whose hearing such profane cursing and swearing shall
be uttered, to convict the offender on his
own knowledge of the offence.

Sec. 35. *And be it further enacted,* That Voluntary es-
if any gaoler or keeper of a prison shall cape.
voluntarily suffer any prisoner committed
unto him to escape, he shall suffer and undergo the like pains, punishments and penalties, as the prisoner so escaping. was sentenced to suffer and undergo; or in case
such prisoner so escaping shall not be, at the
time of such escape, a convict, then the gaoler
or prison-keeper, voluntarily suffering such
prisoner to escape, shall suffer and undergo
the like pains, punishments and penalties, as
the prisoner so escaping shall or may by
law be subjected to for the crime or crimes
wherewith

wherewith he fhall ftand charged, if he had
been convicted thereof. *Provided always,*
that if the prifoner efcaping fhall be charged
with or convicted of any crime, the punifhment whereof is by law capital, the gaoler
or prifon-keeper, permitting fuch voluntary
efcape, fhall be fined not exceeding three
thoufand dollars, and be imprifoned not
exceeding fix years.

Sec. 36. *And be it further enacted,* That
if any gaoler or prifon-keeper fhall, through
negligence, fuffer any prifoner, accufed or
convicted of any crime, to efcape, he fhall
be fined not exceeding one thoufand dollars,
and be imprifoned not exceeding one year.
Provided always, that if any prifoner, who fhall
ftand committed for debt on *mefne procefs*
or execution, fhall efcape from prifon againft
the confent and without the permiffion of
the Sheriff or prifon-keeper, and the Sheriff
or prifon-keeper fhall, within three months
next after fuch efcape, recover the prifoner
fo efcaped, and return him back to prifon
again, the Sheriff or gaoler fhall be liable to
nothing further than the coft of any action
which may have been commenced againft
him for fuch efcape.

Sec. 37. *And be it further enacted,* That
if any perfon fhall directly or indirectly,
by any ways or means howfoever, without
the knowledge or privity of the gaoler, convey any inftrument or other thing whatfoever to any prifoner, or into any prifon,
whereby any prifoner might break the prifon, or work himfelf unlawfully out of the
fame, or in any way thereby efcape, the
perfon fo offending fhall be fined not exceeding five hundred dollars, and be imprifoned not exceeding one year. And if
it

it shall so happen that any prisoner shall make his escape, by means of any instrument, tool, or other thing so conveyed, without the knowledge and privity of the gaoler, the person so conveying the same shall be liable to pay all such sums of money as the prisoner stood committed for, and shall suffer all such punishments, pains and penalties, as the escaped prisoner would be liable to, on the charge or conviction on which he stood committed, unless such prisoner would have been liable to capital punishment, in which case the person assisting in such escape as aforesaid shall be fined not exceeding three thousand dollars, and be imprisoned not exceeding five years.

Sec. 38. *And be it further enacted*, That every convict, who shall escape from his imprisonment, and be retaken and recommitted, shall continue in prison for such term of his imprisonment as remained unexpired at the time of his escape, and moreover shall undergo such additional imprisonment as the Court, before whom the original conviction was had, shall, on conviction for such escape, order and direct, not exceeding six months.

Convicts escaping.

Sec. 39. *And be it further enacted*, That if any woman shall endeavour privately, either by herself, or the procurement of others, to conceal the death of any issue of her body, male or female, which if it were born alive would by law be a bastard, so that it may not be known whether it were born dead or alive, or whether it were murdered or not, every such mother shall be fined not exceeding three hundred dollars, and be imprisoned not exceeding one year, or shall suffer either or both said punishments, at the discretion of the Court. And

Concealing the death of a bastard child.

if

if the Grand Jury ſhall, in the ſame indictment, charge any woman with the murder of
her baſtard child, and alſo with the offence
of concealment of its death as aforeſaid, the
Jury, by whom ſuch woman ſhall be tried,
may either acquit or convict her of both
offences, or find her guilty of one, and not
guilty of the other, as the caſe may be; and the
concealment of the death of any ſuch child
ſhall not be concluſive evidence to convict
the party indicted of the murder of her
baſtard child, unleſs the circumſtances attending it be ſuch as ſhall convince and ſatisfy the minds of the Jury, that ſhe did wilfully and maliciouſly deſtroy and take away
the life of ſuch child.

Sec. 40. *And be it further enacted,* That

Marrying a ſe-
cond huſband or
wiſe, the former
living.

if any perſon, being married, or who hereafter ſhall be married, ſhall marry any other
perſon, the former huſband or wife being
alive, or ſhall continue to live ſo married,
the perſon ſo offending ſhall be ſet on the
gallows for the ſpace of one hour, with a
rope about his or her neck, be fined not
exceeding one thouſand dollars, and be impriſoned not exceeding two years; or ſhall
ſuffer all or any of theſe puniſhments, at the
diſcretion of the Court.

Proviſo.

Proviaed, That this act, or any thing
therein contained, ſhall not extend to any
perſon whoſe huſband or wife ſhall be con-
tinually remaining beyond ſea by the ſpace
of ſeven years together, the one of them in
either caſe not knowing the other to be living within that time. *Provided alſo,* that
this act, or any thing therein contained,
ſhall not extend to the wife of any man
who ſhall voluntarily abſent himſelf from his
ſaid wife by the ſpace of ſeven years together, without making ſuitable proviſion for
her

her fupport and maintenance in the mean
time, if it fhall be in his power fo to do.
Provided alfo, that this act, or any thing
therein contained, fhall not extend to any
perfon who is or fhall be divorced at the
time of fuch marriage, nor to any perfon,
for or by reafon of any former or prior
marriage, made within the age of confent.

Sec. 41. *And be it further enacted,* That
every perfon who fhall wrongfully or mali- Burning houfes, &c.
cioufly burn, or otherwife deftroy, any dwelling-houfe, barn, warehoufe, fhop, mill,
malt-houfe, out-houfe, any public building,
or other building whatever, or the frame of
any fuch building, the burning whereof
fhall not amount to arfon at the common
law, fhall be fined not exceeding two thoufand dollars, and be imprifoned not exceeding three years.

Sec. 42. *And be it further enacted,* That
every perfon who fhall wilfully and mali- Burning ftacks of corn, &c.
cioufly burn any ftacks of corn, hay, grain,
ftraw, corn-ftalks or hufks, flax, fences,
piles of wood, boards, timber or other lum-
ber, fhall be fined not exceeding one thoufand dollars, and be imprifoned not exceeding one year.

Sec. 43. *And be it further enacted,* That
every perfon who fhall be convicted before Affault and bat- tery.
any one or more Juftices of the Peace or
Wardens of an affault or battery, or both,
fhall be fined not exceeding four dollars,
or be imprifoned not exceeding twenty
days: But if it fhall appear to the Juftice or
Juftices to whom complaint of an affault or
battery fhall be made, that neither of the
punifhments aforefaid is adequate to the offence, it fhall be the duty of fuch Juftice or
Juftices thereupon to bind over the offender.

er, with one or more sufficient sureties, in a recognizance, for his appearance at the next Court of General Sessions of the Peace in the county wherein said offence shall have been committed. And if any person shall be convicted before any Court of General Sessions of the Peace, or before the Supreme Judicial Court, of making an assault with an intent to commit murder, rape, sodomy, burglary or robbery, he or she shall be fined not exceeding one thousand dollars, and be imprisoned not exceeding two years. And any person convicted before either of said Courts of any other assault or battery, or both, shall be fined not exceeding one hundred dollars, and be imprisoned not exceeding six months, or shall suffer either or both of said punishments, at the discretion of the Court.

with intent to commit murder, &c.

Sec. 44. *And be it further enacted,* That if any person shall by force set at liberty or rescue any person convicted or charged with any other crime than murder of the first degree, he or she so offending shall be fined not exceeding one thousand dollars, and be imprisoned not exceeding two years.

Rescuing convicts other than of murder.

Sec. 45. *And be it further enacted,* That if any person shall cut out the tongue, or otherwise dismember any beast, maliciously or of purpose, or shall maliciously and of purpose kill, destroy or wound the beast of another, such person shall be fined not exceeding one hundred dollars, or be imprisoned not exceeding two months, or shall suffer both said punishments, at the discretion of the Court ; and shall pay to the owner of such beast treble damages, to be recovered by an action of trespass.

Dismembering, &c. beasts.

Sec.

Sec. 46. *And be it further enacted,* That every perfon who fhall clandeftinely take and carry away any corn or fruit out of any field, garden or orchard, without the privity or confent of the owner thereof, or fhall root up, cut down, or otherwife deftroy, any trees, roots, fruits or other vegetables, growing in any garden or orchard, without permiffion of the owner thereof, fhall, if convicted before any two Juftices of the Peace or Wardens, be fined not exceeding ten dollars ; or if convicted before the Supreme Judicial Court, or Court of General Seffions of the Peace, fhall be fined not exceeding fifty dollars, and be imprifoned not exceeding one month, or fhall fuffer either or both faid punifhments, at the difcretion of the Court ; and fhall moreover pay to the party grieved treble damages, to be recovered by an action of trefpafs.

Clandeftinely taking fruit, &c.

Sec. 47. *And be it further enacted,* That in every indictment to be profecuted againft any perfon for wilful and corrupt perjury, or for fubornation of or incitement to perjury, it fhall be fufficient to fet forth the fubftance of the offence charged upon the defendant, and by what Court, or before whom, the oath or affirmation was taken (averring fuch Court or perfon or perfons to have a competent authority to adminifter the fame) together with the proper averment or averments to falfify the matter or matters wherein the perjury or perjuries is or are affigned, without fetting forth the bill, anfwer, information, indictment, declaration, or any part of any record or proceeding, either in law or equity, other than as aforefaid, and without fetting forth

Indictments for perjury, and fubornation of perjury.

the

the commiſſion or authority of the Court or perſon or perſons before whom the perjury was committed, or was agreed or promiſed to be committed.

Benefit of clergy abolished.

Sec. 48. *And be it further enacted,* That all claims to diſpenſation from puniſhment by benefit of clergy, ſhall be, and hereby are, forever aboliſhed; and every perſon convicted of any felony, heretofore deemed clergiable, ſhall be fined and impriſoned at the diſcretion of the Court, excepting in thoſe caſes where ſome other ſpecific penalty is preſcribed by this act.

And whereas it may happen that perſons, from obſtinacy, may, on their arraignment, refuſe to plead to indictments or informations found or exhibited againſt them, or challenge more of the perſons ſummoned or returned as Jurors on their trials, than they are legally entitled to; and it being inconſiſtent with principles of juſtice, that ſuch obſtinacy ſhould ſubject any perſon to capital or other puniſhment, where all the effects of a plea may be otherwiſe obtained, and the illegal challenge be overruled:

Prisoner standing mute, &c.

Sec. 49. *Be it therefore enacted,* That if any priſoner ſhall, upon his or her arraignment for any crime or offence whatever, ſtand mute, or not anſwer directly, or ſhall peremptorily challenge above the number of perſons ſummoned or returned as Jurors for his or her trial, to which he or ſhe is by law entitled, the plea of not guilty ſhall be entered for him or her on the record, the ſupernumerary challenges ſhall be diſregarded, and the trial ſhall proceed in the ſame manner as if he or ſhe had pleaded not guilty, and for his or her trial had put himſelf or herſelf upon the country, any law, cuſtom

or

or ufage, to the contrary thereof in any wife notwithftanding.

Sec. 50. *And be it further enacted,* That when any perfon fhall be indicted for any high and aggravated crime or mifdemeanor, by the Grand Jury, and upon trial of the iffue, it fhall appear to the Petit Jury that the perfon accufed is not guilty of the whole crime charged in the indictment, but is guilty of fo much thereof as fhall fubftantially amount to a crime of a lower nature, the Petit Jury may find the indicted perfon guilty of fuch part only, and not guilty of the whole indictment; and the Court fhall proceed to fentence fuch convict for the crime of which he is found guilty, according to law. *Perfons indicted may be found not guilty as to part, &c.*

Sec. 51. *And be it further enacted,* That if any perfon fhall hereafter be convicted of any crime committed before the paffing of this act, he or fhe fhall be fentenced to undergo fuch pains and punifhments, as by the laws now in force are prefcribed and directed, unlefs fuch convict fhall openly pray in Court, before whom fuch conviction fhall be had, that fentence may be pronounced, agreeably to the provifions of this act for the like offence; in which cafe the faid Court fhall comply with the faid prayer, and pafs fuch fentence on fuch convict as they would have paffed, had the faid offence been committed fubfequent to the paffing of this act. *Convicts of crimes, committed before the paffing of this act, &c.*

Sec. 52. *And be it further enacted,* That no perfon fhall be profecuted, tried or punifhed, for any crimes or offences whatfoever, excepting thofe hereafter mentioned, unlefs the indictment for the fame fhall be found or inftituted within three years from the *Time within which indictments are to be preferred.*

the time of committing the crime or offence, or incurring the fine or forfeiture.

Proviso.

Provided, That the aforesaid limitation shall not extend to the crimes of murder, arson, counterfeiting, forgery, polygamy, rape, robbery, horse-stealing, or other theft, or any of them ; and *provided also,* that nothing herein contained shall extend to any person or persons fleeing from justice.

No conviction to work corruption of blood, or forfeiture of estate.

Sec. 53. *And be it further enacted,* That no conviction or judgment for any crime or offence whatever, which hereafter shall be had or rendered within any of the Courts of this State, shall work corruption of blood or forfeiture of estate.

Deodands abolished.

Sec. 54. *And be it further enacted,* That whenever any death shall happen by casualty or accident, there shall be in future no forfeiture of any personal chattel, or the value thereof, as a deodand.

Crimes at the common law, not provided against by this act.

Sec. 55. *And be it further enacted,* That any crime or offence, being such at the common law, and for which no punishment is prescribed by this act, shall and may be prosecuted and tried, adjudged and punished, by fine or imprisonment, or both, as an offence at the common law, any thing in this act to the contrary notwithstanding.

Accused persons, where to be tried.

Sec. 56. *And be it further enacted,* That persons accused of any crime or crimes, shall be proceeded against either in the Supreme Judicial Court, or the Court of General Sessions of the Peace of the county wherein the crime or crimes charged may be committed, unless in cases where by law special provision is or shall be otherwise made.

Fines, where to be paid.

Sec. 57. *And be it further enacted,* That
all

all fines not ſpecially appropriated, ſhall be paid into the general-treaſury, to and for the uſe of the State.

Sec. 58. *And be it further enacted,* That all perſons ſentenced to impriſonment, ſhall be impriſoned in the common gaol of the county in which the offence ſhall be committed : *Provided nevertheleſs,* that whenever, in the opinion of the Supreme Judicial Court, the common gaol of any county in which any priſoner ſhall be confined, or by law ought to be confined, is inſufficient to hold the ſaid priſoner in ſafe cuſtody ; or whenever, in the opinion of ſaid Court, there ſhall be ſufficient cauſe to apprehend that a reſcue and liberation of ſaid priſoner will be made, either by foreign enemies, or by riot and lawleſs violence, it ſhall be lawful for ſaid Court, by order thereof, to remove ſuch priſoner to any other county gaol in the State, until ſuch priſon ſhall be rendered ſafe and ſufficient, or until ſuch reaſonable apprehenſion of the reſcue and liberation of ſaid priſoner ſhall ceaſe.

Sec. 59. *And be it further enacted,* That the puniſhment of death ſhall be inflicted by hanging the perſon convicted by the neck, until dead.

Margin notes:
Convicts, where to be impriſoned.
Proviſo.
Puniſhment of death.

An Act to prevent unneceſſary Expence to the State.

Section 1. BE *it enacted by the General Aſſembly, and by the authority thereof it is enacted,* That when complaint ſhall be made to any Juſtice of the Peace or Warden, of any aſſault or battery, or any theft or other crime within the juriſdiction

Margin notes:
1785.
1798.
Complainant to enter into a recognizance.

rifdiction of Juftices of the Peace to try, the faid Juftice, before he fhall grant any warrant or other procefs to apprehend the perfon or perfons accufed, fhall take a recognizance from the complainant, with fufficient furety to profecute his faid complaint with effect, or in default thereof to pay all lawful cofts which may accrue to the State, or to the perfon or perfons accufed; and in cafe the complainant fhall not profecute his complaint, or if the defendant or defendants upon trial fhall be acquitted, the Juftice of the Peace or Warden, to whom the complaint fhall be made, or the Juftice's Court, before whom the caufe fhall be tried, fhall tax and allow all

To pay cofts, in cafe.

lawful cofts againft the complainant: And in default of payment of the fame within three days after the taxation thereof, the Juftice or Court as aforefaid fhall iffue an execution againft the complainant, and his, her or their fureties, returnable in forty days.

Sec. 2. *And be it further enacted,* That

Appellant to produce a copy of recognizance, &c.

if after a trial as aforefaid, before a Juftice or Juftices of the Peace, an appeal fhall be had to the Court of General Seffions of the Peace, the party appealing fhall bring into the Court appealed to, together with a copy of the cafe, a copy of the recognizance given by the complainant as aforefaid, and if the defendant or defendants fhall there be acquitted, the faid Court fhall tax the cofts, and iffue execution as aforefaid.

An

An Act relative to Slaves, and to their Ma- 1766.
numiſſion and Support. 1774.

Section 1. BE it enacted by the General 1779.
Aſſembly, and by the autho- 1784.
rity thereof it is enacted, That for the future 1785.
no Negro, Mulatto or Indian ſlave ſhall be 1798.
brought into this State; and that if any No ſlaves to be brought into the
ſlave ſhall hereafter be brought in, he or ſhe State, &c.
ſhall be and hereby is rendered immedi-
ately free, ſo far as reſpects perſonal free-
dom, and the enjoyment of private property, in the ſame manner as the native Indians.

Provided nevertheleſs, That this act ſhall not Proviſo.
be deemed to extend to the domeſtic ſlaves
or ſervants of citizens of other States, or of
foreigners, travelling through the State, or
coming to reſide therein; nor to ſervants or
ſlaves eſcaping from ſervice or ſervitude in
other States, or in foreign countries, and
coming of their own accord into this State.

Sec. 2. *And be it further enacted,* That
if any perſon ſhall bring into this State any Penalty for bringing ſlaves
ſlave or ſlaves, with intent that they may into the State.
thereby become free, or ſhall be aiding or
abetting therein, he or ſhe ſo offending
ſhall forfeit and pay the ſum of three hundred dollars for each ſlave ſo brought in, to
be recovered by action of debt, one moiety thereof to and for the uſe of the State,
and the other moiety to and for the uſe of
the perſon who ſhall ſue for the ſame.

Sec. 3. *And be it further enacted,* That
if any perſon ſhall conceal any Negro or Mu- For concealing ſlaves.
latto ſlave, or ſhall in any manner aſſiſt ſuch
ſlave in eſcaping from the lawful authority
of his or her maſter, the perſon ſo offending ſhall forfeit and pay the ſum of three
hundred

hundred dollars, to be recovered by action of debt, one moiety thereof to and for
the use of the State, and the other moiety
thereof to and for the use of the person who
shall sue for the same.

For forcibly car-
rying off slaves.
Sec. 4. *And be it further enacted*, That
if any person or persons shall forcibly or
fraudulently, by themselves or others, carry
off or transport, or attempt to carry off or
transport from this State, any person bound
to slavery by the laws of this State, against
such slave's consent, such carrying off or
transportation, or attempt to carry off or
transport. shall operate against the person or
persons so offending, as a total defeazance
and forfeiture of all their right, title and
claim to such slave.

On proof, a cer-
tificate of eman-
cipation to be
given.
Sec. 5. *And be it further enacted*, That
upon due proof being made by such slave,
or any other person in his or her behalf, before any Justice of the Peace or Warden, that
such an attempt hath been made as aforesaid, it shall be the duty of said Justice to
give under his hand and seal a statement of
the facts attending such transaction, and a
certificate of the total emancipation of said
slave, by virtue of which statement and
certificate, the said slave shall forever
thereafter be liberated and emancipated
from the claim and power of the persons
concerned in said attempts.

Sec. 6. *And be it further enacted*, That
nothing shall be deemed evidence of the
consent of a slave to be transported out of
the State, except a certificate of two or more
Justices of the Peace or Wardens in the
town where such slave may reside, to the
following purport, *viz.*

WE

WE the subscribers, Justices of the Peace in the town of   county of   and State of Rhode-Island and Providence Plantations, do hereby certify, that   a slave, about   years of age, heretofore belonging to   and usually serving   in this town, hath appeared before us at two several times, three days asunder, in the absence of   owner, and under no apparent restraint or duress, hath fully at each time declared   consent to be sold to   of the town of   county of   and State of   and to be forthwith carried to said town, to reside with said   in a state of slavery. Witness our hands, this   day of

Provided always, That in case any slave shall become criminally and notoriously unfaithful, and the owner thereof shall alledge and make proof of the same at the Court of General Sessions of the Peace in the county where such slave may reside, the said Court, after hearing said slave or his counsel, said slave being present in Court, may authorize and empower the said owner to transport said slave to any part of the United States.

Sec. 7. *And be it further enacted,* That if any person shall transport, or cause to be transported out of this State, any slave or slaves contrary to this act, the person so offending shall forfeit and pay the sum of three hundred dollars for every slave so transported, to be recovered by action of debt, one half to and for the use of the State, and the other half to and for the use of the person who shall sue for the same.

Provided, That nothing herein contained

H h h h   shall

[Marginal notes:]
Form of certificate of a slave's consent to be transported.

Proviso.

Penalty for transporting slaves.

Proviso.

shall be deemed or taken to extend to the masters or owners of domestic servants or slaves, being citizens of other States, or foreigners travelling through the State, or coming to reside therein; nor to the masters or owners of servants or slaves escaping from service or servitude in other States, or in foreign countries, and coming of their own accord into this State.

Persons born after 1784, free.

Sec. 8. *And be it further enacted*, That no person born within this State on or after the first day of March, A. D. 1784, shall be deemed or considered a servant for life, or a slave; and that all servitude for life, or slavery of children to be born as aforesaid, in consequence of the condition of their mothers, be and the same is hereby taken away, extinguished, and forever abolished.

Children of slaves, how supported.

Sec. 9. *And be it further enacted*, That every child born on or after the said first day of March, A. D. 1784, whose mother is or shall be a slave, shall be supported and maintained by the owner of the mother, until such child arrive at the age of twenty-one years, *provided* the owner of the mother shall, during that time, hold her in slavery.

Children of other blacks, how maintained.

Sec. 10. *And be it further enacted*, That other children of black or coloured parents, born on or after the said first day of March, A. D. 1784, whose parents are unable to support them, shall be supported and maintained by the towns where they are legally settled.

Proviso.

Provided nevertheless, That the respective Town-Councils may bind out such children as apprentices, at any time after they arrive at the age of one year, and before they arrive

rive at their respective ages of twenty-one, if males, and eighteen, if females.

Sec. 11. *And be it further enacted,* That all persons holden in servitude or slavery, who shall be emancipated by those who claim them, shall be supported in the same manner as other paupers, if they shall become chargeable; *provided* they shall be, at the time of their emancipation, under the age of thirty years, and of sound body and mind, to be judged of and determined by the Town-Councils of the towns in which they may reside. And that all persons holden in servitude or slavery, who may not be of the description last mentioned, and shall be manumitted or emancipated by their owners, or who shall not be emancipated according to the provisions of this act, shall be maintained and supported at the cost and charge of their owners, their heirs, executors or administrators, if they shall ever become chargeable to the town or towns in which they shall reside.

Slaves under the age of 30 emancipated, how supported.

Over that age, how supported.

An Act for breaking up disorderly Houses kept by free Negroes and Mulattoes, and for putting out such Negroes and Mulattoes to Service.

1770.

WHEREAS it often happens that free Negroes and Mulattoes keep very disorderly houses, and entice servants and others to spend their time and money in gaming, drinking, and other vicious practices:

Preamble.

Be it enacted by the General Assembly, and by the authority thereof it is enacted, That upon complaint being made to any Town-Council in this State, of any free Negro or Mulatto

Disorderly houses kept by Negroes, &c. to be broken up, and they bound out.

Mulatto who shall keep a disorderly house, or entertain any person or persons at unreasonable hours, or in an extravagant manner. such Town-Council be and they are hereby empowered to examine into the truth of the complaint, and if they shall find such free Negroe or Mulatto guilty of the same, they may, if they think proper, break up from house-keeping such Negro or Mulatto, and bind out such free Negro or Mulatto to service for any term not exceeding two years. That the wages of

Wages, how to be applied.

every free Negro or Mulatto so bounden out, which shall remain after the expiration of his servitude, and which shall not have been expended in maintaining him and his family, be paid to such Negro or Mulatto, unless the Town-Council shall deem it most for the interest of the town, and of such Negro or Mulatto, to reserve the same for the maintenance of himself and his family.

1750.

An Act to prevent all Persons within this State from entertaining Indian, Negro or Mulatto Servants or Slaves, or trading with them.

Penalty for selling liquors to Indian servants, &c.

Section 1. **B**E it enacted by the General Assembly, and by the authority thereof it is enacted, That no person or persons whosoever shall or may presume, by him or herself, or themselves, or any other for them, directly or indirectly, to sell, give, truck, barter or exchange, with or to any Indian, Mulatto or Negro servant or slave, any strong beer, ale, cider, wine, rum, brandy or other strong liquor, by what name or names soever called or known, on penalty of forfeiting a sum not exceeding

fifteen

fifteen dollars for each offence, to be re-covered by bill, plaint or information, in any of the Courts of Record in this State, one half thereof to the perfon that fhall inform and profecute for the fame, the other half to and for the ufe of the town where the offence fhall be committed.

Sec. 2. *And be it further enacted,* That no white perfon, Indian, Mulatto or Negro, keeping houfe in any town in this State, fhall entertain in his, her or their houfe or houfes, any Indian, Mulatto or Negro fervant or flave, without the confent or approbation of the mafter, miftrefs or owner of fuch fervant or flave, firft had and obtained, or fhall fuffer any fervant or flave to have any dancing, gaming, or diverfion of any kind, in his, her or their houfe or houfes, on penalty of forfeiting the fum of twenty dollars, to be recovered and appropriated in manner as aforefaid, for each and every offence, or fuffer one month's imprifonment. And every fuch free Indian, Mulatto or Negro, tranfgreffing as aforefaid, and duly convicted thereof, fhall not be permitted or fuffered to keep houfe, but fhall be by the Town Council of the town wherein the offence fhall be committed, turned out and difpoffeffed of fuch his, her or their houfe or houfes, and fhall be put into fome private family, to work for the fpace of one whole year; the wages accruing by faid fervice to be for the benefit of the town where the offence fhall be committed.

Not to be out after nine o'clock.

Sec. 3. *And be it further enacted,* That no Indian, Mulatto or Negro fervant or flave fhall be abfent from the family whereto he or fhe fhall refpectively belong, or be

For entertaining them.

be found abroad, in the night time, after nine of the clock, unless it be with the consent of his or her respective master, mistress or owner.

If found out, may be taken up and whipped.

Sec. 4. *And be it further enacted,* That all Justices of the Peace, Constables, watchmen and others, being householders, are hereby respectively empowered to take up and apprehend, or cause to be taken up and apprehended, any Indian, Mulatto or Negro servant or slave, that shall be found abroad after nine of the clock at night, and shall not give a good and satisfactory account of his or her business, and forthwith convey him, her or them, before the next Justice of the Peace (if it be not late in the night) or commit him, her or them, to the common prison until morning, and then cause him, her or them, to appear before a Justice of the Peace, who is hereby ordered and directed to cause such servant or slave to be publicly whipped by the Constable ten stripes. *Provided always,* that the master, mistress or owner of such servant or slave have notice thereof given him or her; and if such master, mistress or owner of such servant or slave will pay the sum of three dollars, to and for the use of the town where such offence shall be committed, that then, and in that case only, such servant or slave shall not be punished as aforesaid.

Proviso.

Penalty for trading with Indian servants, &c.

Sec. 5. *And be it further enacted,* That no person whosoever shall buy, sell, or otherwise trade with any servant or slave, or receive any thing from a servant or slave, without leave first had and obtained from the master, mistress or owner of such servant or slave, on penalty of forfeiting the sum of three dollars for each offence, and

and the thing or things received, or value thereof, to be recovered by complaint in writing before a Court of Justices or Wardens, one half to the informer, and the other half to the master, mistress or owner of such servant or slave. And whosoever shall be suspected of receiving any thing from, or trading with, any servant or slave, contrary to the true intent and meaning of this act, and shall refuse to purge him, her or themselves by oath, shall be adjudged guilty, and sentence shall be given against him, her or them, accordingly.

A Law made and passed by the General Assembly on the fourth Monday of Dec. A. D. 1783. 1783.

An Act to prevent Impositions upon Indians of the Narragansett Tribe.

WHEREAS it is represented unto this Assembly, that unjust advantages are frequently taken of the Indians of the Narragansett tribe within this State, by inducing them to sign and execute notes, bonds and other instruments, for the payment of money, or delivery of articles, whereby they are often involved in the payment of large debts which are not *bona fide* due. To prevent which,

Preamble.

Be it enacted by the General Assembly, and by the authority thereof it is enacted, That in every action already brought, or which shall be brought, on any note, bond or other instrument, given or entered into by any of the said Indians for the payment of money, or delivery of articles, proof shall be made of full and just value having been paid for the same, before judgment shall be made up by any Court of law in favour of the person

Actions against Indians, how maintained.

c 2

or perfons bringing fuch action; and for want of fuch proof, fuch action fhall be difmiffed with coft.

1790.

An Act directing the Keepers of Gaols in this State to receive and fafe keep all Prifoners committed under the Authority of the United States.

Preamble.

WHEREAS by an act of the Congrefs of the United States. at the feffion begun and holden on the fourth day of March, A. D. 1789, it was refolved, that it be recommended to the Legiflatures of the feveral States to pafs laws making it expressly the duty of the keepers of their gaols to receive, and fafe keep therein, all prifoners committed under the authority of the United States, until they fhall be difcharged by due courfe of the laws thereof, under the like penalties as in cafe of prifoners committed under the authority of fuch States refpectively; the United States to pay for the ufe and keeping of fuch gaols, at the rate of fifty cents per month, for each prifoner that fhall, under their authority, be committed thereto, during the time fuch prifoner fhall therein be committed, and alfo to fupport fuch of faid prifoners as fhall be committed for offences:

Whereupon this Affembly, in full confidence that Congrefs will make provifion for the fupport of poor prifoners committed for debt, as otherwife humanity will call upon the inhabitants of the county towns to fupply their neceffities, which will prove unreafonably expenfive and burthenfome, *do enact, and by the authority thereof it is enacted,* That the keepers of the refpective gaols in the

Gaolers to receive prifoners committed under the authority of the United States.

counties

counties of Newport, Providence, Washington, Bristol and Kent, be and they are hereby ordered and directed, and it shall be expresly their duty, to receive and safe keep therein all prisoners committed, or who shall be committed, under the authority of the United States, until they shall be discharged by due course of the laws thereof, under the like penalties as in case of prisoners committed under the authority of this State, and upon the terms in the said resolve of Congress expressed.

An Act for preventing Fraud in Fire-Wood and Charcoal expofed to Sale.

1698.
1798.

Section 1. **B**E *it enacted by the General Affembly, and by the authority thereof it is enacted,* That all fire-wood expofed to fale in this State shall be four feet long, meafuring to one half of the kerf, and shall be fold by the cord, and that the cord shall be eight feet long, four feet wide, and four feet high, well stowed, and closely laid together.

Length, &c. of fire-wood expofed to fale.

Sec. 2. *And be it further enacted,* That whofoever shall fell or expofe to fale any wood that is not of the length aforefaid, shall, upon due conviction thereof before any Juftice of the Peace of the town where fuch offence shall be committed, forfeit all fuch wood fo expofed to fale, the one half to the informer, and the other half to and for the ufe of fuch town, to be levied by warrant of diftrefs, to be granted by fuch Juftice before whom fuch offender shall be convicted. And that in every town in this State, where fire-wood shall be expofed to fale by the cord, the freemen of the town

Penalty for felling wood not of length.

Iiii shall,

shall (if they think fit) annually choose and elect one or more persons to be corders of wood, who shall take the same engagement to his or their office as other town-officers do, and shall have eight cents per cord for every cord by him or them corded, to be paid by the seller of said wood.

Baskets for measuring charcoal, how much to contain, &c.

Sec. 3. *And be it further enacted,* That all baskets used in measuring charcoal, exposed to sale in any town in this State, shall contain two bushels; that the basket be well heaped, and also be sealed by the sealer of weights and measures of the town where the person so using the same shall usually inhabit or reside, or of the town where the same shall be sold; and every person who shall measure charcoal offered for sale in any basket of less size, or not sealed as aforesaid shall forfeit and pay for each offence fifty cents, to be recovered in manner and to the use aforementioned, and such basket shall be destroyed.

INDEX

I N D E X.

A.

From

Duty

Any

   K k k k   May

In

In

Maintenance,

M.

Mut,

Partition,

P.

United

Oo

FINIS.